WESTWARD BEFORE COLUMBUS

by

Kåre Prytz

Translated by
Liv Myhre & Charles De Stefano, Ph.D.

NORSK MARITIMT FORLAG AS

Kåre Prytz:
Jegernes kvinne, 1968
På fremmed kyst, 1969
Lenken 1971
Bisettes senere, 1972
Lykkelige Vinland, 1975
Demringen, 1978
På stigende kurs, 1984

© H. Aschehoug & Co. (W. Nygaard), Oslo 1990
English edition 1991: Norsk Maritimt Forlag A/S
P.O.Box A, Bygdoy, 0211 Oslo 2, Norway.
Phone: 472-43 75 75, Fax: 472-43 84 49.

Printed in the U.S. by Courier Stoughton, Inc.

Translation Copyright © 1991 by Liv Myhre

ISBN: 82.90319.13.4

Distributed in the U.S. by Norumbega Books,
P.O. Box 1267, Weston, CT   06883.

TABLE OF CONTENTS

THE MYSTICAL LAND IN THE WEST

For at least five thousand years people in Europe believed there was a continent on the other side of the ocean to the west. But we are venturing onto shaky ground when we try to find any verifiable contact between the continents. The learned Spanish archbishop, Isidor, who lived in Seville around the year 600 and was an expert on Arabic history, tells us that the cultures of the eastern Mediterranean knew a good deal about a world to the west. But that claim is somewhat suspect in light of their belief in the existence of the mythical kingdom of Atlantis, alleged to have sunk into the ocean during a catastrophic earthquake.

It has been pointed out that there are similarities between Egyptian and Mexican methods of pyramid building, and between Mayan culture and the ancient culture of Israel. Asian researchers suggest that Central America may have had substantial cultural contact with the Orient, via the Bering Strait, at the time of Christ. But the East Asian horse people never ventured anywhere without their animals, and America was still without horses when the Europeans arrived in the Middle Ages.

Irish legends point to the existence of contact with America in the first millennium A.D. Some American researchers claim to have found stone huts, or possibly stone passages, that may be the remains of a pre-Christian European culture in New England.[1] Their manner of construction, and the placement of window openings in the structures, seem to have been based on ancient sun worship and astronomy, reminiscent of the mysterious Stonehenge in England.

Common to all the interesting evidence, is the fact that there are no reliable «reports» of journeys to the continent west of the ocean. The first person to return home after he and his crew had drifted to America in a storm, was the Icelandic merchant Bjarne Herjulfsson, in the year 986 A.D. The voyage is described in the Icelandic saga collection, Flateyarboken.[2]

Bjarne and his men were on their way to the newly discovered Greenland during the summer, when they ran into a storm west of Iceland, bearing down from the north. Medieval sailors always steered away from the wind in bad weather. History is full of dramatic accounts of such voyages. An Italian, Querini, was sailing from Crete to a harbor on the French Atlantic coast in the fall of 1431 when he encountered a lengthy storm off Gibraltar. In January the following year he ended up shipwrecked in Lofoten in northern Norway. The Dutch India-farer, «Akrendam», drifted in the same direction in a storm in the 1700s and broke up off Runde on the coast of Möre in western Norway. In 1970 one of the world's richest finds of gold and silver coins was made on board this wreck.

Bjarne Herjulfsson is believed to have used a ship 25–30 meters long and 7–8 meters wide, with about the same sailing characteristics as the Viking ships. During trial voyages with replicas of the Gokstad Ship, sailors have been able to maintain an average speed of about 7.5 knots for long periods of time when scudding away from bad weather.[3] Bjarne's ship probably gained extra speed from the Labrador and Greenland currents, both of which are stable and strong. According to the saga, the voyage lasted 10–12 days before the storm abated. At that point they were in a hurry to head up to the 60th parallel, where Greenland was located.

In order to practice efficient and reliable latitudinal sailing, the Norse seafarers used a piece of translucent stone, cordierite. With the help of this stone they could determine the position of the sun in cloudy weather. The method is best described in the saga of Olav Den Hellige (St. Olav's Saga) in Flateyarbok:[4] During a visit to a farmer named Raud in Österdalen in Norway, the king was told during the evening feast that the farmer's son, Sigurd, could tell the position of the heavenly bodies, even in cloudy weather. The next day it was snowing hard, and King Olav asked Sigurd to tell him exactly how high in the sky the sun was. Sigurd located it precisely. The king then took the sun stone and held it up high, and he saw how the light sparkled from the stone, indicating the location that Sigurd had given.

This method was rediscovered and used by the world's leading airline companies in the 1950s, when they began scheduled flights over the North Pole.[5] In addition to this stone, the Norse seafarers probably had a compass-like dial that made simple latitudinal navigation possible. Up until the 1600s it was common for navigators to count quickly to sixty to measure short intervals of 30 seconds when estimating speed.[6]

The saga of Bjarne's voyage reads almost like a «log book»,[7] based on the same simple systems and tables used by the Phoenicians, Arabs and mariners in European countries. There were Greek terms in the Nordic tables as well.[8]

The British researcher Dr. G.M. Gathorne-Hardy, has studied all the details of Bjarne's account after they had turned around and started the

8

voyage home, and has offered the following interpretation:[9]

After sailing for one «dögr» to the north, they reached a flat land that seems reminiscent of the area of Cape Cod on the American east coast. It is important to note in this context that a «dögr» refers not to time, but to a distance of 144 nautical miles.[10] They kept the land behind them on port side, and continued on a northeasterly course for two «dögr» (288 nautical miles) across the Gulf of Maine. Here they discovered a new land (Nova Scotia), that was hilly and forested. The wind died down while they were sailing along this coast, and for a while they were completely dead in the water. The men wanted to sail toward the coast and go ashore. But Bjarne was not interested. He was not an explorer, and all he owned in this world—a cargo of wares from Norway—was stored in the hull of his ship. They had already lost a lot of time. The crew complained that they needed both water and wood for their on board hearth, but Bjarne said they didn't need either.

Then the wind quickened. Unfortunately the saga doesn't specify how much time they spent sailing by the lands they saw; we are only told the distance between each. The ship was now in open ocean for 4 «dögr» (576 nautical miles) before they reached a new land that is believed to have been Newfoundland. They apparently sailed the inner channel, because the description says that this was an «island land», as opposed to the two previous ones. There were mountains as well. But Greenland it was not, so Bjarne decided he did not want to go ashore.

They headed out to sea on a southwesterly wind that increased in strength to a gale force storm. The ship was going so fast that Bjarne ordered the sail reefed. This was done with the help of ropes sewn into the sail. For a while Bjarne was afraid they would lose the rigging entirely, so this must have been quite a storm.

The old long ships were incredibly agile in difficult weather. They had to leave some canvas up so as not to lose speed and risk being overcome by the seas that came rolling in from astern. Experience with Viking ship replicas that have crossed the Atlantic indicates that the ships bob like corks on the crests of the waves as long as they don't lose speed.

The saga states that they were mired in this weather for four «dögr», or 576 nautical miles. They wouldn't have to worry about running out of firewood under those conditions. Even if the ship was watertight, the sailors would still be drenched by the seaspray that whipped across the stormy ocean. Usually a ship was considered seaworthy when it didn't have to be bailed out more than three times in two days. But on this occasion it is likely that the bailers spent considerable time in the special «bailing room».

Navigation apparently presented few problems. They headed straight to South Greenland, and saw at once that the mountains there agreed with the description they had been given before departing from Iceland. After that it was easy to find Herjulfsneset, where Bjarne's father had begun building the large farm that was to become the focal point of this district, and which was the first and last station for traffic between Europe and the polar region.

Roughly estimated, according to this description, Bjarne and his men must have sailed two to three weeks after turning back from the American coast. This was not a substantial disruption in travel plans when compared to a number of other recorded Atlantic voyages. Querini, for example, didn't sight land for two months and eight days from the time he left Spain until he ran aground in Lofoten.

The distant polar island of Greenland was, as we will see later, a medieval Klondike, except that the first colonists had to cross the entire North Atlantic to reach the nearest forest. As soon as they had discovered America, they were able to get timber and wood only four «dögr» sailing from their front door.

The discovery of these lands robbed Eirik Raude of some of the glory of having found Greenland. He fled there permanently after a series of killings and feuds in Norway and Iceland, and established himself as a kind of absolute ruler on behalf of the Norwegian crown. The sagas describe how he did considerable advertising for the new land by giving it an enticing name. However, this cannot be accurate, because as early as 831 Pope Gregor IV wrote to the papal legate of the Nordic countries, Ansgar, that Greenland (Groenlanders) was to be administered by the archbishopric of Hamburg.[11] It is also stated in The Eirik Raude Saga that the land had been sighted by others before him.[12]

Eirik Raude's oldest son and Greenland's «crown prince», Leiv Eiriksson, went to Norway to see King Olav Trygvasson in Nidaros, Norway, in the year 999. En route he was storm driven all the way to the Hebrides, not an unusal occurrence in the Atlantic Ocean. While waiting for a southwest wind, Leiv became involved in a love relationship that would turn out to be quite bothersome for him. He met the somewhat older, but very beautiful and attractive Torgunna, a woman of high birth. The Örbygjasaga (in Flateyarbok) makes particular mention of her luxurious bedding. Among the gifts she received was a narwhal tooth that was very costly—and prized as a powerful stimulant and aphrodisiac. Leiv was not inclined to take her away with force, as she asked him to, because he was afraid of her brothers. But it may also be that he didn't think she would adjust to the harsh daily life on Greenland. The result of the romance was a son, Torgils, who was handicapped, possibly with Down's syndrome.[13] The boy was later taken to Greenland, and grew up at Brattalid.

The stay with Torgunna was short enough for Leiv to get to the king that same fall. Here he was well received. Among other things he became an honorary member of the king's «hird»—the hand-picked noblemen who were both the king's guard, closest advisors and drinking companions. But his majesty also preached Christianity to Leiv, «the way he did to all heathens», as it is stated in The Olav Trygvasson Saga.[14] Leiv and his crew allowed themselves to be converted, and Leiv promised to introduce Christianity on Greenland. He was given a priest to take back, and received gifts from the king, among them an Irish slave couple.

Eirik Raude's saga states that Leiv returned to Greenland with considerable authority from the king. But in September of that same year (1000), King Olav Trygvasson fell at the battle of Svolder.

Eirik Jarl, who had played a pivotal role in the naval battle at Svolder in which the king was killed, became the next ruler of the young and large Norwegian kingdom. At this point Bjarne Herjulfsson paid an unexpected visit to the new king. Bjarne had lived in seclusion on the farm he and his father owned for about 14 years after his storm driven discovery of America. He was received just as well as Leiv had been by the previous king, and he, too, joined the king's hird. But during the winter he spent at court, he had to endure much chiding because he had not explored the new land that he had found to the west.

Bjarne's journey to the court in Nidaros suggests some rivalry with Eirik Raude that is further substantiated by the fact that the Raude family at Brattalid decided to lay claim to the land that Bjarne had found. Leiv visited Bjarne after he returned home, bought his ship, and hired 35 men for a voyage expected to take a year and a half. If Bjarne was not inclined to «give» his land away, he had no way of preventing it. He must have been close to 50 years old, and according to local reckoning, in the process of turning into an old man.

When the Raude family later had their own saga recorded, not a single word was written about Bjarne Herjulfsson's voyage.

The Land of Timber and Grapes

Leiv Eiriksson planned to claim the new land, and made preparations to be gone for one and a half years. The size of the crew indicates that the ship had at least 16 pairs of oars. As mentioned, such a ship would have been about 25 meters long and about 7 meters wide.

Since Bjarne's description of the course he had sailed was so good and thorough, it appears that Leiv's voyage was not especially eventful. They held so much to starbord that they probably sighted southern Labrador and Newfoundland first. A group rowed ashore in their small boat, but the visit was a short one. The rocky coast was not very inviting, so they continued to the southwest. Soon stripes of warmer and greener water began to mix with the cold, gray polar water. This belt between the Gulf Stream and the Labrador Current was, and is, one of the best fishing grounds in the world.

They named the American coast north of the Gulf of St. Lawrence Helluland—«The Stone Land». They continued to the next land Bjarne had described. It was flat and forested and had sandy beaches that sloped gently up from the sea. The collected descriptions of distances and other details indicate that the land was located in the area between the Gulf of St. Lawrence and the Gulf of Maine. Leiv named it Markland—«The Forest Land» or «The Wilderness Land».

After exploring this area, they set out to sea again. They sailed for two «dögr,» or about 290 nautical miles, to the southwest, until they reached a new land south of the Gulf of Maine. At the mouth of a bay they anchored off an island to stretch their legs and get their bearings. The weather was wonderful, the vegetation luxuriant, and the air fresh—they even thought the dew tasted sweet. After a time they went back on board and sailed past the island into the bay beyond.

The Vinland Saga in large part consists of practical observations, with precise sailing directions and navigational details for those who might follow later. They followed a course straight west through the sound between the island and a headland that stretched north from the mainland to their south.

They were not fortunate in their choice of approach, because the water was shallow and the tide falling. A dangerous situation arose when they ran aground. When the ship finally lay high and dry, considerable weight was resting on the 20 meter long keel. The men reached land in their shore-boat, and waited. They realized that this must be the outlet of a very large river. When high tide returned, they made it back to the ship, which was undamaged.

Under such circumstances it would have been sensible to establish a base by the mouth of the river, the way all the world's settlements have begun. But at this point they made a choice that the saga does not explain. They sailed up the river instead, and passed through a quiet stretch where the water flowed calmly. Beyond this «lake» they went ashore.

They were quite satisfied with conditions there, and built temporary huts. According to the saga, the salmon were bigger than those they were used to catching at home on Greenland. Obviously quite a lot of fish was needed to feed 30 men, but we are not told how the river fishing was done.

People have searched for Leiv's base camp site on the coast of New England for centuries. But this is all the information the saga gives: A «fjord» laying in an east to west direction, with a protruding headland on the shallow south side, and one or more islands at the mouth of the fjord. And a large river that runs into the fjord. That's as far as anyone has gotten.

The saga provides no running narrative about that summer. At this point the discoverers knew little or nothing about their surroundings. But what we are told after this point they could not have known without having made additional forays south along the coast.

They stated that there was no frost in this land during the winter, and that the grass did not wither much. At home they had to gather fodder all summer in order to bring the animals through the winter. The only problem with the land was that it was so far from home. In the Greenland saga of the Flateyarbok the following observations are made about the journey: «Days and nights were more equal in length than at home on Greenland and on Iceland. The sun was in «dagamálstad» and «eyktarstad» on Skamdagen [the shortest day of the year, December 23]».

Dagamál was a well-known point in the morning sky, and in Norway a number of «Durmål Peaks» have been established. They are always 60 degrees east of south, seen from a particular farm or hamlet.[15]

The opposite point in the sky, which the saga calls eyktarstad, is explained in the following way in the Icelandic book of legal codes, Gragás:[16] «It is eykt when the sky between south and west is divided into three parts, and the sun has gone two parts, and there is one left.» That means a point 60 degrees west of south. This agrees with a piece of information in Snorre Sturlasson's Heimskringla («World Description») which states that the beginning of the winter-half of the year (October 18) occurred on his farm at Reykjaholt on Iceland when the sun went down in «eyktarstad» (in eykt position).[17]

A modern mathematical treatment of Leiv's observations was done by Dr. Almar Næss in his book Hvor lå Vinland («Where Was Vinland») with material provided by Gustav Storm, professor of history; Hans Geel-muyden, professor of astronomy; the navigational expert M.M. Mjelde, and the British scientist G.M. Gathorne-Hardy.[18] The conclusion they reached was that the information concerned sunrise and sunset at the inlet of Chesapeake Bay in Virginia on the 23rd of December. The latitude was determined to be 36° 54' north.

In that location the shortest day of the year is 9 hours and 27 minutes, while in Leiv's home district on Greenland it was only 5 hours and 29 minutes. As early as the 900s the Norse seafarers had «Rim» tables (old Norse navigational system) for the sun's declination for every day of the year, and for sunrise and sunset on important days, such as midsummer and midwinter, and spring and fall solstice. Today we can verify a number of the distances and latitudes given in the Viking «Rim» edition, and in Landnámabok.[19] The observations do not necessarily mean that this is where the expedition was on the 23rd of December.

Leiv's statement only explains how far south the expedition reached, just as we today would indicate the latitude. But the fact that they found the green grass and the absence of snow unusual, indicates that they were travelling in the middle of winter. At the 36th parallel «Solarsudr» began—the latitude of the north coast of Africa. As we will see later, this was to become the most well-known latitude in the history of America's discovery.

It is not clear whether they built permanent houses before or after their journey south, but once at home in base camp they set about exploring the nearby area. Half the crew would make day trips. These explorers, who came from Iceland and Greenland where trees were rare or non-existent, seem to have been uncertain about what the forests might hide. They may have suspected that the land was inhabited, because they were given specific instructions not to split up and never to spend the night outside the main camp. Half the crew always stayed behind in camp, where they spent their time cutting wood and making planks and other things that were needed at home on Greenland. The limited capacity of the ship made it necessary to do as much of the finish work as possible on land.

The reason they waited until winter to make a trip south may have had something to do with the most important event that took place that first summer:

One evening Leiv's «foster father»*—an old slave from Germany— disappeared without a trace. Leiv was furious with the group that had let this happen, for the man had been Leiv's servant since he was a small boy. They searched for him an entire night, but didn't find him until the next day. He was extremely agitated and spoke only German at first. But then he explained in Norwegian:

«I didn't go very far, but I have some important news to tell you. I found grape vines and grapes!» «Is this true, my foster father?» said a doubtful Leiv. «It is true,» said the slave, who was a man of many talents. «Where I was born, there was no shortage of grape vines and grapes.»

The man had a comical appearance—almost a clown face. Everyone laughed at his southern gestures and excitement at having spent the night with the precious plants of his childhood—before his life had been ruined by the marauders from the North.

Dried grapes were one of the most valuable food articles of antiquity and the Middle Ages. They are mentioned in the Book of Numbers (6.3) and First Samuel (25.18). The great seafarers and caravans brought raisins, almonds and beans along as provisions on long journeys. For the Greenlanders, whose closest field was nearly a thousand miles across dangerous ocean, it was sensational to find this wonderful resource. The significance of the discovery is also stressed in the text of the saga—they were able to sleep the first night after their find, but the next day the work routine was changed. They decided they would spend alternate days picking grapes and cutting timber. The saga scribe was impressed, too, noting that they were able to fill the shore boat with grapes in just a single day. The grapes were easy to preserve. The sun took care of that—whether before or after the grapes were picked.

A later lay [heraldic song] tells about the production of wine in America. But this was something largely unimportant in a society suffering from lack of food, persistent hunger, harsh discipline, and which observed a drinking practice that was deeply ingrained in the Nordic culture. They drank infrequently, but when they did, they drank heavily. Drunkenness was scorned in everyday Viking life.

*Foster father in this context means a man-servant, someone who had taken care of Leiv since childhood.

There is a brief reference in the saga to «self sown» wheat, but grain is not mentioned in any of the sagas as being part of the cargo on the return voyage.

The most important thing about America was the unlimited availability of timber. Without a secure and steady supply of lumber the Greenland society could not survive. Even so, when they left for home in the spring, Leiv gave the land south of Cape Cod the name Vinland after the grapes that grew there. In Old Norse both grapes and raisins are called «vin-ber», and it is the term almost always used in the sagas.[20]

A few clergymen with foreign background used the name Vinland det gode («Vinland the Good»). But there are no three-word Norwegian place names, and in the Norse tongue the name frequently used was «Landit Goda», later «Landegode».[21]

Leiv's expedition really didn't go all that far. The distance between Greenland and Chesapeake Bay was no farther than from the Norwegian capital of Bergen to Gibraltar, where the Vikings had gone every year for summer plunder. We are familiar with a voyage similar to Leiv's. In the summer of 1526 the explorer Magellan's navigator, Estevan Gomez, sailed from Europe to Labrador, down along the entire east coast of America, and back to Europe, with a ship that was far slower and less maneuverable than the Viking long ships.[22] In the 1500s, countless British, Portuguese and Dutch ships sailed on summer expeditions all the way to Greenland, the banks of Newfoundland, and Labrador.

Until the steam engine came into use, there was no faster ship on the ocean than the Viking long ship.

1. Fell, 1976
2. Flateyarbok, which includes the Vinland saga, was written down by two priests on parchment made from the hides of 125 calves during the years 1387–94. It is kept in the national library of Iceland in Reykjavik.
3. Magnus Andersen in 1893, and the Viking expedition Norway-US in 1957.
4. Column 466.
5. Ramskau, 1982.
6. Hewson, 1951, p. 155.
7. Alfrædi islenzk, I-III.
8. Morcken, 1968.
9. Gathorne-Hardy, 1921.

10. A <u>dögr</u> of sailing was the distance a ship sailed with an average speed of 6 knots for 24 hours. See Gathorne-Hardy, in Næss, 1954, pp. 175–89. Also see Morcken, 1968.
11. Nordenskiöld, 1883, p. 40.
12. The saga of Eirik Raude, hand written on parchment, dates back to approximately year 1200.
13. Henriksen, 1988, p. 214.
14. Halldorsson, 1958.
15. Werenskiold, in Næss, 1954.
16. <u>Grágás</u>.
17. Snorre Sturlasson (1179–1241) was an Icelandic historian, politician and «skald» (heraldic poet). <u>Edda</u> is his most famous work.
18. Næss, 1954.
19. <u>Landnámabok</u> is the story of the settlement of Iceland from 870 to 930. The book was begun by Are Frode in 1100. Modern edition: Benediktsson, 1969.
20. Heggstad et.al., 1975.
21. Nansen, 1911, p. 283.
22. Quinn, et.al., 1971, p. 68.

TORVALD EIRIKSSON'S LONG JOURNEY

After his voyage, the thirty year old Leiv was the «hot name» among the Greenlanders. At least the saga says that he was lauded as wise, rich in friends, and a very lucky man. His luck was demonstrated on the return voyage when he rescued the crew and the cargo of a ship loaded with lumber that was sinking off the coast of Greenland. The shipwrecked captain's young wife, Gudrid, later married Leiv's brother, Torstein. She was the granddaughter of a liberated Irish slave of high birth, and is said to have had a lovely singing voice. Yet all the loud praise still did not overshadow the fact that Leif had merely visited the land that Bjarne Herulfsson had seen first.

Leiv's father was pleased that his son had visited the new land. But the joy, he said, was dimmed by the fact that Leiv destroyed the old beliefs on Greenland by bringing «the hypocrite» (the Christian priest) from Norway. Eirik Raude was now a much reduced man. His wife refused to live under his roof because he insisted on believing in the old gods. And he had to accept a church being built on the grounds of his own farm.

Leiv's younger brother, Torvald, didn't mince words when commenting about the Vinland voyage. Leiv and his 35 men had explored far too little of the area during the voyage, he said. The expedition had become bogged down with grape picking and tree felling.

Leiv was the very opposite of his brutal father, Eirik Raude. And on this occasion he once more reaffirms the impression we have of him. He backed off.

«Go to Vinland yourself,» he said. «You can borrow my ship and the houses I built there. Take thirty men with you and explore all you want.»

Torvald accepted the offer, and for the third time the same ship headed to America. Torvald Eiriksson must have been in his mid-20s when he left on his big voyage. He was third in line to become chieftain on Greenland, because there was another brother between himself and Leiv.

In the hard, competitive society of Greenland, honor, fame and being well travelled were important. And now the possibility was open to Torvald to become an even greater seafarer than both his father and his brother. He was the only true explorer among the Vinlandfarers—the others had gone for practical reasons.

On long voyages the Greenlanders primarily stocked dried meat and fish, butter and cheese, and a type of sour milk that could withstand long storage. The ships had their own cooks. The old Norse rules of the sea established that a cook was to be a slave or a man of low birth. It was accepted practice to cuff him if he didn't stock enough food, but the beating could not be so hard as to permanently injure him.

In Viking times men worked four hour shifts both at sea and when farming. They continued this routine on their ships even after the advent of Christianity, when four three-hour day watches and four night watches were prescribed, as mentioned in the Gospel of St. Mark (6.48).

We may assume that several of the men had participated in Leiv's expedition and were familiar with the wine grapes. When they passed the bowl of sour milk around, they probably spoke of the wine that the German grape expert Tyrk had made. It is not very difficult to make wine «on the spot». If you crush the grapes, nature takes care of the rest. In the grape juice, the must, there is sugar, and in the skins, yeast. From yeast and sugar you get alcohol.[1] The quality is another matter.

The journey was not recorded—they already knew the way. At last they arrived at Leiv's camp—a few wooden huts on a huge continent. That they found their way, says something about how skilled they were at navigation.

In the fall they beached the ship to be tarred. That was very important this far south, because toredo worms were carried north with the Gulf Stream—something Leiv probably had noted. The toredo worms are common south of 30°N, but they are occasionally found further north. The Spaniards were later to pay a dear price for not taking such precautions. The saga about Karlsevne's voyage also tells of a tragic journey on which it was suddenly discovered that the ship was worm-eaten and sinking.[2] Luckily the shore boat was tarred and unharmed, but it could hold only half of the men. They divided into two groups, and drew lots over who was to be saved. When an Icelander in the «losing group» was gripped with intense fear of death, the captain, Bjarne Grimjolfsson, gave him his place, went back to the ship, and drowned.

As mentioned, Torvald and his men lived in Leiv's house some distance up the calm and navigable river. It is difficult to imagine this as a good fishing ground. Yet the saga states matter of factly and without hesitation that Torvald's expedition caught all the fish they needed for the winter. They couldn't have fished anywhere else, because their ship was beached for the winter. Fishing nets are not mentioned at any time in the sagas. We have to wonder what kinds of fishing methods they used. In addition to requiring a daily catch of at least 30 kilos, they needed to smoke and dry provisions for 31 men for at least half a year.

Muddy Waters and Barren Islands

The story of Torvald's voyage is «the forgotten saga» in the history of Viking explorations. He was merely going to investigate new lands and new oceans. Both the ones who went before him and those to come after mostly stayed put and sought out high-grade wood, lumber, skins and provisions. But Torvald became a loser in his short life, and history is reserved for those who survive to tell their tales. The saga about these 31 youths for a long time seemed disconnected and truncated.

Historians agree that Torvald's journey began where Leiv's ended. Here we will try to retell the story of the second summer in the New World, based on information in the saga, correlating it to later maps and Norse geographical knowledge.

When spring came, the expedition split up at the tip of Vinland, at 36°N. Here Torvald gave orders for the men to take the shoreboat and explore the land along the shore to the west during the course of the summer. The west side of Vinland would mean the west side of the Delaware peninsula, thus placing them in the Chesapeake Bay.

Torvald himself, with most of the crew, was going to search for coasts that neither Leiv nor any other Norseman had ever seen. The existence of Indians was still unknown. The Norse seafarers, the pioneers of the Atlantic, always sailed far off the coast in unfamiliar waters.[3] Thanks to a deep oak keel the long ships were eminently suited to close-haul sailing. When Magnus Andersen crossed the Atlantic with the ship «Viking» in 1893, his long ship replica maintained an average speed of 5.2–5.7 knots for several days, with the wind at six points off the bow (8 points is abeam). The famous and often used Vinland ship probably had a deeper draft, but was not necessarily a poorer sailer for that reason.

It turned out to be especially important to stay off the coast south of Chesapeake Bay, because this is where they would encounter the Gulf Stream, a hundred mile wide current headed north at a speed of 3 knots. As a result, the Carolinas were never recorded on any maps pre-dating Columbus. But according to the veteran sailors I have consulted, the expedition could not have avoided seeing Grand Bahama Island if they were sailing outside the Gulf Stream. The Vinland seafarers knew the mainland as far south as Georgia and Florida, as we shall see later. But in this connection we are confounded by the fact that the saga scribes used the words «islands» and «lands» interchangeably. The way the Europeans saw it, all the lands in America lay out there in the ocean somewhere.

Among the observations they made was that the land was heavily wooded. The forest went almost down to the water, and there were white, sandy beaches. This is a description that would generally fit most of America's east coast. The Bahama Islands were forested by pine to the water's edge at that time, as is still the case on Andros Island, where dangerous shoals kept colonists away.

But then we are told of more specific observations. On these islands there was no sign of any kind of animal life. The only islands in the Western world that had no animal life, were the Bahama Islands, the Antilles and the Caribbean islands. The participants in Columbus' expedition were just as baffled by this phenomenon when they came here five hundred years later. When a small Indian population finally established itself there, some groups among the Caribes resorted to cannibalism for meat. They actually hunted other tribes in order to eat them. Female prisoners were used to breed babies for human consumption, or so it is claimed in the report from Columbus' second voyage.[4]

When Torvald was there, the humans had yet to arrive. But on one of the western islands they found what they thought was a «kornhjelm» made of wood. A «kornhjelm» was a round roof of tarred skin, fastened on poles, used to dry grains and grass during harvesting in Scandinavia. On Mecia de Vilastede's world map of 1413 it is stated that «in Norway they make good tarpaulins for haystacks from whaleskin».[5] On the island, wood thatch probably was used for the roof. This still remains the predominant hut type of the Caribbean area. It did not exist on the mainland, where rectangular roofs were used up to the Carolinas. Farther north huts were built with walls.[6]

Apparently they were not impressed with this area. The saga states that there were many islands, and the sea very shallow. That information

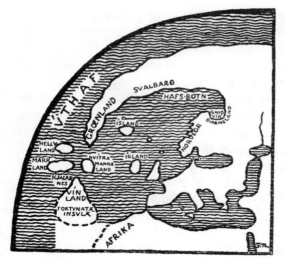

The world view of the Vinlandfarers, according to a map drawn by Fridtjof Nansen. There is continuous ice from Asia and the north of Europe to Greenland. America, or "Fortunatæ Insula", is connected to Africa in the south.

is correct. A characteristic sight here are all the dark coral reefs that stick up everywhere. On Great Bahama Bank, more than 60 miles across, the depth is anywhere from 3 to 9 meters. The shallows are very dangerous, and the lookout and the pilot had to exercise extreme caution. In the clear water the shadow of the ship moved gingerly over the sandbanks, sailing over dunes and shallows and steep drops—and where the bottom could suddenly be dangerously close to the keel. The saga twice stresses that there was no sign of life. In the fall they returned to spend another winter in Leiv's camp, after bringing back the men who had gone to Chesapeake Bay in the shore boat. The explorers had determined the extent of the American coast. What remained was to explore the coast that was rumored to stretch all the way to Africa.

During the third summer Torvald and his men sailed eastward. They sailed «north of the land», according to the saga. In keeping with the old and familiar world view, he was now supposedly near the world's southernmost coast, which was thought to be a continuous stretch of land between Cap Bojador near the Canary Islands and the southern part of Florida at 27–28°N—only interrupted by a furious current where the ocean spilled off the edge of the world somewhere between the Canary Islands and Florida.[7]

In order to understand Torvald's voyage we need to look at some ancient sources. The Icelandic abbot, Niculas of Thverå, who died in 1159, wrote:

«South of Greenland lies Helluland. Thereafter Markland. From there it is not far to Vinland the good, which some believe is connected to Africa. And if this is so, then Mare Oceanum must be located somewhere between Vinland and Markland.»[8]

The explanation for the last sentence was that water was thought to rush out of the world through the straits between the Canary Islands and Florida, and would necessarily have to flow in somewhere in the north.

In the world view presented in Gripla, Markland is called «Skræling-land, where the natives are».[9] Furthermore it states that Vinland is believed to be a land that extends to the west off Africa.

In the Latin Speculum Regale we can read the same thing.[10] And in Historia Norwegiæ from the 1200s we are told:[11]

«This land [Greenland] was found and settled by the Icelanders, and built on the Catholic faith. It represents the end of Europe to the west. And the land almost touches "the African Islands", where the backflowing ocean enters.»

Fridtjof Nansen felt that the name «Africanae Insulae» was used instead of Vinland.[12]

The wealth of European literature about the old world view in essence implies that no ships should venture south of 27–28 degrees. If they did, they would be sucked by the ocean current out over the edge of the world and would never return from the darkness, the fog and the horrible maelstroms.

The Greek Christian, Ptolemy, had argued against this view a thousand years earlier and had given a convincing description of a round earth in his great work, Almagest, though it was probably unknown in Scandinavia. When paganism was replaced by Christianity, the ancient and primitive world view gained support from the holy man Lactantius, «the Christian Cicero», who once and for all proclaimed:

«Could anyone be so foolish as to believe that there are antipodes that stand feet to feet with us—men who walk with their legs up and their heads hanging down? That there could be a place on earth where things have been turned upside down: Where trees grow backwards, and rain and snow fall upward? The heretic view that the world is round, is the reason for the fable about antipodes whose feet are higher than their heads. Such men in their madness are full of delusions, and deduce one delusion from another.»

On their voyage «eastward north of the coast» between the continents, the young Norwegians were the first to navigate a ship in the Bermuda Triangle, the final resting place for hundreds of sailing ships which later were to break up in the big and heavy seas on the northeast side of the islands. And they were the first to experience the meaning of the name «The Grave of Sailing Ships». They met with bad weather and were tossed so hard against a reef that their keel broke in two.

It is recommended in Spectrum Regale that an ocean going ship should bring the following: At least 200 alen (1 alen = 2 feet) of homespun to make sail repairs. Needles and thread, and ropes to sew into the sails. Iron rivets for riveting, axes to cut ship planks, a special iron for planing, drills and «all other tools needed for ship building».

Bringing the ship on shore for repairs was not an easy matter. The much smaller Gokstad ship weighed between 8 and 10 tons after it was excavated and dried. Torvald's ship must have weighed at least 10–12 tons. When it was finally brought out of the water, it had to be raised before the repairs could be made. The entire keel was removed. A very large tree had to be cut in the forest, and thereafter hewn as a keel and fitted. Even with modern tools it is a big and difficult job that must be done with precision. They probably didn't bring enough tar for caulking, so we must assume that they also had to burn tar. The saga states that they stayed for quite a while after the shipwreck. They probably spent most of the summer there.

During the long stay—around the evening camp fires in the balmy darkness—they also had time for reflection. This island kingdom, without game, was no place to live. We get a sense of their loneliness when we read the stories. There was no question of colonizing. The provisions diminished as the weeks passed, and there were no rivers where they could catch fish as they were accustomed to doing. When they had the keel fitted, they decided to turn back. They returned to the mainland.

But even if the voyage ended badly, Torvald had still found a land of «his own» in the new world. Leiv had his houses up in Vinland, and

Torvald wanted to build a place of his own, or «sin heim» (his home), to use the saga phrase.

They now sailed along the east coast («austr firir landit»), and explored the inlets of several large bays. But they found them poorly suited for settling. This is understandable—the first European botanists to come here, described the area in this way:

«Large coastal areas were swamps and tidal basins, with gloomy and dark muddy water under large cypresses and marsh vegetation. Here and there were vast swamps, with groups of trees and small islands. The large oak trees were draped with hanging mosses. From the depths of this jungle came a cacophony of strange birds—one of them the screech of the trumpeter swan.»[13]

At long last they found a bay they liked. It must have had a fine harbor, because all they had to do was put down the gangplank and go ashore.

«This is a beautiful place,» said Torvald. «This is where I'll build my house.»

The whole crew came along when Torvald chose his building site. Norse farmers were always particular about building their farms on hills where they could keep an eye on the shore, to avoid being suprised by possible enemies coming by water. They also had a deep appreciation for the free and panoramic view from up high—as evidenced by Gunnar of Lidarende's eloquent praise of «de fagre lier» (the fair hillsides).[14]

All we are told about Torvald's settlement site in America is that it was on a wooded headland—probably a steep pine forested slope by the fjord, since the water was so deep they could sail right up to land with their ship.

After this they went on board again, says the saga. And then they discovered something peculiar. On the other side of the headland they saw «lumps» in the sand. Further text in the saga gives reason to believe that what they saw was on the other side of an inlet, because they left the headland in order to investigate what these strange things might be. They apparently proceeded with caution, and surrounded the area. When they came closer, they saw that it was three small boats. And under each boat three men were hiding.

This is the first historical report of a meeting between Native Americans and white men, and the meeting was brief and violent. Eight natives were taken prisoner, while the ninth managed to escape in his boat.

Indians living in southeastern North America had strict rules of con-

25

duct when taken prisoner. They were to behave with haughtiness and under no circumstances show humility in front of an enemy. They were expected to act with contempt till their last dying breath.[15]

The encounter ended in tragedy. The eight natives were killed. After the killings the Greenlanders went back to their homestead and conducted a closer investigation of the surrounding region. Further into the bay they discovered some mounds that they believed were made by men. They must have observed these buildings from afar. In order to be able to identify the mounds as huts, they would have had to be no more than a few hundred meters away. Initially the Greenlanders made no attempt to approach the mounds. They were tired, the saga reports, and decided to take a rest in the warm forest. They all lay down and fell asleep.

Their guess was right—the mounds indeed meant that there was a dwelling place deeper into the bay. Ethnographers and archaeologists have confirmed that the people who lived there, were the only ones along the entire American coast to construct mound houses.[16] It was a greatly reduced branch of the great mound culture that existed in the distant past along the Mississippi and the Ohio—where more than twelve thousand such mounds have been identified. Of the one million Indians believed to have lived in North America around the year 1000, it was only the tribes in the southeast that were devoted to battle and warfare. They could safely do so because they were farmers as well, and secured a fairly stable existence—even though there were no livestock or work animals at that time on the American continent. The Spanish explorer de Soto was another who observed the immense dirt mounds in their camps.[17]

In the 1960s and 70s I personally made a systematic investigation in an effort to identify the location where the Vinlandfarers could have experienced such a sight.[18] The mound culture was present in a very limited coastal region, and thanks to very thorough archaeological cataloging in the United States, it is possible to determine that the group of mounds to which the saga refers was located in Savannah Bay in Georgia.[19]

The following may have occurred:

As soon as they passed the place where Fort Jackson is now located, they came to a dry and wooded area—which became more and more attractive the further inland they sailed. The course of the river has changed somewhat over time, but then there were headlands, with a nice view of the bay and the surrounding territory.

They could not have chosen a more dangerous place on the entire American east coast. At the head of the bay was the village of Deptford,

26

The large mounds that Torvald Eiriksson's expedition came across, were only found along a 150 kilometer stretch of the Georgia coast. Here all large and small mounds are noted on Henry Clay Shetrone's map. The northernmost visible mounds were found near present day Savannah.

and to the south the village of Oemler on Wilmington Island. The Cedar Grove mounds, associated with a third Indian village, were not far away. On the hill where downtown Savannah is now located, was the village Haven Home around the legendary burial mound «The Indian Kings' Tomb». It was leveled in the 1930s, after excavations had uncovered 44 prominent Indian persons—all cremated. That this was a lively region can be presumed from the reports of roads found leading to the burial mounds.[20] On a map from 1740 the entire area along the south side of the bay is called «Indian Land», and immigrants from Salzburg in Austria had become their neighbors.[21]

The most important center was the mound complex «Irene» on a large island flanked on each side by outlets from Pipemaker's Creek in Savannah Bay, about 3 miles from downtown Savannah. They were the only mounds found that were located by the bay.

The archaeologist Clarence B. Moore, who first mapped the mounds, reports that one of the seven mounds was the largest platform mound ever found along the Atlantic Ocean.[22] It is reported to have been 16 to 20 feet high and 120 feet long when it was first reported. It is possible that each new generation continued the building from where the last one had left off.

Professor Joseph R. Caldwell concludes that this was the ceremonial center of a large region, where all the seven mounds in the complex originally had buildings and palisades on top.[23] Clear evidence of palisades has been found, indicating that the center had monumental form and must have been visible from a great distance upon entering the bay.

Dr. Antonio Waring's many years of excavations brought out a number of items that may have been used for bartering—knives, fishing implements, sinkers for fishing nets, etc. The calm currents carried good materials for making pottery, which was extensively produced in the area. Dr. Waring also feels that it must have been a trade and bartering center for a sizeable inland region.

And where there were mounds, there were also organized societies. Lacking work animals, the building materials had to be carried to the mounds in baskets. The construction of one of the mounds, at Ocmoulgee National Monument near Macon, Georgia, is estimated to have required over one million baskets of dirt. It is the same size as the largest of the Savannah mounds.

When attacks were mounted by the mound people, or when they were defending their tribe, a young chief would step in to take the place of the regular chief. Before they attacked, they would always conduct a characteristic ecstatic ritual on the village ceremonial ground. The chief would perform a war dance, expressing the fighting spirit in movement and cries. Finally all the men would join in a rocking, hopping circle dance.[24] There are also suggestions that the southeast Indians increased their thirst for battle with a drink that made them agitated, much like the Norse «berserkers» used dried toadstools to work themselves into such a blind rage that the wildest and most uncontrolled began chewing on their shields.

When the news of the foreign intruders spread among the Indians, the whole bay area no doubt began to mobilize.

In the first phase of an attack it was common for the Indians to proceed quietly, and to yell at the top of their lungs when the attack got under way.

This is how Torvald and his men experienced it:

There was a cry so shrill that they all woke up, and they interpreted the cry in this way—«Wake up Torvald, and all your men, if you value your life. Return to the ship with your men, and head out of the fjord as fast as you can.» They ran to the ship. When they got on board they saw «countless small boats» approaching from the bay.

«We must raise our shields along the side of the ship and defend ourselves as best we can,» said Torvald. «But we won't go on the offensive.»

Against such an onslaught it would make no sense for 31 men to counter attack. Besides, the Norsemen were not warriors, just second generation colonists. Bloody feuds were common in those days, but that meant fighting against a small band of men—never against a swarm of well-prepared warriors. The sagas also tend to omit the fact that feuds were fought by slaves, who were forced to maltreat, torture, blind, castrate and otherwise mutilate family enemies. The treatment of the last heathen king of Hedmark, Rörek, is a typical example. When Eirik Raude trashed the farm Valtjov on Iceland, it was his slaves who were ordered to do the destruction.

The men stood on board their ships defending themselves with shields against the shower of incoming arrows. Nothing more happened. And suddenly the Indians ceased their firing, turned around, and disappeared in a way that the Greenlanders interpreted as flight.

When the attack was over, Torvald asked if anyone was wounded. Everyone had escaped without injury.

«I have a wound under my arm,» said Torvald. «An arrow entered between my shield and the gunwale and went into my arm. Here it is—I'm going to die. Get ready, and leave this place as soon as you can. You can take me to the headland where I planned to build my home. Maybe I spoke the truth earlier when I said I would be here for a while. Bury me there, and place one cross at my feet and one at my head. And from now on you must call the land <u>Korsneset</u> («Cross Ness»).»

Torvald simply stated what everyone realized but was unwilling to say. They were too far from Leiv's homestead to take his body there for burial. In the heat of the south they could not keep a body for many days before it would begin to rot and make life unbearable for the men on board. It would have been different had they been sailing in cooler northern waters. The way things stood, there was no other solution than to bury him in the distant land.

And there Torvald was put to rest. The Indians did not reappear, but there was no telling what they might have in mind once they had a chance to restock their quivers.

The strict rules in the land beneath the Polar Star required that a chieftain of Torvald's stature—the son of Eirik Raude—must be given a real and visible grave. The final journey was very important in the transitional period between the old and the new faith.

After the events as reconstructed above, and Torvald's subsequent death struggle, it would seem natural that they would have stayed the night. The body would have to be carried to the headland once life had ebbed away, and the night comes early so far south. A rushed burial of a chieftain would be out of character with what we otherwise know of Viking culture.

At this point I believe the original saga was probably more detailed than the version with which we are familiar, and which says nothing about who became chieftain when Torvald died. This was vital information in earlier times.

Could these events have taken place farther north?

Some very small mounds have been found on Little Island across the border in South Carolina, about 30 miles north of Savannah. But archaeologists conclude that they are from a later era.

Farther north than that, mounds have never existed along the Atlantic Ocean.[25] Thorough and accepted scientific studies of American Indian tribes have concluded that such an organized and massive attack by

Indians could not have taken place north of the Carolinas in the year 1000.[26]

Unfortunately, none of the seven mounds have been preserved. Much of the soil was used as ballast when the colonists blocked the eastern outlet of Pipemaker's Creek. In the 1700s a governor built a private family crypt into the side of one of the largest mounds, and from the other mounds earth has been taken for centuries to create the harbor and for other building projects. When a military unit was camped in Savannah during the last world war, the last and largest of the mounds was leveled and forgotten. With the help of Ivar Lövald, president of Wilhelm Wilhelmsen Shipping, and the Savannah Port Authority, I was still able to identify the site when I visited. Today Garden Spot Truck Terminals No. 20–21 are located where the mounds once stood.

Torvald's traveling companions continued on their way to Leiv's house. The shipwreck that summer had been a serious reminder to stay away from land if they wished to get home safely. It's not hard to understand that under the circumstances they made no attempt to chart the coast line of the Carolinas. In Leiv's camp they were able to stay for the grape season, and cut timber and dry it before heading home the following summer. No other types of food, such as corn for instance, are mentioned. A cargo of dried grapes would be more than welcome among the fish and meat eating Greenlanders, where vitamin C deficiency and scurvy were serious threats.

The Scandinavian seafarers were the best the western world had seen since the time of the Phoenicians, according to the oceanographer Rachel Carson. With unfailing precision they made their way through waters that were ravaged by storms, fog, darkness and ice.[27] Their accurate distance table, Rim, and the «sun stone» have already been mentioned. In Historia Norwegiæ we learn that Ingolf and Hjoleiv came to Iceland by «testing the ocean with weights»—in other words, sounding the depth. This glimpse into their methods shows how meticulous they must have been in their navigation. In the 1300s, when cartographers entered the picture, they found that precise positions were available—including both length and width—of the lands the Vinlandfarers had seen in America. This would lead us to suspect that they were familiar with the main elements of trigonometry, or triangulation.

However, when Norwegian scientists in the last century began to reconstruct our history after 450 years of occupation and an in absentia government, we had become the most historically source-less country in

Europe. The Vinland voyages were very low on the list of research priorities, and the saga about Torvald at the very bottom. Apart from a few specialists, neither Norwegian nor American archaeologists had yet heard of any native culture that built mounds visible from the Atlantic Ocean. For this reason alone, the account was practically unintelligible. No maps confirmed Torvald's visit south of Virginia. Had such a map been found, it would have shown some of the Bahama islands and the coast of Florida and Georgia. But it simply did not exist.

It was also assumed that our forebears could not have traveled in waters that seemed so infinitely far away—even though the distance from Leiv's camp site to San Augustine in Florida is no farther than from Stavanger to Lofoten in Norway. And the voyage was shorter than the journeys they made from the Eastern Settlement on Greenland to the northernmost hunting grounds at around 73–76°N, where the Greenlanders sailed every summer. Off the coast of Greenland they had problems with both ice and wind, and had a far shorter summer than the one Torvald experienced in the warmer land to the south.

Nor did anyone know that Torvald's journey had long since been duplicated. In the summer of 1588 the Spanish captain Vincente Gonzales sailed from San Augustine in Florida up the coast to Chesapeake Bay. He went as far as the Susquehanna River—and returned to Florida six weeks after setting out.[28]

If we leap ahead to our own century, heavily loaded fishing sloops sailed every summer from North Norway to Bergen and back. They went south in the late summmer with their cargo of dried fish, and never had problems returning home in the course of the fall.

Professor A.W. Brögger, the foremost Norwegian expert on the seafarers' lives and journeys, warned the overly critical sceptics. In 1937 he wrote, in his book Vinlandsferdene («The Vinland Voyages»):

«The critical researchers, who choose to be on the safe side, are afraid to place Vinland too far to the south. They seem to think it best to err on the side of caution and place it as far north as possible. Such «caution» only masks inability to comprehend. It is unmethodical and illogical, seen against the background of Viking society. Once the young seafarers had found their way to America, no southern limit stopped them. There is no reason in the world why they should not have reached both Virginia and Carolina, and gone even further south.»

He couldn't have been much closer to the truth.

The Failed Funeral Voyage

The brother of Leiv and Torvald Eiriksson—Eirik's middle son—planned to make the long journey to bring Torvald's earthly remains home. He was obviously prepared for battle against Indians, since he chose 20 of the scrappiest men he could find. His young wife Gudrid also went along, but we don't know whether she did so voluntarily. As soon as they were clear of Greenland, their difficulties began. They were caught in a storm, and as usual had to steer away from it. They were followed by more bad weather that blew them off course in the Atlantic.

In the late summer it became apparent to them that they would not be able to make the voyage, and on October 20 they managed to reach the northernmost of the two Greenland communities, The Western Settlement, 625 miles north of the southern tip of the island. Torstein owned one half of a farm there. The other half was owned by Torstein Svarte, who had not yet converted to Christianity.

By this time the travelers were battered and exhausted, and the saga gives a grim description of a disease that attacked the ship's crew and took many lives in the polar gloom. The description seems to point to scurvy. Later in the winter Torstein Svarte's wife, Grimhild, and Torstein Eiriksson both became ill and bedridden. First Grimhild died, or feigned death. While her husband was gone to find a burial shroud, she came back to life, sat up in bed and reached for her shoes. A rather unclear description in The Saga of Eirik Raude seems to imply that Torstein Svarte used an axe to put an end to her and the horror when he came back to the house. It seems a love triangle was in progress in the middle of the misery.

Torstein Eiriksson «died» shortly thereafter, but nobody seemed to notice. Gudrid sat on a stool by his bed. Torstein Svarte then took her in his arms and led her to a bench across the room from her husband's «body». He promised to go with her to Eiriksfjord and to take the dead crew back to be buried there. He furthermore promised her several servants to cheer her up. It seems this was a proposal, and that Gudrid was fond of him.

At this point Torvald Eiriksson sat up in bed and screamed, «Where is Gudrid?» Three times he screamed, and Gudrid quietly asked Torstein Svarte if she should answer, but he advised her against it. Instead he sat down on the stool by the bed with Gudrid in his lap and asked what Torstein Eiriksson wanted of his wife.

At first the «dead» man was silent. But then he livened up again, and used the last minutes of his life to ruin the romance in progress. He warned Gudrid about marrying a Greenlander, because he knew she was destined to marry an Icelander. She and the Icelander would have a long life together and have a large family of strong, fair, good, healthy and lucky men. When she got old she would travel to Rome and after her return home she would live out her life as a nun.

When Torstein's coffin and the dead sailors were taken home to the family grave at Brattalid the next spring, only Leiv remained of Eirik's sons. His position as the highest leader of Greenland required that he remain at home.

At Brattalid on Greenland the Danish archaeologist Knud J. Krogh has examined a grave containing the bones of 13 humans, buried after the flesh had rotted from their bones. Their average height was 1.77 meters, or 4 centimeters taller than the average height of people buried in Greenland graves. We are told that Torstein chose especially strong and big men. Were these the men Krogh found?

Torstein Svarte sold all he owned and went south with Gudrid. He lived in Eiriksfjord the rest of his life, alone but well respected. He was never able to marry Gudrid—Leiv said no.

Other attempts to find Torvald Eiriksson's grave in the distant land were never made, even though the exact location was known by the Greenlanders.

1. Vinbladet, no.3, 1989.
2. The story about Torfinn Karlsevne's journey is an addition to the Flateyarbok's Vinland saga, but the sequence of events comes from another, unknown saga.
3. Gathorne-Hardy, 1921, p. 241.
4. The diary from Columbus' second voyage. See Jane, 1930.
5. Nansen, 1911, p. 459.
6. Driver, 1961.
7. Grimberg, vol. II, 1957, p. 103.
8. Grönlands Historiske Minnesmerker, volume III, p. 218.
9. Ibid, page 222.
10. Kongespeilet (Speculum Regale) is an Old Norse textbook for young men. The edition dating from about 1200 is based on a much older, unknown source. It addresses morals, behavior, astronomy, geography, sailing directions, etc.

11. Historia Norwegiæ is a brief Latin description of Norway from the end of the 1100s or the early 1200s. The oldest known copy (from about 1450) was found in Scotland in 1849.
12. Nansen, 1911, p. 291. See also Björnbo, 1909, p. 229, and Storm, 1890.
13. Summary from Lowery, 1911, volume I.
14. From Njál's Saga.
15. La Farge, 1956.
16. Caldwell, 1952.
17. Hodge and Lewis, 1907.
18. Prytz, 1975, pp. 40–46.
19. Waring, 1972. Paper no. 7 describes this group of burial mounds. See archaeological map of Savannah Bay, page 153.
20. Waring, 1972, paper no. 7.
21. From Ausfürliche Nachricht von den Salzburgischen Emigranten..., Viertes Stück (1740).
22. In 1897 and 1898 the archaeologist C.B. Moore published thorough descriptions of all the mounds along the coast of Georgia. See summary in Caldwell, 1952.
23. Caldwell, 1952.
24. Tunis, 1953.
25. Caldwell, 1952, p. 317.
26. The perimeters are drawn on a wellknown map by Norman McOuwn, University of Chicago, after an original by George L. Trager, University of Buffalo. See reduced copy in Encyclopædia Britannica, under «Indians.»
27. Carson, 1952, p. 179.
28. Lowery, 1911.

COLONIZING AMERICA

[Note: <u>The Vinland Saga</u>, as so many sagas in <u>Flateyarbok</u>, is an abbreviated version. <u>Eirik Raude's Saga</u> and <u>Hauk's Book</u> both have a more detailed description of the voyage. The following incorporates details from all three sources.]

Leiv decided that Gudrid should marry a rich and much traveled merchant from Iceland, Torfinn Karlsevne, who had become a welcome guest in the Raude family because of his generosity. They lived at Brattalid during the winter following their wedding. A lot of time was spent talking about the warm and fertile «grape land», and it was decided that they would colonize America. Torfinn Karlsevne became the leader of an expedition of 160 people, half of them Icelanders and half Greenlanders. Eirik Raude's daughter Fröydis and her husband Torvard were among them.

On a summer day three ships headed out of the fjord from Brattalid with their shore boats in tow. The hillsides were covered with flowers and buzzing insects.

They followed the strong Greenland Current nearly 400 miles up the desolate and windblown coast, to the northernmost Western Settlement.

Thanks to the light northern nights and temperatures around 5–6° Celsius, they could sail around the clock. When the sun disappeared below the northern horizon for a while, the metallic reflection of the sky lit the ocean. Puzzled seals stretched their necks. Far out to sea the whales blew. And between the ice floes the summer's crop of new birds swam. In the Western Settlement they took on board several more settlers before they continued on to the Greenland Current, which makes a turn into the Davis Strait. The distance over to Baffin Island is about 250 miles, but they had not yet reached that point when they entered a new and strong current, the Labrador Current, which flows in a southerly direction. It was just as cold and if possible even more ice-filled than the current near Greenland. They had to stay clear of enormous icebergs, only a fraction of which were visible above the water line; they were very dangerous because they could create near tidal waves when they split. The smaller blocks of ice probably were not that problematic. The ships had side rudders that enabled them to make sudden turns and sail with precision.

The saga says they had a good wind blowing from the north. But the coast off Labrador is a difficult course to sail, with shallows and reefs that made it necessary for them to stay many miles off the coast. The nights became darker as they sailed south. It seems they took the time to go ashore along the way, because we are told that they saw many animals, arctic foxes among them. They used the name Helluland («Stone Land») for Labrador.

Past the southern tip of Labrador they changed course from south to southwest. To their southeast they passed an island, Newfoundland, that they called Bear Island, because they saw a bear there. They continued southwest for two «dögr», and this information would indicate that they sighted the south coast of the Gulf of St. Lawrence. Bjarne Herjulfsson had estimated the distance there from Nova Scotia to be two and one half «dögr».

Unfortunately the saga tells us nothing about their stops along the way. The animals obviously had to graze, and 160 people needed food and drink. A combination of hunting and fishing was undoubtedly necessary en route.

When they finally set out to sea again, they were able to verify Bjarne's and Leiv's information that it took two «dögr» to cross the Gulf of Maine to the northern coast of Vinland. They apparently stayed a bit to the right to make sure they didn't sail past Cape Cod, but found themselves instead on the coast of the Gulf of Maine. When they discovered their mistake they at once began to tack back. They had landed on the starboard side, says the saga. It was a desolate country with no harbors, and they advanced slowly on a southwesterly wind. Every time they came about, they were met with the same sight—sandy beach after sandy beach. They named them Furdustrendene («The Endless Shores»). They obviously kept way off the coast.

The saga tells us that they eventually came to a headland where they found a ship's keel. Nansen concludes that this is a misunderstanding on the part of the saga scribes.[1] The many references to places called «Kjölnes» (the Vinland sagas have several) means that the land is formed like a keel. What they were searching for was Cape Cod, which looked very much like the keel of a long boat, and which extended 38 miles into the Gulf of Maine. Today we can see the striking keel-shape both from maps and from airplanes. Not to mention when driving in an automobile in this now so popular vacation spot.

They were approaching the goal of their journey: Leiv's homestead.

The voyage was no doubt beginning to wear them out. It was crowded on board, with hungry animals that mooed and bleated for food, and with all the equipment brought along for the first stage of colonization. The coast had several small inlets—not bays—and they sailed into one of them to let the men and animals gather strength after the long sail.

Torfinn had borrowed the Irish slave couple that King Olav Trygvasson had given to Leiv Eiriksson. The purpose was quite devilish. The Irish were told to head inland, to run as fast as they could for three days, and to come back to give a report of what they had seen. The Vikings had designed an ingenious way to make sure they did as they were told. They were given no clothes, just a hooded, sleeveless garment open on both sides, fastened with a button between the legs. What this meant was that they would freeze unless they kept running. The garment was so cleverly designed that there was no way to modify it to make it feel warmer. This gives us a less than flattering view of conditions for the slaves of the Norsemen. Two youths are left in the wilderness to fend for themselves as best they can. Not a single word is wasted in the saga on any compassion for them.

The two came back and reported that the land looked fertile and promising. The expedition now advanced further, until the bay they were seeking finally came into view. This is where Leiv's houses stood. The Vinland saga reports that Torvald borrowed Leiv's house, and later repeats that the expedition entered the bay where Leiv had his houses.

Leiv Eiriksson had run aground when he headed straight west past the headland that protruded from the southern mouth of the bay. The heavily loaded immigrant ships had therefore been warned against repeating this maneuver. They chose to go in by an island that lay in the middle of the inlet. But here another problem arose. There was such a strong current on both sides of the island that they had difficulty maneuvering. All the American bays seemed to be sandy and had unpredictable channels running crosswise. The saga says nothing about what they did to control their ships, but most likely all the men had to take to the oars to

38

bring them safely through. All long ships had a ship's chest/seat for each of the crew at every oarlock. The texts seem to suggest that they tried both sides of the island with disappointing results. But they all ended up on shore, without losses.

On the island they passed, there were so many birds that the following spring they were barely able to take a step without crushing an egg. They called it Fugleöya («Bird Island»). The Greenlanders named the bay Straumfjord («Current Fjord») because of the strong current that made sailing it so difficult.

Leiv's huts lay further up the river. And again we are amazed at how 160 men and women could head straight there and find all the food they needed. The saga mentions briefly that they lived by hunting and fishing, emphasizing the latter. They benefited from cow's milk, because the grazing was plentiful. But with an average of 53 immigrants on each ship, they were overloaded even before taking on board the livestock and the fodder they needed. It is unlikely that they could have had more than ten cows on each ship. Sheep, goats and slaves also needed to be accommodated. And the cows probably didn't produce much after the long sea voyage.

The climate was just as Leiv had described. The nice, warm autumn, so typical of this part of America, made them optimistic and perhaps a little too sanguine. They made no preparations for the winter, something that would otherwise be unthinkable for a northerner.

They made a grievous mistake. During the winter they were hit by one of the cold spells that are also typical of the northeastern part of America, where no high mountains block the polar air when it heads south, accompanied by heavy snow. The river probably filled with icy slush. No game moved in the snowy forests, and food became scarce. Most dangerous of all was the fact that the snow prevented the animals from grazing, for without livestock their plans to colonize were doomed. In a mad rush they headed for the island they had seen when they arrived. The climate was milder there, apparently without snow, because the animals did well, we are told. They had hoped to catch birds or animals or hunt marine mammals, but had to subsist on fishing instead. They suffered, even if no one starved to death.

A Contest Between Whitechrist and Thor

The relationship between the expedition members was not good. In addition to everything else, they also had to deal with religious differences. One of the leaders, Torhall Veidemann, kept to the old faith. But the majority was Christian, and gathered in prayer to ask God to help them find food. When their «prayers were not answered as quickly as they would have liked», as the saga puts it, Torhall headed into the woods in an attempt to make contact with the pagan god, Thor.

Torhall was not well liked by most of the colonists, particularly by the leaders. He blatantly disregarded accepted customs and codes of behavior, enjoyed picking quarrels and never pulled any punches when speaking his mind. He didn't usually live in the Greenland settlements, but spent most of his time in the hunting grounds of the desolate north. Since he owned his own ship he must have hunted and traded on a grand scale.

Greenland's discoverer, Eirik Raude, was an admirer of the rough and daring Torhall. The two of them did not give in when the Greenlanders accepted Christianity, and both died in the old pagan faith. The similarity between them is obvious, except that Eirik was an extrovert and Torhall didn't speak very often and had a formidable appearance.

When Torhall did not return from the forest, a search party was sent out to look for him. On the third day he was found in religious ecstasy on a rocky ledge. His mouth was wide open, his nostrils flaring. He was rolling around on the ground staring at Thor's sky while he scratched and pinched himself and spoke in tongues. This is one of the very few descriptions we have of Norse ecstatic worship. What the search party saw, was a hedonistic profession of faith. When they brought him out of his ecstasy he was furious. He demanded they stay out of whatever he was doing—it was none of their business.

Shortly afterwards a whale beached itself on the island. None of them had seen that kind of whale before. They cut it up, and the meat was cooked. But it made them all sick.

Then Torhall Veidemann told them that he had prayed to Thor to help them with food, and that he took the beached whale as a sign that his god had granted his prayer, while their White-Christ hadn't done a thing!

This created great commotion among the settlers. The rest of the whale was tossed into the sea, and they prayed to God to forgive them the sin Torhall had led them to commit.

Shortly afterward they were able to catch all the food they needed in the sea. Something similar was experienced much later by the English colonists. In April enormous schools of herring would come up the New England coast, so thick that they could practically scoop them out of the water.[2] When spring came they moved upriver once more, where the fishing continued as before. There was plenty of game in the forest, and out on Bird Island they could pick eggs when the migrating birds returned. We are also told that they varied their diet by rowing out to sea to fish—probably at the same time they were gathering eggs.

An event took place that summer that was a special moment in American history—Karlsevne's wife, Gudrid, bore a son, Snorre, the first «white American».

But the leaders were unable to agree on where they should settle permanently. They couldn't occupy the land that Leiv owned. Some years back they had all colonized Greenland by each claiming their own fjord. Torhall Veidemann and nine others decided to go east beyond the keel-shaped cape, and look for good land in that direction. Karlsevne was inclined to go south, since he felt the land would get wider as they traveled south. Fridtjof Nansen writes that they based their belief that the coast continued in an eastern direction on the Icelandic geographical world description—that Vinland was connected to Africa.[3] They agreed to go looking in both directions. While Torhall was carrying drinking water on board his ship, he recited a lay he had composed, reminding everyone how he had been promised the most delicious wine before they left Greenland. But all he'd had so far was cold water.

Nine men were not enough to maneuver the ship through the swift currents at the mouth of the bay. The saga describes how the others went with them and helped them get safely out of «the sound». The endlessly shifting shoals, dunes and channels in the middle of tidal currents made it difficult to know what to expect. On the day of departure, when Torfinn Karlsevne and the others helped maneuver his boat through the sound, Torhall added another verse to his lay just as he hoisted the sail after their efforts. He announced that he was now headed home, while the high and mighty chiefs were welcome to stay on the sandy beach and eat all the whalemeat they pleased!

The main expedition continued south, apparently after spending two weeks in a place they called Hop—an inlet by the mouth of a river—where they found nothing extraordinary. The saga narrative makes it seem as if all the colonists came along. As usual, The Vinland Saga gives no indication of distances sailed. We are only told that they sailed «for a long time», but not whether they sailed far.

They headed into an inlet toward the mouth of a river. But the sandy bank by the river could only be crossed at high tide, so they had to wait for a while. And now, for the first time, we are told the reason why it was so important for them to head upriver as quickly as possible. They had to find the highwater point where schools of fish turned, swimming back and forth between fresh and salt water. At that point, where a tributary met the main river, is where they always found the best fishing.

In this case, being in a new place, they were in a great hurry to catch fresh fish for the 150 remaining colonists, and for slaves and servants. As a quick solution they dug hollows in the sand where the fish would be trapped when the tide went out again. Then they could catch the fish in the pools with spears until the next tide came in with a new supply of fish in a few hours. The saga says that all the creeks were teeming with fish. What we would have liked to know, is how they constructed their permanent fishing traps.

«Fishing pools» in the sand sometimes occur naturally, and are a phenomenon especially noted in Acadia National Park in the Gulf of Maine.

All the sagas agree that they found wild wheat growing in the fields, and wine grapes on the hillsides. They immediately set about building permanent housing. Some located their houses on the banks of the calm river, some farther away. In other words, a community of 150 free adult men and women. They were in no hurry to work the fields, for in addition to all the fish, there was plenty of game in the forest.

One of the purposes of this colonization seems to have been to export lumber to Greenland, because the saga says that Torfinn ordered them to begin felling trees and that the timber was to be hewn and dried— presumably with shipping it in mind.

Skirmishes With Indians

Soon after they had arrived at their new site, they had a peculiar experience. Nine small boats appeared, carrying strange, dark men with tangled hair. While sitting in their boats, they waved sticks at the colonists, perhaps in an attempt at greeting before coming ashore. They walked around and looked with curiosity at the colonists, before disappearing to the south in their boats.

The winter in Vinland turned out as Leiv had told them it would—fair and mild, and without snow. Normally one has to go far down America's east coast to find such a climate. But along the coasts of New England the winters are often mild, and snowless.

Early one morning in the beginning of spring the Indians reappeared. They were apparently the same Indians. One saga says they came in boats, another that they came walking out of the forest. Karlsevne and his people seem to have been a little wary, because they took out their shields to be on the safe side. But things stayed peaceful this time also.

According to all known Norse laws and customs, no guest was to leave without being served a meal. As late as 1433, the Italian sea captain Querini and his crew traveled across Norway-Sweden from Trondheim to Öresund and were given free room and board everywhere.[4] And when the flock of Indians appeared at Karlsevne's door, the same rule applied, even if the guests in this case were only «skrælings». The women carried out «budrått»—meaning milk, cheese and butter. The Indians had no experience with livestock, and they took a fancy to the unfamiliar food. They soon returned to barter with furs and pelts, and were particularly interested in red cloth. Some tried to trade for swords and spears, but this was forbidden by Karlsevne.

To begin with the natives were given a piece of cloth 9 inches wide in exchange for a black pelt. But after a while the supply of red cloth became low, and they had to cut a narrower swatch to keep the trade going. This made the Indians even more eager. For a piece of cloth as narrow as a finger they bid more than the one pelt which had been the going rate to begin with. The long strips of cloth they tied around their heads as decoration.

The Greenlanders had no need for, or interest in the pelts for their own use. But they were goods that would fetch a fine price in Europe.

While the trade was going on, Karlsevne's ox came charging from the forest «with an ominous roar», probably a mad animal. It gave the natives a terrible fright. They ran for their boats and paddled off as fast as they could.

In the imagery of eastern Indian tribes, fabled animals were a prominent element. A number of scientists confirm that the sight of unfamiliar animals could cause the Indians to become paralyzed with fear.

In 1493 Columbus witnessed a group of Indians on Haiti go nearly crazy when they saw five Spanish horses. This fear of animals was soon exploited, and the results exceeded even their boldest expectations. The Spaniards brought bloodhounds across the ocean, which were far more efficient than soldiers in the battle against Indians, whose resistance collapsed when the dogs were let loose. And the Indians—who easily could have killed the dogs—let themselves be ripped to shreds by the scores. To hunt Indians with dogs actually developed into a sport. Champions, like the notorious «Berserrico», sired a line of dogs that were renowned for being particularly adept at tracking Indians, and for spreading insane terror with their murderous sprees. It is part of this horrendous chapter in American history that the dogs actually ate their victims, and drank their blood.

It would be tempting to present more such anecdotes, but let us return to our settlers.

The Vinland Saga version of this story gives the impression that the Indians did not paddle away immediately, but that they headed to Karlsevne's farm where they wanted to be let into the houses. Karlsevne ordered his men to keep them out.

The time of neighborly coexistence was over. Karlsevne took no chances and built a fence—a palisade made of logs—around the farm. The Indians were fully aware of the purpose of the fortifications but were still hungry to trade—they were «kaupföre», as the saga says. When they returned the next time, they threw their bows over the fence to signal their peaceful intentions. Gudrid was sitting in the doorway with little Snorre when a young Indian woman came over and sat down next to her, trying to repeat what Gudrid was saying. Even so, it ended badly. An Indian tried to take, or perhaps just touch, the weapon of one of the Greenlanders. He was immediately killed. The others then threw down their cloth and bartering goods and disappeared.

The Indians stayed away for a while. One saga says for three weeks. The Norsemen made preparations for a fight.

They were right. The Indians struck the settlement early one morning. The boats carrying the attackers came «as thick as a fast current toward land». The Indians were hollering and screaming, waving sticks «at the sun».

When they came ashore, both sides shot with bows and arrows. The attackers also had what the saga calls «valslynger»*. They hoisted a ball the size of a sheep's belly up a pole, and catapulted it into the field of battle. It made a terrible noise when it fell, and Karlsevne and his men were sufficiently chastened to withdraw further upriver. They also reported that they had been attacked from land.

The Englishman William Wood, whose acquaintance we will soon make, was on very good terms with the Indians in New England in 1630–33. He writes that their «Toma-hauks» were poles two and a half feet high, with a round object the size of a soccer ball at one end. He does not specify any measurements.

44

*A primitive type of buzz bomb, probably made from a blown-up moose bladder.

The Indians became curious when they found an iron axe next to one of the fallen settlers. One by one they tried it. First they used it on some trees, and were visibly impressed. Then one of them tried it on a rock, and the blade broke. They lost interest in the axe and tossed it aside.

One of the more robust women in this community of settlers, Eirik Raude's daughter Fröydis, became both frightened and angry when she saw the Norsemen beginning to yield. She raged at them for being frightened of the natives. But no one listened. Fröydis therefore set after the fighters, who had retreated to a steep hill in the forest. On the way she found Torbrand Snorresson lying dead, with a stone axe in his head. She picked up his sword, but suddenly found herself surrounded by Indians. Swiftly she drew a breast from her dress, and pretended to sharpen the sword on it. The Indians were so taken aback by this incomprehensible gesture that they ceased fighting, ran back to their boats and disappeared.

Even if the settlers later decided that there hadn't been as many fighting Indians as they first thought, they now decided to abandon the colony. The land was as fine as anyone could wish for, but there would be so much fighting with those who were there already that they would live in constant fear and conflict, said Karlsevne in addressing the colonists.

His assessment was correct. They were much too far from home to be able to carry on a war with the Indians. Their source of supply was simply too far away, and at any rate was nothing more than a small society of settlers hanging on to a green strip below the ice and glaciers of Greenland.

Many thorough, but unsuccessful attempts have been made to find the location of Karlsevne's community in Vinland. It is strange that neither Leiv, Torvald or Karlsevne saw any sign of Indians near Leiv's settlement. The group must have been quite small, and confined to the region around «Hop».

On the return trip to Straumfjord in the fall they came across a place where five natives were sleeping, rolled up in furs, with provisions consisting of animal marrow mixed with blood. All five were killed. One of the sagas reports that they suspected the Indians of being spies for the natives they had just fought.

1. Nansen, 1911.
2. Wood, 1634, p. 34.
3. Nansen, 1911.
4. Helland, 1906, volume XVIII.

ENGLISH DOCUMENTS CONFIRM LOCATION OF LEIV EIRIKSSON'S STRAUMFJORD

When they were about to enter Straumfjord again, the settlers apparently decided to find an approach other than the two previous ones which had been fraught with such difficulty. Since both the southern and middle courses had been tried with poor result, they decided to attempt a northern approach. And now they made a strange discovery:

Standing on a headland the ships passed, was a large herd of deer. The ground was a solid crust of droppings because the animals seemed to gather there, the saga reports.

The information about «hjorteneset» («Deer Point») has not been subject to much commentary from researchers and historians. We've had the feeling that it was the place and not the deer that was important. And yet this one detail may solve the centuries old mystery of precisely where the Norse expeditions had their permanent camp in Vinland.

While reading some English documents about the colonization of the Boston area from around 1630, I noticed a description of a similar headland. I therefore began to delve into the ample materials that exist about the English colonization in America. Very soon I had the sense that for 350 years we could have had the answer to where Leiv's camp was located, simply by referring to a book published in England in 1634. I wouldn't dare call it a discovery—it is a coincidence of understandable circumstances. The detailed texts of our Vinland sagas have been fairly unknown, except in Scandinavia and certain Norwegian-American regions in the United States, just as we Norwegians have been unfamiliar with the excellent source material in the book New England's Prospect, published in 1634 by the Englishman William Wood who lived with the Boston colonists during their first three years. His astute observations are of solid journalistic quality, even by modern standards. But most interesting to us is the fact that he describes, point by point, the same details that the sagas report about the fjord where the Vinlandfarers had their headquarters. It is so similar, in fact, that we may marvel that there are several hundred years between the observations, experiences and practices of the Norse and English colonists.

About the peculiar deer point, William Wood writes that it became an important source of help and «refreshment» for the first English colonists who came there in 1630. The point was a narrow promontory, eight kilometers long, that protruded from a peninsula on the north side of the inlet to Boston, directly to the east of present day Logan International Airport. Both the large peninsula and the narrow point extending into the bay provided excellent grazing land for deer, he explains. But the area was menaced by roaming packs of wolves that chased the deer south, where the headland became narrower and narrower. At the very tip there was a sound the width of an «arrow shot» (140–150 meters).[1] Here the deer would swim out to an islet, leaving the wolves stranded on the other side of the «moat». Some days the colonists took as many as sixteen deer on the islet.[2] The peninsula with this islet was quickly given the name «Deer Isle», the name it still carries today. Eirik Raude's Saga says only that the animals would stand there during the night, while another saga version claims that the animals tended to gather there during the winter. Again we turn to Wood:

«The winter is the best time for deer there, because the northern districts of the region become too cold for them. The animals prefer to stay near the sea, so they can swim out to the islet when they are frightened by wolves. It is hard to say how many deer there would be if it weren't for the packs of wolves. Further inland they [the deer] tend to band together in threes, and graze about a mile apart. If the wolves find one, the other two escape.»[3]

No similar phenomenon has ever been described in any other location on the American east coast. Wood adds that the most prevalent animal in New England was the moose, and that only 40 miles north of Boston the moose dominated the terrain, while being almost unknown in the Boston area.

All by itself this piece of information would be insufficient evidence. But the descriptions confirm, piece by piece, the other details the sagas offer about Straumfjorden. For instance the fact that the British did not dare sail in because of the unpredictable tidal currents on both sides of Long Island. It almost certainly meant running aground.

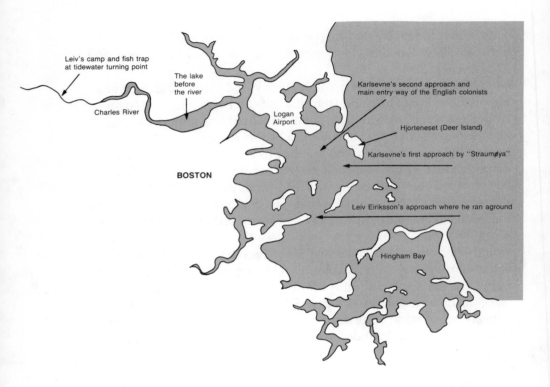

The description of the bay where Leiv Eiriksson built the «Vinland Camp» in America is precisely the same as the one English colonists gave of the Boston area. Leiv ran aground when he tried to sail past a peninsula protruding from the south. Karlsevne's three ships encountered difficulties in the tidal currents when they tried to enter the bay near an island farther out. The next time they sailed in by a headland where they saw a huge herd of deer crowded together. The English colonists were afraid to sail directly into the bay too, and the channel by Deer Island also became their main entry way to Boston.

In Wood's account we even find the answer to why Karlsevne's three ships seem to have had no more problems after they discovered the headland with the deer. All we are told in the saga is that «they were now back in Straumfjord, where they had all they needed».

Wood explains why, and illustrates it with a map: The long and narrow point of land was, as we have been told, broken by a small sound. Whoever saw the headland with the deer, would also see the sound the deer swam across when they fled from the wolves. This channel, in its well protected location, solved the problem of the difficult entry. Wood writes:

48

«The point on the opposite side [from which the animals swam] is called "Pulling Point" because this is the canal the boats usually choose to enter the bay. The tides here are very strong. They are forced to put people ashore to haul the boats through the sound. Hence the name "Pulling Point".»

The name still exists.

By «hauling» it is probably meant that the tidal water was the pulling force, while the men with the ropes made sure the boats did not cut loose and run aground in the narrow channel. To this day this is a dramatic place when the spring tides come in and the northeast wind whips up waves of 12–13 meters.

Vinland and Leiv's campsite are inextricably tied to grapes and the picking of grapes, in all the Norse sagas. The excitement over grapes is no less exhuberant in the English accounts, and the colonists did exactly the same thing that their Norse predecessors had done. They immediately began picking and drying the valuable «corinths»—which they felt were not as good as those available in England, writes Wood.[4] The colonization period yielded a great deal of material about the grapes, which fully supports the Vinlandfarers' excitement over this noble plant. James Dawies, Henry Hudson and Samuel Champlain were all pleased with the abundance of this fruit that was so easily accessible.

From the saga we know that the islands of Straumfjord had a better climate than the mainland. William Wood and, later, Governor William Bradford confirm this. The latter writes:

«The next island [in the inlet] is called Long Island, so named because of its length. Other islands in the bay include «Nodles Island», «Round Island» and «Governor's Garden», where a fruit garden and a grape arbor and many other plants were cultivated.»[5]

He further mentions «Slate Island», «Glaffe Island» and «Bird Island». They all had forests, fresh water and extensive grazing land, he writes. Karlsevne's saga also tells us that the animals did well when they were taken out to an island during the first hard winter. We learn both from Wood and the Governor's diary that the British brought rams, goats and pigs out there while the crops were growing.

If we compare the Norse sagas, a map of Boston harbor from the colonial period, and a modern map, there is great consistency. The peninsula that pointed north from the south side of the bay, and which Leiv passed, is the narrow, nine kilometer long «Hull», with Nantusket Beach on the lee side. In the middle of the bay the large «Long Island» sits across the inlet. This must have been the island with all the birds. Over time sedimentation and dredging have tamed the once so unpredictable currents. From the north side of the bay the pointed «Deer Island» still stretches eight kilometers south. But in the small channel where Karlsevne finally found an acceptable approach, and where the English colonists and their successors hauled or steered their sailing ships in and out of Boston harbor, traffic has died down. Today there is a bridge and a road over the sound. Modern ships sail past the monumental light house on the tip of «Deer Island», well marked by visual and electronic guides. Boston has one of the best and most trafficked harbors on the entire Atlantic coast.

The main concern of the Vinlandfarers was the fishing possibilities further upriver. Both Wood's book and the minutes from the English colonists' town meetings provide an explanation why the Vinlandfarers were in such a hurry to sail up to the high water mark.

By the calm «lake» in the Charles River, where the Vinland-farers' camp presumably was located, according to descriptions, the Englishmen found an old fish trap below a stone dam where the tide turned. Twice in twenty-four hours huge numbers of fish streamed in from the ocean with the high tide. The normal catch in a twenty-four hour period (two high tides) was one hundred thousand fish. The British repaired the trap two years after they arrived. The method of fishing was as simple as could be: When the high tide crested, they closed the return path for the fish in the dam, and scooped them up. From the British descriptions it seems that the main catch consisted of America's popular and robust bass, the Micro-peterus salmoides. Today the fish has an average weight of a little more than one kilo.

When Karlsevne's group returned to Straumfjord, they realized the mountains they saw there were the same they had seen at Hop. And that the mountains were an equal distance from both places (as stated in both Hauk's Book and Eirik Raude's Saga). Professor Gustav Storm took this to mean that the mountains they saw to the west in Straumfjord, were the same they saw to the east when in Hop.[6] But beyond that historians have given up trying to understand this «meaningless» description. It may actually turn out to be a rather interesting supplement to Norwegian maritime history: I interpret this sentence to mean that Karlsevne used triangulation in his navigation. This would not be all that surprising, since

50

a pair of compasses thought to have navigational uses were found in the excavated Oseberg Ship, dating from about 850.

The method of triangular calculation, or trigonometry, was common among Hindus, Arabs and Greeks at the time of Christ, and was further developed by the geographer Ptolemy in his work <u>Almagest</u> in the 3rd century A.D. Triangular measurement was never forgotten, and it would be hard to believe that the Vikings had not learned it during their sailing of the Mediterranean. What the saga reports, in my opinion, is that Straumfjord (Boston), Hop (Rhode Island Sound), and the mountains (the Appalachians) form an equilateral triangle. This is fairly accurate. Anyone who knew this simple and ingenious navigational technique would also be able to determine length, width, direction and approximate distance from any location they had observed either from the ocean or from land.[7]

Back in Straumfjord Karlsevne sent out a search party in an effort to find the psychopath Torhall Veidemann and his eight companions, but they were never found. The Vinland saga tells us that they spent the last fall gathering timber and drying grapes and pelts, to load on the ships going home.

Though there was an abundance of everything they needed in Boston Bay, the situation became untenable because the bachelors insisted on sexual relations with the married women. How the women felt about this, we are not told. Gudrid was already married to Torfinn Karlsevne at Leiv Eiriksson's order.

When the colonists started home the following summer, they came upon some natives along the way and they captured two small boys who were taken back to Greenland. The boys told them they were part of a group that had no permanent homesteads.

During later excavations on Karlsevne's farm at Sandnes in the Western Settlement on Greenland, a lump of anthracite coal, indigenous to Rhode Island, was found. It is one of only two locations on the east coast of the United States where such coal is found.[8] Later an Indian arrowhead was found in the western part of the church yard. It is very possible that it may have been lodged in one of the bodies buried there.[9]

It has been noted that the saga scribes consistently used the term «hudkeiper» when referring to the boats used by the natives. Since «hud» means skin, it was assumed that they were talking about Eskimos with kayaks. This is not so—a «hudkeipe» just means the opposite of a wooden boat fashioned from a dugout tree. The term «hud» is still used in boat building, whether the skin is steel, wood, leather or plastic.

From a commercial point of view, Karlsevne's voyage was a success. He sailed to Norway and sold all the wares brought from America. The saga mentions furs and items made from rare types of wood that had been carved on Iceland. When Karlsevne was ready to return to Iceland, a man from Bremen asked if he could buy his «husasnotra». What this was, we don't know. Guesses include a navigational instrument, a container for the safekeeping of valuables, or a figurehead. Linguists have been unable to come up with a definitive answer.

What made this particular item so attractive, was the fact that it was fashioned from Vinland mazer. North America's most valued tree was a type of cedar, with a heavy red and white grain, used to decorate houses, caskets, chests, boxes and «staffs», according to the English reports 600 years later.[10] Karlsevne didn't know what kind of wood it was, nor did he want to sell it. But the German didn't give up, and for the dizzying sum of a half mark gold piece, Karlsevne finally decided to part with it.

He bought a large farm when he returned to Iceland, and lived there the rest of his life. When he died, his wife Gudrid and his son Snorre took over the farm. But when Snorre got married, Gudrid went on a pilgrimage to Rome, just like her husband had predicted during that terrible winter up in the Western Settlement. Thus many people in Europe had a chance to meet someone who had experienced America personally. Upon her return she became a nun, and spent the rest of her life in quiet solitude and meditation. Her name is inextricably tied to the history of both Greenland and America.

Nightmare in Vinland

The timber in America was a tempting resource. Mazer from the protuberances of trees was not only a unique material to use for bowls and troughs and plates, because it didn't crack, but it was also used for sacred vessels in churches.

The English colonists immediately began the production of bowls and plates when they came to America in the 1600s. In Europe the items were so much in demand, and so expensive, that mazer was chosen by the nobility for drinking vessels and jewelry boxes. Even the gavel of the British Parliament is fashioned from American mazer.

This may have been the reason why Fröydis Eiriksdatter raised the issue of sending another expedition. She was able to interest the captains and crew of a ship that arrived from Norway in a new journey, and they agreed that the profit would be equally divided. The captains of the ship were two Icelandic brothers, Helge and Finnboge. They also had five women on board.

This time Fröydis wanted to go to Leiv's house in Vinland, where no Indians had been seen. Otherwise it would have been natural to head back to Karlsevne's homestead where she had already spent time and where houses were still standing after the first attempt at colonization.

Leiv Eiriksson said no when she asked permission to take over his houses in Vinland. But he did give her leave to use them temporarily. He was obviously aware that Fröydis was both ruthless and cruel—something she was to demonstrate to excess during this expedition. It became apparent from the very start. She smuggled five more men aboard her ship than the thirty fit sailors each ship was supposed to carry.

They had reviewed the sailing directions, and knew precisely where to find Leiv's houses in Vinland. The Norwegian ship, somewhat larger than the one Fröydis had, sailed ahead of the Greenlanders. They were already in the process of settling into Leiv's houses when Fröydis arrived.

Convinced she had the advantage with five more men, she chased the Norwegians out, claiming she was the only one who had permission to use Leiv's houses. The others protested, but had no choice but to begin building a camp on another site. Fröydis immediately set her men to work cutting and hewing wood.

The relationship between the two groups grew strained, both because of Fröydis' behavior and because the Norwegians had to spend their time building shelter instead of concentrating on securing valuable cargo for the return journey, which is how the Greenlanders spent their time.

Helge and Finnboge of the Norwegian ship tried to encourage friendly competitions between the two groups throughout the winter. They tried to get the popular Norse game of «knattleikar» started. But Fröydis was intent on spreading ill will among the men. At some point during the winter months there was a complete break between the two parties.

In the end Fröydis discovered that there was not enough room for her cargo on her own ship. Early one morning she got up and went barefoot to the camp of the two brothers, and offered them such a high price for the Norwegian ship that Finnboge decided to accept the offer. Fröydis then went back to the Greenlanders, with ice cold feet, claiming that Helge and Finnboge had violated her. She demanded immediate retribution. It was unthinkable to let such a violation go unpunished.

All the Norwegian and Icelandic men were killed before they had a chance to get out of bed. Fröydis' husband refused to kill the five women. Fröydis then grabbed an axe and did the deed herself.

In early spring they left for home with both ships and reached Eiriksfjord on Greenland in the beginning of summer. Fröydis threatened to kill anyone who breathed a word of what had happened. But Leiv tortured three of the expedition members until they confessed, whereupon Fröydis was cast out of the Eiriksson family.

The Rich Forest Land

What has been described above are the main features of what the Norse sagas and a number of other sources report about the voyages of discovery from Greenland to the east coast of the North American continent. The division of America into the three regions of Vinland, Markland and Helluland is reiterated in an old Icelandic handbill,[11] with reference to European locations. It says:

"West in the ocean from Spain, which some call Gigunnagap, there is first the land of Vinland the Good (the southern tip of Virginia is on the same latitude as Gibraltar, 36 degrees). Thereafter comes Markland. Thereafter a wilderness where the skrælings live. After that there is wilderness all the way to Greenland."

There are no descriptions of the three American lands that contradict this description. All of the sources place them south of Greenland.

If we try to pin-point the location of the three countries relative to European latitudes, Vinland stretches from Gibraltar to France, Markland from Bordeaux to Brest, and Helluland from the southern tip of England to Oslo. Newfoundland is on the same latitude as the middle of England.

In all the accounts much is made of the grapes in America. The German geographer, Adam of Bremen, wrote in his four-volume work Descripto insolarum aguilonis from 1070 that Vinland is a large «island» in the ocean south of Helluland and Markland.[12] And that in Vinland it is possible—or should be possible—to make really good wine. He refers to information learned from the Danish court. But remember that Karlsevne's "husasnotra" was sold to a merchant from Bremen, and that Gudrid had been on a pilgrimage to Rome, so at least some information about the land must have been known in Europe.

After the first few voyages Vinland was not given much attention and is mentioned only in passing—just like the rich hunting grounds of the far north. It was still very far away. Are Frode (born 1067) in his monumental work Islendingabok, talks passionately and matter-of-factly about the natives in America.[13] It was apparently something everyone was expected to be familiar with and therefore required no further explanation.

For the Norse communities on Greenland—between three and five thousand people—the forests of North America became an absolute necessity. The walls of a Greenland house were typically constructed from stone and peatmoss, while the roofs had to be made from wood and bark. Even if they initially found driftwood along their beaches, bark had to be brought from America to make the roofs waterproof. We know for certain that they continued to go there for another 350 years. The people who plied those waters were average seamen and hunters, and the sagas didn't bother recording their adventures. The sagas are the histories of the upper classes of Norse society.

At times the traffic must have been considerable. Some of Greenland's sixteen churches had at least one wall made of wood. And in one instance we are told that Grim and Sorli came to Iceland with lumber from Greenland.

Runic stones have been found that tell about Greenlanders spending winters in the area of the Northwest Passage, in hunting camps owned by wealthy farmers. The saga about Skald-Helge even indicates that they had something resembling a «social life» there during the dark winters.[14]

Wintering in North America was also necessary. Lumber had to be dried for months, and thereafter hewn—or «whittled», as the Karlsevne saga puts it—before being transported across the ocean. The grapes had to be dried. They also hunted extensively. The summer skins were of no value, so the fur animals had to be trapped during the winter. From the few inventory lists that have survived from the records of the harbor of Bergen—Norway's old capital—we learn that the ships from Greenland brought skins of marmot, otter, beaver, wolverine, lynx, sable and black bear. None of these animals were found on Greenland—such animals had to be trapped in North America. When archbishop Eirik Valkendorf announced that he intended to send an expedition to Greenland, he said it was a land of silver and gold ore, or «gull-muld» (gold soil).[15] Canada is one of the world's richest sources of silver, and sand containing gold dust can be found along the entire northeast coast of North America. Gold is also found on Greenland.

No systematic attempts have been made to find traces of centuries of Greenlander activities on the North American east coast. Since the colonization in the 1600s, most of the areas in question had been, or were in the process of being built up. But there are four places in North America that with certainty can be designated as former Greenland «colonies». One is Ungava Bay at the mouth of the Hudson Bay, just west of South Greenland. Here Canadian and American archaeologists have found a number of permanent Norse settlements. Then there is the north tip of Newfoundland, where Anne-Stine and Helge Ingstad have found remains of long houses, a forge, and several loose items of Norse origin.[16] But the primary area of activity for the Greenlanders seems to have been the Gulf of Maine. Here two rivers, the Penobscot in Maine and the Charles in the Boston area, figure prominently in the Norse activities that spanned the entire Massachussets peninsula, including Newport, Rhode Island, on the Atlantic side. The Penobscot River ran through a veritable Eldorado for hunting, and it was accessible from the north via the Gulf of St. Lawrence.

The manuscripts and maps of the French explorer, Allefonse, in the Bibliothéque Nationale in Paris, note that houses were in existence in the Boston area when he arrived in 1543. But the people who had occupied them, were gone.

1. See Kulturhistorisk Lexikon för Nordisk Medeltid, volume XIII, p. 314.
2. Wood, 1634, p. 40.
3. Ibid., p. 21
4. Ibid., p. 40.
5. Ibid.
6. Storm, 1891.
7. See Scott, 1958, for the history of trigonometry.
8. Ingstad, 1959, pp. 266–70.
9. Ibid.

10. Wood, 1634, p. 17.
11. Den eldste Noregshistoria, p. 88.
12. Ibid.
13. Holtsmark, 1967.
14. Rimasafn, p. 161.
15. Henriksen, 1988, p. 355.
16. Ingstad, 1975, p. 116.

NORDRSETUR—THE LAND OF RICHES BENEATH THE POLAR STAR

The migration of people from Iceland and Norway to the distant and barren Greenland just before the turn of the millennium resembled a gold-rush.

Ivory was then the dearest commodity in the world, along with gold, jewels, enamel and dyes. Walrus tusks were more desireable than elephant tusks, because they had a better color, and a clarity that the African ivory could never match.

An enterprising farmer from North Norway, Ottar, went all the way up to Kvitsjöen in the 800s and bought walrus tusks from Russian trappers for export to Europe. He later was in the service of King Alfred of England, who personally recorded the story of this Norwegian entrepreneur. The original signed by the king in his elegant hand writing is kept in the British Museum.[1]

The modest and unreliable supply of walrus tusks from North Norway didn't begin to meet the demand. A veritable fever was raging—we hear for instance of Floke Vilgerdsson who went to Iceland to become a farming settler, but became so preoccupied with the rich catch at sea that his livestock starved to death during the winter. A little later in the 800s, a wave of immigrants from Norway and the outlying islands was to follow.

The real coup was made by the outlaw murderer Eirik Raude, who sought refuge on Greenland.

Life was a lot harder there than on Iceland. They were dependent on a reliable supply of commodities from the outside world to survive, and paid dearly for it. The excavation of scrap piles reveals that the colony would have perished very quickly if it hadn't been for the sensational supply of walrus tusks. This commodity was of such vital importance that the Greenlanders, even in later Christian times, brought walrus heads back from the hunting grounds and buried them in the church yard to win favor from the animal's «spirit».[2]

Were these hunters half pagans who brought the heads into the church yard under cover of darkness? Hardly. It probably happened in full daylight—and as part of everyday Christian practice, sanctioned by the local priest.

Walrus tusks were so valuable in Europe that just like gold and silver, they were buried in the ground as treasures, hidden from marauding enemies. We know that art pieces made from walrus tusks were sent as gifts from the Scandinavian kings to other regents.[3]

All over Europe, but centered in Scandinavia, the art of walrus ivory carving flourished.[4] Beautiful sculptures were made, and plaques and reliefs appeared as decoration on the finest furnishings, relic chests, and other church art. Both Romanesque and Gothic art made from walrus ivory was common in European churches and monasteries. Perhaps the most famous of these ivory works of art is the Norse board game with carved figures, intricately carved hunting horns, and King Magnus Barefoot's scabbard made of walrus ivory and gold.[5] Among the most beautiful art pieces we know of are the chests from Ammin and Bamberg in the so-called «Jellinge» style. At Gardar on Greenland a beautiful crozier of carved walrus ivory was found. All over Europe artists were working on ivory from Greenland. There were some in Scandinavia as well. On an elaborate hunting horn from the 1200s in Museo Nazionale in Florence we find a runic inscription: «Reinaldr made me.»[6]

The daughter of an Icelandic priest, Margrete, became famous for carving the crozier for the venerable archbishop of Nidaros in Norway, around the year 1200.[7]

In 1327 a ship came to Bergen with a cargo that included 130 lispound of walrus tusks, which were sold for 12.7 pounds of silver. This was a considerable fortune for just a small part of the total cargo. All of it was a tithe to the pope. Compared to the expenses incurred, Greenland emerged as an extremely lucrative bishopric of the Roman Catholic church.

The Unicorn Becomes A Reality

In addition to walrus tusks and whale bone for larger works, European shipping had an almost unlimited need for strong ropes that would not deteriorate in salt water, as ropes made of animal hide did. Walrus ropes from Greenland were unmatched throughout the Middle Ages.

The biggest sensation of all was the narwhal with its straight, twisted horn, several meters long. Rumors circulated that this was the unicorn that had been thought to live in Africa or India. Some narwhals came south to Upernavik on the upper Greenland coast during the winter.[8] But their true home was in the farthest reaches of the north.

The tusk was finer than the finest ivory, and was ideal for making jewelry and health-bringing talismans. Everyone thought it contained medicinal agents and hidden powers that could bring back lost vitality and potency. The price was enormous, and it retained its value. For 300 years a narwhal tusk was kept as a special attraction in the cathedral at Nidaros.[9]

There is an aura of adventure about the Greenland hunters up in the far north. Wealthy Greenland farmers raised permanent buildings in several locations, where hunters and outlaws lived all year round. The agriculture on Greenland was never more than a supplement to the primary hunting culture.

Björn Johnsson reports that even the well-to-do farmers sometimes wintered both at Greipar (on the Greenland side) and on the Kroksfjord moors (on the Canadian side) together with their professional hunters. The famous Skald-Helge visited a community of outlaws on the Greenland coast as early as 1017. For obvious reasons it made sense to hire outlaws as trappers since they couldn't return to their home communities anyway.

Their profession required a good deal of courage. The walrus was killed by attacking it on the beaches with spears and lances. The technique was to kill the animals closest to the sea first, creating a barrier that blocked the path of the others. We have no numbers from Greenland, but there are some available from Svalbard: In 1606 Stephen Benner and his crew killed 600 walrus in six hours. In 1616 twelve men with lances killed 1000 walrus near Egede Island. In 1688, 1000 animals were killed in the course of seven hours.[10]

The few times details of the Greenland hunts are mentioned, we are told that the hunters operated in boat teams of 12–15 men. The profit from such a successful hunt would be a fortune in tusks and hides. The men who performed this dangerous work probably didn't get to keep much themselves, even if Europe was insatiable and the prices were good.

The Bird Worth Twenty Women

The king of Norway, who was easily accepted by the Greenlanders as their ruler when the shippers and merchants became too greedy and unreliable, also got his share. The Greenland hunters were able to supply him with a snow-white falcon (Falco rusticolus), which exceeded in speed and beauty all other hunting falcons in the world. Before the time of guns, hunting with trained falcons was a favorite sport of kings and princes. The German-Roman emperor Frederick II (1194–1250) wrote a book about this sport. The falcon wore a leather hood over its head. It was removed when the hunter sighted a bird he wanted to catch, and the falcon would then attack. Some falcons were also trained to fly above the owner's head and single out its own prey. The white falcon was so valuable that kings had a monopoly on all that were caught. While the king sponsored trading in regular falcons, the white ones were reserved for gifts in connection with the king's diplomatic activity.[11] They were the ultimate gift.[12]

The white falcon is the only bird mentioned in Historia Norvegiae. The Egyptian Abul-Hasan Ali Ibn Said, writing in the 1200s, stated that the sultan of Egypt paid 1000 dinars for a white falcon. The merchants took on great risk with such trade, particularly because of the problems of the long and difficult transport. The sultan therefore also paid 500 dinars for dead white falcons delivered to him. In Bergen harbor, Arab traders waited to buy trained falcons from the training facility there. The Black Death was followed by near panic in the falcon trade, because the ship traffic to Greenland stopped. An Arabic proverb states that one trained falcon was worth twenty women.[13] Just as with the narwhal, hunters had to go all the way up to 70–80°N to find the white falcons.

The distant north had yet another precious commodity—white bear skins. They looked so sensational on the royal floors that historians felt compelled to mention them on several occasions. The Italian Querini in 1432 was very impressed with a polar bear skin he saw in the cathedral at Nidaros. Ibn Said, the Arabic writer, also mentions the beautiful polar bear skins that were brought to Arabia.

Hunting polar bears was even more dangerous than killing walrus. The hunters attacked huge and quick animals with spears.

Not surprisingly, the earliest Norse distance tables in existence note the distance from Europe to Greenland, where all these treasures could be found. In a supplement to Adam of Bremen's world history from 1070, it is written in Latin:[14]

«From Norway to Iceland is 14 'tylfter' miles. [One 'tylft' is 72 nautical miles, and thus the distance to Iceland is given as 504 nautical miles.] From Iceland to «The Green Land» is about 14 tylfter miles. From Hvitserk [the mountain the seafarers headed toward when they sailed to Greenland] to Sunderbondt [the southern tip of the Norse settlement] it is 10 tylfter miles [369 nautical miles]. From Sunderbondt to Norderbondt [the northernmost settlement, in Vestbygden] it is 11 tylfter miles [400 nautical miles]. And from Norderbondt to Hunenrioth it is 17 tylfter miles [612 nautical miles]. And there men live to hunt white bears and tusk whales.»

The place name Hunenrioth comes from a German source, and probably refers to birds, or «hens». Its stated position is the location of present day Upernavik, at 73°N. This is where Greenland's best rookery and winter hunting grounds for walrus, polar bear, and white fish are located. It is also the most profitable hunting area in modern Greenland. Near the inlet there—at the top of an island 300 meters high with a view in all directions—there are three cairns, just like those found at the inlets of important Norwegian harbors in the Middle Ages. Pietro Querini, who sailed down the Norwegian coast after his shipwreck at Röst in 1432, wrote that the cairns indicated the deepest channel leading into the harbors.[15]

Near the cairns in Upernavik an Eskimo named Pelimut in 1824 found a small stone with the following runic inscription:[16] «Erling Sigvatsson and Bjarne Tordsson and Eindride Oddsson raised [or cleared] these cairns on Saturday before «gangdag», and made the runes too.» It is dated 1333. According to our calendar, the date would be May 2nd. The inscription also includes several «lönnruner», which were magical symbols or secret messages only skilled rune makers could understand. With the help of computers modern experts, especially in America, are trying hard to break these codes.

Skald-Helge wrote in the 1000s that the hunting ground of Greipar was at the northern end of Greenland.[17] The name Greipar may refer to the fact that the coast was formed like the palm of a hand, or a mitten, with the well-known and oddlooking mountain «Devil's Thumb» as the thumb and the Melville coast as the inside of the mitten.

But very early on the Greenlanders discovered a new hunting area. Straight across the narrow Smith Sound lay the Canadian islands, where they could hunt all year around for both narwhal, white falcons, walrus and polar bear. This area was called «Kroksfjordheiene» (the Kroksfjord

Moors). Nansen thought the name meant «the flat plateau by the crooked fjord».[18] The polar explorer Roald Amundsen followed in the wake of the Greenland hunters when he entered the Northwest Passage in 1903, and unsuspectingly confirmed this interpretation. In his book Nordvestpassasjen («The Northwest Passage») he describes his meeting with the Canadian islands in this way: «The fog stayed with us all the way to Cape Warrender. Here it lifted, and in the fine, clear weather we could observe the land. It is completely different from the wild and jagged mountains of Greenland. Most prominent is the plateau shape.»[19]

The few names we know from the old Greenland hunting grounds are all based on observations of a practical nature.

On the Canadian side the Greenlanders met an animal that no white men had ever seen before—the musk ox. In the church of the Norwegian archbishop, the cathedral at Nidaros, and in the royal chapel in the capital of Bergen, musk ox heads were mounted on the walls.[20]

But yet another surprise awaited them. One of the islands was inhabited by strangers: Eskimos. We don't know if they were there when the Greenlanders first arrived, but they were later. In the first reference to them in Historia Norvegiae we read, «to the north there are small people that they call skrælings». The sources imply that they believed the Eskimos belonged in a homeland «beyond» the North Pole, and that the Eskimo groups that the Greenlanders had met lived in an «outpost» of their country.[21]

Rafn assumed Kroksfjordheiene to be Lancaster Sound between Baffin Island and Devon Island at 74 degrees north.[22] P.A. Munch reached the same conclusion.[23] Gunnar Isachsen, who participated in the «Fram» expedition to this area in 1898–1901, suggested it was Jones Sound on the north side of Devon Island.[24] Here a number of eider duck brooderies were found, which were man made contraptions intended to encourage the eider ducks to lay eggs, thus providing the hunter with both eggs and down. The Eskimos were not interested in such things. The Danish Polar scientist Knud Rasmussen writes that a group of Eskimos wintering on the north side of Jones Sound in 1918 found a stone that according to their description must have been inscribed with runes. They said the stone had an inscription, but not with letters. It had strange symbols they didn't understand. The report was given to station master Peter Freuchen of Thule by the Eskimo couple Itsukusuk and Arnajaq, «who are both truthful and reliable people».[25] Not many people venture into those regions, so there's not much hope the stone will ever be seen again.

Professor Fridtjov Isachsen and Gunnar Isachsen[26] conclude that the central part of Kroksfjordheiene appears to have been Devon Island at the entrance to the Northwest Passage, at 73–75°N. During the few excavations done in this area, European medieval artifacts have been found.[27]

Until modern times the Igulik Eskimos have had their narwhal season in this area in late spring, when large numbers of whales entered the fjords and bays during the breaking up of the ice. Hunting was always done with hand harpoons.[28] Here a lucky buyer could get rich in a hurry if he arrived at the right time.

In the beginning the Greenlanders could catch whatever they wanted, because the animals had no fear of man. Egil's Saga describes Egil Skallagrimsson's first time on Iceland: «Whales came up to land in large numbers in those days. You could hunt as many as you wanted, because the animals lay safe and calm on the hunting grounds, unaccustomed as they were to men.»[29]

Leif Lundgaard, for many years an inspector in the Canadian Northwest Territory, which also includes the old Kroksfjordheiene, told this author that none of the animals of the uninhabited polar regions have any fear of man, and it is therefore necessary to enforce very strict regulations to protect them. Inexperienced people can for instance misunderstand the interest of a polar wolf or misjudge a polar bear's intentions.

But once the animals were attacked, it quickly became a matter of life and death. We often hear about the rich catches, but never about what happened when a spear broke during a battle with a walrus or a polar bear, or when the wound was not deadly, or when the hunter stumbled in the heat of the battle.

Commerce with this medieval Klondike was initially the province of the Norwegian aristocracy, who held the sole right to export to Europe the wares upon which the society in the polar regions depended. Royal families, like the Ring family of Ringerike and Ketil Kalv's family from Ringnes in Stange, became major shipowners. One man who died on a trading expedition to Greenland, was probably Finn Fegin of the Ringnes family, the nephew of Olav den Hellige. «The Hönen Stone», found on a farm in Norderhov in Ringerike in the last century, probably describes that event. It appears that the ship was storm driven all the way to the north Canadian coast. A Norwegian translation by Sophus Bugge, reads as follows: «They drifted across the ocean, over vast distances, in need of food and clothing, toward Vinland, and up to desolate areas of the north. Evil can take the place of happiness, and a man dies young.»

Another Norwegian rune expert, Magnus Olsen, agrees in the main with this translation, but is of the opinion that it says «windswept ice», and not Vinland. We'll never have the answer unless the stone reappears some day. In 1820 it disappeared. It is thought that it ended up in the foundation of a barn, in a fireplace, or a chimney.

The Eskimos—A Mystery

As described above, the narwhals migrate to the edge of the permanent ice during the summer, and in the summer of 1266 hunters from Kroks-fjordheiene followed them north—farther north than anyone had ever gone before. A priest on Greenland, Haldor, notified a priest of King Håkon's court about this, because the hunters had not encountered any Eskimos or Eskimo dwelling places north of Kroksfjordheiene. He there-fore assumed that the Eskimos who frequented Kroksfjordheiene had a shorter route, other than to the north, to the land where they belonged.[30] It was an ominous message—about a mystical heathen land somewhere in the icy desolation.

After hearing this, the church sent an expedition north, under the leadership of several priests. They went to the hunting grounds on the Canadian side in one or more boats, each with three pairs of oars. This was an ideal vessel because it could be pulled up on land in pack ice. In the beginning they encountered fog and a southerly wind. According to the account, the weather cleared when they reached Kane Basin. Their description seems accurate and comprehensible. The land was flat, and they saw both whales and bears. To the south they observed Greenland with glaciers as far as the eye could see. They found some old Eskimo camps, but no Eskimos. They dared not set up camp on shore, for fear of polar bears.

At the end of the sea, where the ice cap began at 82°N, they turned around.[31] No one could live farther north than that. Nansen thinks the purpose of the journey was to determine the range and the extent of the Eskimos.[32] From then on there was a definite uneasiness about the exis-tence of these diminutive people.

The expedition could still see the tops of glaciers far to the south when they turned back. After having sailed for 4 «dögr» (432 nautical miles) they encountered some Eskimo dwellings on some islands «south of the gla-cier». The glacier is associated with Greenland throughout the account, so this must be after they passed Thule (where an American military base is now located) on their way south. At that point they had the glaciers of Greenland behind them. On the 25th of July they sailed 36 nautical miles and reached Kroksfjordheiene.

The midnight sun was out when they returned to Kroksfjordheiene, but the temperature still dipped below freezing during the night. When the sun was to the south it was still very low on the horizon, and at midnight it was like the sun in the northwest back home. A number of attempts have been made to interpret these observations. If we assume they meant the height of the sun in the two locations on the same day of the year, the latitudinal position of Kroksfjordheiene is 74°34', or about the middle of Devon Island. But usually such comparisons refer to the position of the sun either on the 23rd of December or the 23rd of June—the shortest and the longest days of the year. In that case the location could have been Bylot Island at 73°N.

This expedition to the extreme north in 1266 was probably not the only one.

On top of the small, steep Washington Irving Island at 79°35', Sir George Nares in 1875 found two cairns in 1875.[33] They were built 900 feet above the sea. This is in one of the best walrus hunting grounds in the large Kane Basin, a favored narwhal location in the summertime. Not far from there, Henry Larsen, a superintendent of the Royal Canadian Mounted Police, found a rookery for eider ducks, made by humans. Down and eggs from eider ducks were necessities for the Greenland hunters. Such rookeries have also been found near Alexandra Lake a bit south of the two cairns, but in the same general area.[34] It seems appropriate to mention here the name of the northernmost area—Ædanes, «Eider Duck Point». Across the fjord, on the Greenland side, excavations in 1937 yielded a comb, remains of a coat of mail, a spear point, part of an iron cooking vessel, a game piece of carved whale bone, the bottom of an oak casket, and pieces of woven cloth.

We can assume that the cairns here, as elsewhere, are sea markers that indicated an important hunting ground.

Farther north than this no humans could go, because of the ice.

1. Storm, 1893–94.
2. Holmsen, 1949, p. 126.
3. Pedersen, 1966, p. 9.
4. Rygge, 1972.
5. Kielland, Thor B., in Kulturhistorisk Lexicon för Nordisk Medeltid, vol.I.
6. Ibid.
7. Grönlands Historiske Minnesmerker, vol. II, p. 272, note 3.
8. Salomonsen (ed.), 1981, p. 438.
9. Kolsrud, 1914, p. 70.
10. Ingstad, 1948, p. 56.
11. Lövenskiold, 1972.
12. Diplomatarium Norwegicum, XIX, no. 167.
13. Ingstad, 1959, p. 377.
14. Lappenberg, 1834, p. 851.
15. Querini's travel description is included in Helland, volume XVIII.
16. Olsen, 1932, p. 189.
17. Rimasafn, p. 129.
18. Nansen, 1911, p. 230.
19. Amundsen, 1972, p. 33.
20. Grönlands annaler.
21. Olaus Magnus, 1555.
22. Grönlands Historiske Minnesmerker, vol. III, pp. 881–85.
23. Munch, 1849, p. 218.
24. Isachsen, 1906–07, pp. 20–32.
25. Rasmussen, 1920.
26. Isachsen, G. and F., 1932.
27. McGovern, 1980.
28. Jordens folk.
29. Benediktsson, 1968, vol. II, pp. 77–78.
30. Jonsson, Björn (Grönlands Annaler), with Hauks Book as source.
31. Isachsen, G. and F., 1932.
32. Nansen, 1911.
33. Nares, 1878, Vol. I, p. 88.
34. Isachsen, G. and F., 1932.

MISSIONARY VOYAGE TO
NORTHERN CANADA

The little Eskimo group on Devon Island was apparently a permanent community. The Eskimos had no boats to reach Greenland across the Davis Strait. Up at Smith Sound they could travel across the winter ice. But on the Greenland side they would not be able to go south, because the enormous Melville Glacier blocked their way. A saga story reporting that around the year 1000 Norsemen saw an Eskimo woman in the process of quartering an animal on the ice outside East Greenland, is the only saga reference to encounters with Eskimos on Greenland itself.[1]

The Norse colonists found evidence of people who had been on Greenland before them. Pope Gregor knew about the land 130 years before Eirik Raude arrived there, and we can not discount the possibility that the Irish monks who went to Iceland traveled further west when the Norsemen arrived. Inasmuch as they were a society without women, their colony could only have lasted a generation.

Uneasiness about the mystical Eskimos was given new life around 1340, when it was discovered that the people in the Western Settlement, the northernmost of the two Greenland communities, had disappeared. Canon Ivar Baardssön from Bergen, probably a Greenlander who was in temporary charge of the bishopric at Gardar, immediately sent an expedition north to the sub-arctic settlement «to rid it of skrælings».

The Western Settlement never had more than about ninety farms and four churches. The expedition visited farm after farm. Nowhere was smoke coming from the vents of the hut roofs. All the houses were empty and silent inside. Furniture pieces with carved dragon heads dating back to the Viking era were left untouched.[2]

There was nothing to indicate any fighting. No bodies were found— no skeletons. The ships entered fjord after fjord but were met only by the silence of the dramatic landscape. No pirates had been there, since they only captured the young and ablebodied.

Adults and children, young and old, had given up on the hard life and put out the fires after 350 years—if they had anything to burn in the end—and simply left. The little birch forest had long since been consumed, and the beaches had been swept clean of drift wood. Behind the forge at the bishop's residence at Sandnes they had left a hearth used to burn dyes. There had once been a bishop in residence, but the last one went to Vinland in 1121 and never returned.

An Indian arrowhead and a piece of anthracite from Rhode Island spoke of contact with America.[3] The shovels left behind were made of wood and reindeer horn. Other things left behind included axes, spears, sickles, forge tongs, weaving tools, wooden plates, spinning wheels, shoe lasts, combs, soapstone cooking vessels, bowls and oil lamps. A model boat was found near a sauna. In the church yard the remains of the last 10–11 generations of the community lay buried, many with the customary final farewell placed on their chests—wooden sticks inscribed with runes. One person was buried with a beautiful statue of Christ carved in wood at his side. On the back of five round plates was the inscription «Ave Maria gratia plena».[4]

Herds of cows and goats, sheep and horses wandered about in the fields. Perhaps those who left had planned to come back for them after establishing themselves on the other side of the Davis Strait? Or more likely perhaps, if it turned out to be impossible to settle on the other side, they would have the possibility of returning as long as there was livestock to come back to. They knew that at least some of the sheep would survive, because they were used to being left outside. The search expedition slaughtered as many of the animals as their ships could hold and returned south.

This is thought to have happened in the summer of 1342, because Bishop Gisle Oddsson of Skålholt on Iceland wrote the following in the church diary of 1342:[5] «The colonists of Greenland voluntarily assumed the true faith and Christian religion. After abandoning good morals and true virtues they turned to the people of America.» The name «America» comes from the translation—we don't know which name was used in the original document. The bishop added that an important cause for the emigration was that the distance to America was so much shorter than to Norway.

The decision to give up the settlement and the insecurity of a harsh life in the tree-less sub arctic community was probably not taken on the spur of the moment. Loggers and hunters had had contact with Indians for several hundred years, and the «mixing of blood» probably had been going on for just as long, since Bishop Gisle knew that the transition to Indian life happened voluntarity. There are no surviving sagas or legends about fighting between Greenlanders and Indians in the wilderness. The reason for this may be that the nomadic Indians believed that the land belonged to no one, and that there was enough space and game for everyone. The battles we know of in America were caused by foolishness or accidents involving groups of non-nomadic natives.

The Indian extended families had no rich and no poor—nobody owned the lakes and the forests, nobody had to work for anyone else, and they all took responsibility for one another. This Indian lifestyle probably was not changed in any way, except that a Christian element was added. French missionaries who came to New Brunswick in the 1500s, reported to the Vatican that they met Indian groups who performed Christian rites, according to a report by the Catholic historian, Dr. Jelic, during the Congrés Scientifique International de Catoliqes in 1891.

The Swedish geographer Nordenskiöld points to considerable evidence that white men always become assimilated into the local native culture: «The love of hunting causes the second generation to take on the lifestyle of the natives. And by the third generation most joiners have lost any memories of their roots.»[6]

But certain things that have been learned are slower to vanish, for example the art of writing. George Beste, who participated in Martin Frobisher's third expedition to Hudson Bay in the late 1500s, reported that the natives were familiar with writing, which is noteworthy since they were a preliterate people.

The first part of the 1300s was the golden age of Norse society, and we have many indications of considerable traffic with America. In 1327 the pope's tithe collector, on behalf of the Swedish-Norwegian king, signed a receipt for a bowl with a silver base, the upper part of which was «a nut that had come from the other side of the ocean».[7]

There is no doubt among experts that the mentioned nut was a palm nut. Professor Johan Kielland-Lund, Jr., of the Agricultural College in Norway, states that Florida is the northernmost of the areas where a nut of the size indicated could have been found, although the likely area is probably considerably further south.

It is improbable that a nut used for such a distinguished item had drifted north to the Norse regions. In that case it would have been useless after being so long in salt water. It is also unlikely that no Greenlanders would have ventured south along the coast when they had been visiting America for centuries.

In 1346 a ship arrived in Bergen with an unusually rich cargo. Stories circulated about the fortune, and special mention was made of it in the Icelandic Annals that year.

In 1347 a ship coming from North America met with a storm en route to Greenland. The 18 men on board had to sail ahead of the weather all the way to Iceland, where they created quite a stir because their ship had no anchor. They had actually duplicated Bjarne Herjulfsson's involuntary voyage of 986, in the opposite direction. The next year the ship went on to Norway with its cargo. The authorities in Norway could not have had a more tangible contact with the Greenlanders in America than they did on that occasion.

That the ship reached its destination is indirectly confirmed by the Icelandic Annals of 1348, in which the chieftain Jon Guttormsen is mentioned as having left Norway «together with the Greenlanders». (He was a fugitive from prosecution who was later pardoned by the king, and went back to Norway.)

But regardless of whether Greenland was the pearl in the largest kingdom of Europe, everything was changed in July of 1349.[8]

The crew on a ship that arrived in Bergen from England became ill. They developed black abscesses in the groin area and under their arms, and all died in the course of a few days. It was the Black Death. During the fall and winter of 1349–50 the epidemic killed two thirds of the population of Norway and Sweden. In the cities the funeral bells rang day in and day out. Whole families were wiped out. In outlying areas, where the isolation had left people with little immunity, entire communities and valleys were left depopulated. In the isolated community of Jostedalen, legend has it that only one girl was found alive when people finally arrived. Countless farms ceased operating, simply because there was no one left to run them. «Ödegård» («deserted farm») at this time became one of the most frequently used farm names in Norway. The survivors began a completely new life after the plague. The country's organization had broken down, guilds and regional societies had disappeard. Taxes stopped coming in, because the tax collectors were all dead. There was nothing to mortgage, because there were no buyers for mortgaged properties.

Norway was among the last European countries to be stricken by this Asiatic pestilence. In the previous year 100,000 people had died in Florence between March and July, and mass graves had to be used to bury them all. The intensity of the pestilence was so strong, that even pigs died, wrote Boccaccio in The Decameron, to the great annoyance of modern scientists. In one of the monasteries in Avignon all 66 monks were found dead, without anyone outside the monastery walls realizing that the disease had reached there.[9]

The papacy was on shaky ground after the disaster. Less than a year after the first wave of pestilence in Scandinavia was over, the papal nuncio Johannes Guilaberti came to Sweden to collect the large debt that King Magnus of Sweden-Norway owed the pope. But the king's ability to pay was zero. The suffering was so widespread that Queen Margareta, who lived at Akershus in Oslo, wrote to the king twenty years later pleading for help, because she had no food. The food the farmers were obligated to tithe was not there—because the farmers were dead. The nuncio went home to Rome with very meager results, as the receipts show.[10] And nothing at all was done about the distressing exodus from Greenland to the heathen Indians.

Cultural Interest Awakens

At this time, the French lawyer Etienne Aubert assumed the papal chair under the name of Innocens VI. He warmly supported the novel ideas of the humanists Petrarch and Alvaro Pelajo, and the sudden general interest in history and geography. In Norway there were several who shared their views, who were part of the same university environment. Both archbishop Paal Baardsson and bishop Audfinn in Bergen had the same education as the pope. Bergen's previous judge, Hauk Erlendsen, had himself written down the saga of Torfinn Karlsevne's voyage to Vinland. In the course of half a century, the Icelanders recorded in writing the entire history of the Norsemen. Flateyarboken, which was penned by two priests on parchment made from the skins of 125 calves, also included the account of the Vinland voyages, albeit in a form that seems somewhat abbreviated. It would therefore have been a bit of a scandal for the church, civilization and the papacy if the population of Greenland should turn out to have reverted to heathenism.

Innocens was a stern man. In 1354 the pope's ambassador returned to King Magnus in Västergötland. He meant business. Collector Guilaberti now had orders to go through every single Norwegian-Swedish church and every monastery to make certain that they were operational after the pestilence, but also to empty them of any valuables that could be turned into money. The king was threatened with excommunication. The entire Swedish-Norwegian kingdom, including Greenland, was mortgaged in order to pay the pope his dues. Meanwhile glad tidings arrived. Greenland had not been struck by the pestilence. And now things were set into motion:

On October 28, 1354, the king wrote a dramatic letter to the judge in Bergen, ordering him to outfit a large expedition that was to go to Greenland. The original is lost, probably when Copenhagen burned, but an old Danish translation exists. The judge was given a free hand to requisition anything he might need, including «good men» for leaders and a crew. The king wrote that the expedition was being sent in the name of God, to ensure that the Christian faith which their forefathers had introduced on Greenland would not flounder. It is important to note in this connection that the church itself did function on Greenland. The king and his Belgian queen, as late as 1347, gave 100 marks in silver to embellish the cathedral of Greenland. The problem was the group of Greenland colonists who had left the land and reverted to heathendom on the American side. But throughout history a lot of taxes have been collected in the name of God, so it is reasonable to assume that this was a combined geographical and tax collecting expedition with participants from Sweden, Norway, Iceland and England, and that the Greenlanders, wherever they might be, were to be sought out and made to pay what they owed. Similar expeditions were often dispatched to Finnmark in North Norway, which geographically was as distant and uncharted a region as North America. On some occasions the tax collectors even entered Russian territory.

There weren't many «good men» to be found after the pestilence, so there's nothing to indicate that the expedition ever left. The pope in reality was bankrupt, and in 1356 Guilaberti received authority to begin more aggressive collection tactics in the north. King Magnus Eriksson's kingdom was finally excommunicated because of the high debt owed to the pope.

We hear nothing more about the search for the missing Greenlanders in the few and scattered documents available about this period of history. But when the great geographer, Gerard Mercator, began to draw his map of the world in the 1560s, he came across an account written by the Belgian Jacob Cnoyen, who was attached to the Swedish court in the time of King Magnus.[11]

He wrote that in the year 1360, an able English mathematician and geographer arrived on Greenland as part of an expedition that was to visit «the island lands». This geographer parted from the rest of the expedition and traveled north—«to the places farther away where they practice their magical arts»—heathendom, in other words.

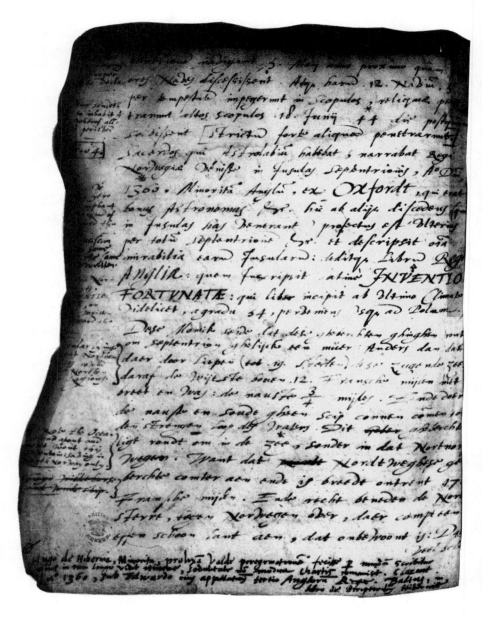

The only preserved version of the book <u>Inventio Fortunatæ</u>, which awakened Columbus' interest in the new world. The author here reports that he met Eskimos in the Greenland hunting fields in northern Canada. Columbus visited the same latitude in 1477. The book also reported about the warmer and more fertile parts of America, and about floating islands in Central America.

altoos so nader, so meer: so laten ...

Fransche mijle niet oveet en is, iaert ...
gheberchte vergadert. Anders en verder

om gheen Landt aen: Maer ...

... is die zee so enghe, dat men ...
van Berr sitt.

Ende dit gheberchte duert in de breede ...
Ende in al den dien Circkel (seide de ...
en was gheen habitatie dan aen die oost ...
daer ... dat smalle landt bescreden ...
waren 23 sieden, boven hier boeten niet ...
waer of die 16 vrouwen waren. Dese ...
seide dat hij in twe ander plaetssen ...
waert ..., een groote stick herdes van scepen ...
ander balken, die in groote scepen ghedient ...
ende heel truncken van boomen die in vorleden ...
tijden ... waren ghehouden, so dat hij ...
... dat daer hier voormaels / habitatie ...
was: maer sij was nu vergaen. Ende dat ...
commerce daer si [Bigmai credo dicti] in ...
... dan 6. gradus breet was (dats 20 dach ...
ende dat men gaen mocht te voete: ende 10. graet ...
lanck: dat is 33 dachvaert. So laghe (seide hij ...
aen dat custende een zuijgende zee daerse 5. in ...
vergaderden, die door de gheberchte commen ...
vanden 19. dorscreven meren. Ende dese zui...
gende zee is wijt bij 12. Fransche mijlen:
Ende over dese zuijgende zee ontrent 4 ...
dach...

Note that in di
place these Norther
they are allmost
... a being of th
lands opposite to
but so as here is
or such one place
East &c an Isth
... the principall
Vnderstand fram
Mare Land, th
place of Land is
from Atlantis or
Asia. or if it
peninsula there
... and so great
by their maya land.

This Inhabited
... deserts are
... dayes breadt way
... more miles that
expedition th...
... foure
... Island 150
of Longitud
place about do.
... latitude
... 3. dayes
... ther
... Begyns of
all places is t
Brytish myle
... to Vnder
great Circkel
and disa...

The historian Richard Haklyut (1553–1616) took this geographer to be the astronomer and mathematician Nicolas of Lynne, and this has since been accepted as fact. Nicolas also worked out a calendar for the period 1387–1461.[12] But Haklyut was a raging nationalist, and anything meaningful to him necessarily had to be English. On the copy that Mercator made of the report of the journey, the recipient, John Dee, wrote in the margin that the geographer in question was the monk Hugo of Ireland. Perhaps it was neither of them. It may simply have been a young English-born monk and geographer who was excited about the newly published book about Marco Polo's long sojourn in China, and who wanted to continue where Marco stopped—to the northeast.

The boat, or boats, with the geographer on board, would have been headed up to the hunting areas to collect taxes and tithes in the form of narwhal and walrus tusks, polar bear skins and falcons. Some years the entire tithe to the papal chair was paid in white falcons. The Vatican was desperate for money. The geographer in question probably came along as an extra passenger, perhaps to keep an eye on the tithes.

During the voyage the geographer wrote down everything he observed, and everything reported to him by men who were geographically knowledgeable. Then he checked the information with his astrolabe (an instrument to determine latitude), and recorded it. In his Cosmographica from 1595, Mercator writes that the geographer «described the lands with a geometrical instrument used to draw accurate maps». This makes it tempting to think that those who provided the information knew the principles of trigonometry. Mercator drew a map of the North Pole based on the information provided by the geographer, and it is a fine supplement to the account itself.

The geographer wrote a book about the expedition. The title was Inventio Fortunatæ—which can mean both «Fortunate Voyage» and «Voyage to the Land of Fortune». Insula Fortunatæ was the name used by many for America.[13] The book, often mentioned in the Middle Ages, no longer exists. But the geographer Gerhard Mercator refers to some of the content in a long letter written in response to a request from a Londoner, John Dee.[14]

Mercator's letter went through a fire, and as a result some lines on top of each page are missing. The account about the lands near the Polar Sea is a difficult one to begin with, and the missing lines add to the problem.

The geographer begins by stating that he had read Marco Polo's book about his journey to China 65 years earlier. Marco wrote that far north of

China there was a kingdom by the name of «Obscur» («polar night land») where a grand khan ruled. After that there was a beautiful and flat land, and a coast named «Bergi». The geographer explained it as follows:

The land of Obscur began north of Norway—on the other side of an ocean bay 12 French miles wide (Kvitsjöen?). It was a very large land, so large that the next flat land lay directly under, or behind, the North Star, seen from North Norway. This would indicate East Siberia. Marco Polo's third land, «Bergi», would then be the American and Canadian arctic regions. All these lands, Norway among them, stretched up to 70°N. Between 70° and 80° there were no known lands, according to the map that Mercator drew.

Furthermore we are told that at 78° there is a mountain range circling the area of the North Pole. Inside this circle the author believed the Eskimos had their homeland. The North Pole land was divided into four «commercial zones» associated with valuable commodities: Ivory, falcons, polar bear skins and walrus. Between these districts are swift north-flowing currents that no ships dare to enter because they would be unable to turn back. Ivar Baardssön, who must have been the geographer's host on Greenland, elaborated on this. In his Greenland description he stated that no ship must pass by Himmelradsfjell («The Mountain That Reaches Heaven»). If they did, they would never return. Keep in mind that the northernmost cairns found on a tiny little island at 79°N, were placed at the top of a steep mountain, 300 meters high.[15]

The geographer's main base in the high north seems to have been «Grockland». The location is the same as Kroksfjordene and Kroksfjord-heiene, centered on Devon Island. I therefore assume that «Grockland» is a Europeanized version of «Krokland». (The geographer used Latin.)

He writes that all the ocean currents make a bend («krok») or turn at this location, and explains somewhat obscurely that this is the best and healthiest land in the entire northern region. The Mercator map, which was based on the information in this book, shows that the island, Grock-land, must be Devon Island, pushed one degree too far to the south -to 73°. The legend on the island is «GROCHLANT insula cuios incolae Suedi sunt origine» («GROCHLAND—the island where the inhabitants are Swedish»). The explanation of course, is that the king was Swedish. In a letter to the court from the pope dated September 13, 1360, Pope Innocens calls Queen Blanca of Norway-Sweden «Queen of Sweden».[16]

The geographer gives us a little help in locating Grochland by explaining one strange phenomenon—the sea on the east side never froze, even in the worst cold, because the currents were so strong there. This is correct. To the southwest of the Thule district, near the Carey Islands at 76.5°N and 72°W, we find the inexplicable phenomenon called Nordvannet («The North Water»), which is never iced over, even if the rest of the Arctic Ocean is frozen solid.[17] But to the west, where there was no sign of settlements, we are told there were four inlet branches that were frozen at least three months of every year.

He also explains that not far from the North Pole there was a magnetic mountain in the sea. It was black and glistening, and it could be seen from the sea. It is somewhat unclear whether he claims to have sighted the magnetic North Pole, or if this is information from people who knew the area. In the summer it could be easily reached.

Apparently he went even further to the north, probably to the old hunting grounds at Vagar and Ædanes at 78°N. There they found planks from large ships, and hewn logs as evidence of «former inhabitants».

They also found remnants of Eskimo camps, and met 23 Eskimos, 16 of them women. At one point in the account it appears they met them on Devon Island, in another place it seems it may have been Smith Sound. A third piece of information states that the island where they met the Eskimos was 6 degrees or 20 sailing days wide, and 10 degrees or 33 sailing days long. That is more suggestive of Ellesmere Island.

He explains that from this area it is not possible to travel to Norway on the other side of the North Pole, because the ocean currents there are impossible to negotiate.

Unfortunately Mercator, who wrote this letter and included the map at the request of Dr. John Dee in London, condensed all the non-geographical pieces of information into a few abbreviated lines in Latin. The doctor was only interested in information about the Northwest Passage. Mercator also repeated pieces of information, making it that much harder to interpret.

This is the first time we find America referred to as «Brazil» in a book. The name appeared «officially» for the first time in reference to an island west of Cornwall in England, on Angellino de Dolorto's Catalan compass map from 1325—thirty-five years earlier. The same map also represented Scandianvia in nearly correct form for the first time. From then on the northeast coast of America was called «Brazil».

The English geographer wrote that the North Pole was an abyss where the water disappeared into the interior of the earth. The abyss was not his idea—it was part of an ancient belief in a devouring whirlpool, and such notions could not easily be dismissed.

The other information about the North Pole remained unchallenged until modern times. The great Norwegian polar explorer, Fridtjof Nansen, as late as 1911 wrote in his book In the Northern Mists:[18]

«The notions about the polar regions are still unclear and vague. While some imagine a continent at the pole, others believe it to be surrounded by islands, with dangerous currents between. Yet others believe there is an open arctic ocean.»

A whole 556 years after the Inventio Fortunatæ expedition, on the 9th of May, 1926, Admiral Richard Byrd (1888–1957) flew from Svalbard to the North Pole and back without seeing any land. This was confirmed four days later, when the dirigible «Norge», with Roald Amundsen, Umberto Nobile and Lincoln Ellsworth on board, crossed the entire Arctic Ocean to Alaska. In 1937 a Russian expedition, led by I.D. Papanin, was carried on an ice floe across the area. They saw no land, but registered an ocean depth of more than 3000 meters. In 1958 the American nuclear submarine «Nautilus» crossed under the polar ice in four days. The crew established that the ocean at the pole was 4000 meters deep, and that the polar basin is divided in two by the high Lomonosov Ridge, which is thought to influence current and temperature conditions in the northern hemisphere.

Jacob Cnoyen—Mercator's source—says he was in Sweden when eight expedition members returned to the Norwegian king in 1364. The text indicates that some «witnesses» came along, who were Greenlanders with knowledge of the American side. The leader of the eight men appears to have been the bishop's man on Greenland, Ivar Baardssön.[19] He presented to the king the astrolabe that the geographer had used. We know from Mercator's copy, kept in the British Museum, that the king of England was given a copy of the book Inventio Fortunatæ, so it would have been appropriate for the «land owner», the king of Norway-Sweden, and the new pope, Urban V, to also receive their copies and their maps. Each one had to be hand written and hand drawn. And several were made. The map maker J. Ruysch noted on a map he made in 1506 that he based his knowledge about the North Pole on the book Inventio Fortunatæ.

When the German-Portuguese geographer Martin Behaim made the world's first known globe a few weeks before Columbus' voyage in 1492, called the «Columbus Globe», he referred to Inventio Fortunatæ on the polar side of the globe.[20]

Mercator only wanted geographical data about the world's «final climate», from 54°N to the North Pole, when he gathered this information. And that is too bad, because Inventio Fortunatæ contained more information about America. Christopher Columbus' son, Fernando, and the 16th century historian Las Casas, both wrote that Inventio Fortunatæ contained astonishing information about two floating islands far to the west on approximately the same latitude as the Cape Verde islands (18 degrees north). This could be the source of an inscription on a map by the Italian cartographer Andrea Bianco, drawn in 1448 (Biblioteca Ambrosiana, Milan). He made the following note in this ocean area: «Authentical islands, 1500 miles to the west». That is a fairly accurate estimate of the distance to Central America.

The second in command on Martin Frobisher's polar expedition, George Beste, writes that Inventio Fortunatæ described America as being very cold up north, «in respect of England», but rich and fertile farther south. Furthermore that one of the wide northern bays mentioned in the book is at about the same latitude as «The Fortunatæ Island»—meaning America.[21] According to the description, the sound referred to is Smith Sound between Greenland and north Canada.[22]

The Scandinavian expedition lasted four years, and we don't know where the rest of the ships went—or how the geographer spent the years 1361–64. In order to find the Greenlanders who had gone to America and turned heathen, they would necessarily have had to travel there.

The French writer Phillipe de Mezières, who in 1360 became chancellor for King Peter of Cyprus and Jerusalem, visited Norway in 1360, the year the expedition left, and in 1366, two years after it had returned. He writes about Norway in two of his books, as in Le songe du vieil pelerin (Paris, 1389) in the style of his day: «...from there they traveled to the kingdoms of Norway, Sweden and Denmark. They were told that one of them, the king of Norway, had an enormous kingdom. And that parts of it were an island in the ocean, so far from Norway and beyond Godeland [Greenland, or Grochlant?] that some ships sent there to collect taxes for him from his subjects took three years on the voyage back and forth.»

The World's First Map of North America

A few months after the expedition returned home, on January 27, 1365, Pope Urban thanked King Magnus for the visit paid him by his chaplain, Halstanus. We don't know if Pope Urban was given a copy of Inventio Fortunatæ, but we do know that he received the world's first known map of the east coast of America.

The Spanish scientist, Pedro de Medina, wrote in his book Libro de grandezas y cosas memorables de Españas (Seville, 1548): «Not far from Madeira there is another island called Antilia, which no man has seen. I found this island included on a very old sea chart. And because there is no information about it, I investigated far and wide to see if information or documents could be found. And on a Ptolemy [map with degrees] with letter and dedication to Pope Urban, I found this island included. According to the map it is 85 leagues at its longest north-south distance, and 28 leagues wide, and is full of rivers and harbors. On the map referred to, it is placed at approximately the same latitude as Gibraltar—at thirty-six and one half degree.»

Unfortunately we are not told who sent the map. But it leaves no doubt that this is the only map known to exist of North America before Columbus. Twenty copies have been found in various Mediterranean countries and in England. Urban V was pope from 1362 to 1370; Urban VI from 1378 to 1389. The recipient of the map must have been the former, because as early as 1367 the brothers Pizzigano of Venice started a map where the name «Antilia» for the first time was given to an island far out in the west Atlantic on the latitude of the Delaware peninsula, at the inlet of Chesapeake Bay. It is tied to a warning: «These statues [columns, cairns?] on the coast of Antilia have been erected to protect sailors. They signify that it is possible to navigate these waters. But beyond these statues lies the sea where the sailors cannot navigate.» It is almost precisely the same warning that the geographer and Ivar Baardssön used in connection with the mountain top in the utmost north—in other words a kind of geographcal marker of the outer limits of the world.

This map is kept at the University of Parma in Italy. In 1977 this author was able to have it photographed with the assistance of Mr. Odd Wibe of the Norwegian embassy in Rome. The map has subsequently been restored by the Italians.

The copies of this map are the only ones pre-dating Columbus on which the name of Antilia appears. The map is not in competition with

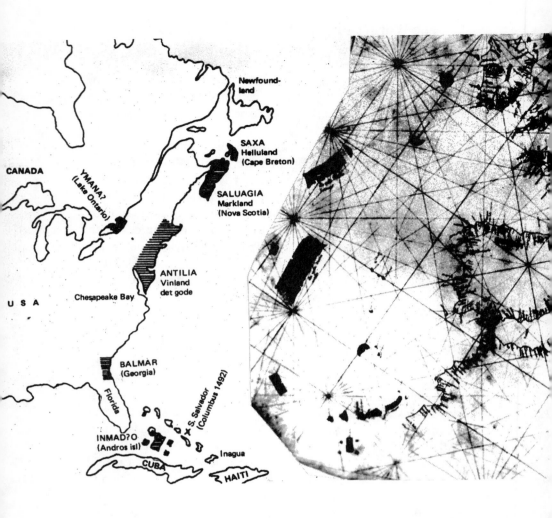

This is the version of Pope Urban's map which Columbus, according to his diary, must have used. Compared to a modern map, «Saxa» becomes Cape Breton, «Saluagia» Nova Scotia, «Antilia» Cape Cod-Virginia, «Balmar» the coast of Georgia-Florida, and «Inmad?o» the Bahama Islands.

other maps of America. The names that are used, do not appear on any other map until the 1500s, when Europeans from lands outside of Scandinavia began their voyages to North America.[23]

82

While the English geographer who wrote <u>Inventio Fortunatæ</u> described and mapped the world from the North Pole down to about 54°, Pope Urban's map continues from 54° south along the east coast of America. It is tempting to think that these two maps, which were made at about the same time, were intended to be seen as two parts of one and the same map. The geographer didn't necessarily have to have visited all locations himself. As mentioned, he made instrument measurements based on oral information as well. Thirty-three years earlier the pope had received the silver-footed bowl made from a nut shell. It doesn't conclusively prove anything, but it does give reason to suspect that someone had been much farther south at some earlier point.

Pope Urban's map starts in the north by marking the eastern tip of Newfoundland, which is called «Isola de ventura». A bit farther to the southwest is the island «Saxa», a name simply meaning «stone». When compared to modern maps on the same scale this could be the stony coast of Cape Breton. But it could also be the island Anticosi at the mouth of St. Lawrence River, and that the name thus indicates the southern point of the northernmost region in America—«Helluland», or «The Stone Land.»

The next «island» on the map is the large «Saluagia». «Salvaggio» is an Italian word which means forest lands where the wild or half-wild natives live. In the Vinland sagas this region is called «Markland», which also means forest land. On the very oldest of the maps «Saluagia» is called «Satan Island». But already in «Gripla», the Norse description of the world, the name «Skrælingeland» is used about Markland, while the Italian Medici sea atlas of 1351—nine years before our geographer's voyage—denotes this area as «Saluagia».

Projecting this map on to modern maps, the area becomes Nova Scotia, or the endless forests between the Gulf of St. Lawrence and the Gulf of Maine. Both possibilities correspond well with a little «island» to the southwest, which compared to modern maps becomes Lake Ontario, the lower of the Canadian lakes. It is very well rendered, including the little peninsula that protrudes from the west. Ships could reach there. This was as far as they were able to go, because the Niagara Falls blocked their way.

Then we come to the map's great land, «Antilia». It starts in the north with Cape Cod at the entrance to the Gulf of Maine, and extends down to the inlet of Chesapeake Bay in Virginia. Long Island appears to be represented as a peninsula. The Bay of Delaware is discernable. And the southern tip of the Delaware peninsula is so accurately drawn that it is no different than contemporary maps of the same scale.

83

The name «Antilia» means «the foremost island»—or the foremost land, because all the American lands are called «islands». In the Scandinavian languages «fremste», or foremost, had the meaning «best». The richest man was the foremost, and the best soil was foremost. This is still true of modern dialects in Norway.

Both in «Saluagia» and «Antilia» there were a number of place names that the Portuguese expert Dr. Armando Cortesao feels do not derive from Roman languages, and he wonders whether they may be Norse.[24] The seven places of Antilia became the most important destination for the explorers, because they were believed to be seven very rich cities. It was not unusual to call Antilia «the Land of the Seven Cities» or «Septe citades».

The most important of these seven names appears to have been «Cua», «Coe», «Choue» etc., apparently also the name of a kingdom. The geographer Johannis de Stobnicza of Cracow in his world atlas of 1512 called the land «Cuba: de bona ventura».[25] Translated: «Cuba: The Good», or «Cuba: The Fortunate». The name Cuba is pronounced «Ko'vâ» in Roman languages (Encyclopedia International). The Norse pronounciation was «Landit Go'ua».

Medieval cartographers placed great emphasis on quoting foreign place names. And when the northeastern America is here called «Terra Cuba» (Ko'vâ) on a number of maps, it seems to be a good rendition of «Landet Goda» (Go'ua).

In the southern part of this land—by Chesapeake Bay—there are two words: «Ansoli» and «Ansodi». The prefix «an» is used in all place names. If we remove the prefix, we have «Soli» and «Sodi», spelled with slight variation. «Soli Sudri» and «Solar Sudur» referred to the latitude of Africa in the language of the Norsemen.[26] In modern Icelandic, Africa is still called «Sudur Alfa»—the southern part.

The latitude at Chesapeake Bay is correctly noted—36°54'. This is the same latitude as Gibraltar and the northern coast of Africa.

European maps, for example Fricius' «Carta Marina» from 1525, called the land in the west «Terra de Cuba—Afrika part». As mentioned, all primary Norse sources call land off the American coast «The African Islands». The Portuguese Hamy map, Martin Waldseemuller's series of «The Admiral» maps (i.e. Columbus), Holbein's world map, and a number of others, use the name «Terra Cuba—Asie partis». In other words, «Asian» land.

On the maps generally known in Europe, the American continent stops at Chesapeake Bay. They apparently are all based on a copy of Pope

Urban's map that Andrea Bianco made in Ancona in Italy in 1436. Common to all of them was a stylized, nearly lifeless, rendition of America.[27] Europe and North Africa are on all these maps an exact copy of the very lively maps that the brothers Pizzigano made in 1367. But it was not possible to give the accurate distance between the continents—the paper was too narrow for that. Therefore the map indicated only 200 leagues, or 1080 kilometers, between the Azores and America.

No one went to the geographical section of the Vatican to make a new copy of the original that we know was kept there.

1. Flomannasaga was written around the year 1300 by an unknown author who had access to numerous sources. The author's description seems realistic and demonstrates considerable local knowledge about Greenland.
2. Roussell, 1941.
3. Ingstad, 1959, p. 268.
4. Roussell, 1941, p. 243.
5. Grönlands annaler.
6. Nordenskiöld, 1883.
7. Munch, 1864, p. 25 and 28.
8. The rating was made by Johanes A. Capestrao (d. 1456) in Kortfattet Geografisk Leksikon. See Haupte Zeitschrift für Deutches Alterthum, IV, p. 488.
9. Grimberg, vol. IX, 1956, p. 266.
10. Diplomatarium Norwegicum, Jan. 12, 1352.
11. Steinnes, 1958, pp. 409–19.
12. Dictionary of National Biography, XIV, p. 418.
13. Nansen, 1911, pp. 290–91.
14. British Museum: Ms. Cott. vit. c. VII, pp. 264–68. Norwegian translation by H.K. Schutter and Asgaut Steinnes available in Riksarkivet, Oslo.
15. Nares, 1878, vol. I, p. 88.
16. Diplomatarium Norwegicum, p. 1360.
17. Solomonsen (ed.), 1981, p. 11.
18. Nansen, 1911, p. 574.
19. Steinnes, 1958, p. 415.
20. Ravenstein, 1908.
21. Nansen, 1911, p. 267.

22. Beste, 1578, and Mercator's map of the polar region.
23. Cortesáo, 1954.
24. <u>Ibid</u>.
25. De Stobnicza, 1512.
26. Fritzner, 1954.
27. See <u>Aschehougs Verdenshistorie</u>, vol. VII, p. 114.

JOURNEYS IN THE DIM LIGHT OF HISTORY

We can not leave the subject of Norse activity in America without mentioning the Kensington Stone. It was found in 1899 by a Swedish settler, Olof Ohman, in Kensington, Minnesota, not far from Alexandria. While clearing his land he found a flat stone with a strange inscription on the underside and along the edge. The stone was entangled in the roots of an aspen tree that had grown over it. It was later determined that the aspen had been growing there for at least forty years. At that time no Europeans lived in the area. Olof Ohman came to the United States in 1881 from Hälsingeland, Sweden. Skeptics doubted the age of the tree, however, and it was destroyed.

No one could decipher the symbols. A local banker sent a rubbing of the stone to a professor of Scandianvian languages at the University of Minnesota. When the professor realized the inscription was runic and that the name «Vinland» appeared in the text, he thought someone was trying to prove that Leiv Eiriksson had been in Minnesota.

In the Minneapolis Journal of February 22, 1899, he wrote that the stone had to be a hoax. Neither Ohman nor his neighbors had any knowledge of or interest in runes. The stone was therefore left in a shed.

Nine years later the Norwegian-American historian Hjalmar Holand came to the area and was told about the find. He visited Ohman, who gave him the stone. Holand interpreted the text on the flat side as follows: «Eight Goths [from Götaland in Sweden] and twenty-two Norwegians on an expedition from Vinland to the west. We camped at two capes [or reefs] one day north of this stone. We went fishing. When we came back we found ten men red with blood, and dead. AVM [Ave Maria] save us from harm [or destruction].»

The text on the edge read: «Ten men have been sent to the sea to look for our ship fourteen days' journey from this island. Anno 1362.» The term «island» is consistently used about all land and regions in America before Columbus, and this has been seen as proof of authenticity.

Holand, who later became a professor of history, spent the rest of his life trying to get the stone accepted as authentic. Linguists argued that the language used was not correct Old Norse. But in 1305–50, Norway-Sweden adopted a standard Old Norse language, and if we look at correspondence from this period, the text on the Kensington Stone is no more un-Norwegian or un-Swedish than contemporary letters, which also often contained English and German words.[1]

Runic characters were not generally used as a written language in the late Middle Ages, but were rather a kind of contemporary «graffiti». Merchants used it among themselves, and it was especially used when people appealed to the higher powers. In addition to the usual runes, there were «secret runes» that could only be interpreted by those in the know, and which were the subject of much superstition and mysticism on the part of ordinary people.

Norwegian, Swedish and Danish rune experts were particularly averse to accepting the Kensington Stone as authentic. They claimed that the symbols were from a far more recent Swedish runic chart, and that the runic writer would have to have been from the turn of the 19th century.

Holand still won much enthusiastic support for his claim, and the stone is today on display at the Smithsonian Institution in Washington, D.C. In Minnesota a special museum was built for it, and the Immigrant Museum in Norway has a copy.

Unfortunately there was a fatal flaw in Hjalmar Holand's argument. He assumed that the day's journeys which the stone mentioned, referred to «dögr» or sailing distance at sea—in this case 14 x 144 nautical miles. If correct, the expedition would have had to come via the long and difficult route across Hudson Bay. But medieval land distances were measured in terms of how far one could travel per day on foot—usually 30–40 kilometers on average. Thus the 14 day journey west from the stone would reach the western shore of Lake Superior, the westernmost of the Great Lakes. Since there were 32 men in the expedition, and more than one ship is referred to, the boats must have been small and light.

When it became generally known in the 1950s that there had probably been a Scandinavian-English expedition in America in 1362, it was immediately assumed that it had something to do with the Kensington Stone, particularly since the Swedish king who would have sent the expedition lived in Västergötland, where the eight men were from, according to the stone. The latest supporting evidence of such an expedition is a note written on a copy of Pope Urban's map, just west of the Canadian lakes, which reads: «Newly discovered land.»[2]

But this has not changed the minds of the rune experts. The Swedish institution, Runeverket, with a new generation of resident experts, continues to claim that we are dealing with a hoax. Norway has no such official experts. The most recent theory about the stone is that a defrocked and drunken priest was the perpetrator. Earlier the farmer himself had been under suspicion.

The dispute flared up again when a code expert from World War II, Alf Monge, supported by O.G. Landsverk, claimed in a number of books and publications that the stone was authentic. An American professor summed up the situation: Nothing has been proved, and nothing has been disproved, about the Kensington Stone. New evidence must be presented before the argument can be settled.

It is worth noting that in addition to the stone, a number of other intriguing items have been found in the Kensington area, inclucing axes, a halberd, and tools from the 1300s. This further complicates the matter.

There were other Europeans in the western Atlantic in the 1300s as well.

The account of the two brothers Nicolo and Antonio Zeno from Venice appeared 20–30 years after Inventio Fortunatæ was published. For many years they had collaborated with an active pirate leader in the area around Greenland-North America. It is unclear whether their pirate's nest was located somewhere on South Greenland or on Newfoundland— Labrador. Their relationship to the Norwegian government was strained. Both brothers were known to belong to the lower ranks of Venetian nobility.

Antonio wrote several letters home to Venice during his piracy period, in which he reported interesting information about the Greenland monastery in Ravnsfjord, that was heated by a warm spring. He also drew a map that was known in the 1400s. Here a land named «Frisland» is noted, later to be associated with South Greenland. As we shall see later, Columbus was familiar with this name. Juan de la Cosa used it on his world map in the year 1500. Many names on the American side are also mentioned, and we recognize several place names from countries in the North Atlantic, Norway among them.

But both the map and the letters came to a sad end when a little boy in the family tore up and destroyed most of them in the early 1500s. Later, as a grown man, he tried to put it all back together as a book. Unfortunately, he made a mess of the map he glued back together, adding «new» islands with names recalled from the letters. The worst thing he did, was to place a very nicely drawn Iceland at the tip of Greenland, while «Frisland» ended up in Iceland's position. The Swedish geographer, A.E. Nordenskiöld, feels that the book and the map still reveal considerably more ship traffic on the northeast coast of America than was generally thought. The map is based on such good observations that it is 300 years ahead of its time, he claims. And it appears that one of the two brothers must have been well acquainted with small communities founded by Europeans on Newfoundland and the Canadian coast. The book offers some well informed descriptions of social conditions on the American side. It describes the Eskimos and their strange kayaks a good many years before they headed from Canada to Greenland.

For our purposes we are more interested in a special event that Antonio Zeno tells us about. A Greenland or Greenland-American fisherman and his five friends were driven south by a storm, and were captured by Indians who lived in a tribe «a thousand miles west of Frisland». There they remained for five years. The Indians apparently had had contact with white men before, because the chief owned a Latin book of which nobody understood a word. The Indians themselves used some unintelligible written symbols. The land was fertile, and the population seemed to live much like the Norsemen did—except that their climate was much warmer. They grew wheat, and they made an alcoholic beverage that was compared to mead. They had their own sign language and were familiar with metals, but not with the compass. The prisoners acquired a certain degree of respect and trust, and they were brought along when a fleet of 12 vessels went on a journey farther south. The purpose of the trip is not mentioned. During the voyage they met with bad weather. In pitiful condition they reached the north coast of a new land and were immediately taken prisoners. Most were killed and eaten by naked primitive people. These natives did not know metals, and used bow strings made of twisted animal hides. The white fishermen's lives were saved because one of them taught the Indians to use fishing nets both in the sea and in fresh water.

The news about the clever hunter from the north spread fast, and he was passed from owner to owner, until he believed he had seen most of this big land during the 13 years he was kept prisoner. It was like a new world, he said. Far to the south there were highly developed cultures which had cities of stone, and temples where humans were sacrificed and eaten. There were also great quantities of gold and silver.

He finally managed to escape to the north, and was able to join the more primitive chieftains whose prisoner he had been earlier. But the ocean prevented flight further north, and he stayed on this coast for three years. Then he was told by the natives that three foreign vessels had arrived. These boats turned out to be from the north where he had first been taken prisoner. They took him along because he had become a useful interpreter after his long sojourn to the south, and they had come to trade. When the three vessels returned to the Indian land in the north, he was allowed to build a ship by which he was able to sail back to «Frisland».

The story seems to be the account of a shipwreck on the southeastern coast of the United States, with a subsequent stay in Mexico, where ritual cannibalistic sacrifices were common in the 1300s, and where the cities and language symbols, and the gold and silver treasures, evoke images of both the Mayan and Aztec cultures.

When the fisherman finally returned home and told about the riches in the south, a large pirate expedition was organized. One of the Zeno brothers was the second in command. The fisherman was supposed to be the navigator, but he died before the expedition left, so they had to make do without him.

Far to the west or southwest they made contact with an Indian tribe that had taken a northerner prisoner. With his assistance it looked for a while like they would be able to maintain contact with the natives, but they quickly became leary of the withdrawn and war-like Indians. Not surprisingly, when they anchored they were subject to a well organized and massive attack, accompanied by yelling, screaming and showers of arrows. Many were killed, and the expedition had to leave the area. The account is almost identical to other descriptions of warring Indians on the coast of Florida and Georgia before Europeans settled there.

After this the pirates sailed out to sea heading southwest, until they arrived at a new and more primitive land inhabited by small Indians. There the expedition decided to establish a colony. Some of those who sailed in «boats that could be rowed» stayed behind. This must mean that the expedition had long ships. But most of the expedition members had had more than enough, and returned home to more northern waters, and finally to Greenland, in their pirate ships.

According to Nordenskiöld the original Zeno map was reproduced by Nikolai Donis in Ulm in 1482 and 1486, but the copies have disappeared.

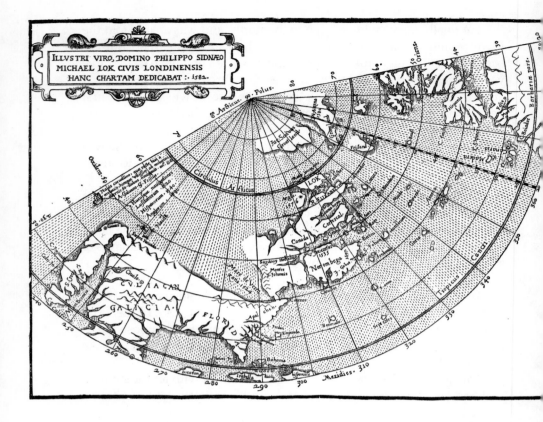

Columbus reported that he sailed 550 kilometers west of «Thule», and that «Thule» was the same as the island «Frisland». The name comes from the medieval Zeno map, and «Frisland» was always considered the southern tip of Greenland—as on this English map of 1582 by Michael Look.

The account of the Zeno brothers was well known in the 1500s. Later on historians tended to doubt the story. But as researchers have gathered more detailed information, the account becomes an interesting challenge to a new generation of historians—and perhaps for computer scientists who may be able to do a better job of assembling the map than the young Zeno did.

The learned Hugo Grotius in the 1600s stated that the Norse Greenlanders had reached Mexico, but he offered no source. Claims that there have been «white Indians» along many of the waterways in the northern and middle parts of South America, are well known and much discussed. Three South American universities are cooperating in gathering material,

but it is proving a difficult task to separate the evidence about these white inhabitants from material about the European colonists who arrived on the continent later. One of the latest developments is the idea that blood tests may yield useful information.

The Tie to Norway Breaks

Even if both merchants and pirates visited Greenland, the need for new blood was a problem for the polar island. According to old church statutes, marrying couples could be no closer than eighth cousins. Most youths were. As early as the middle 1100s the bishop raised the issue with the archbishop in Trondheim, who subsequently asked the pope for dispensation from the rule.

Pope Alexander III then gave permission for marriage between fifth, sixth and seventh cousins. The pope didn't use the name of the land. He only noted that it was 12 days' journey, or 1728 nautical miles, away from Norway. This has caused some to believe that the edict referred to a congregation of Greenlanders in America. But most historians agree that it was the Greenlanders themselves who received this happy news from Rome. The pope's generosity no doubt aided the cause of love, but the Greenlanders still had to do an awful lot of calculating before they were able to figure out whether or not to love each other.

Not everyone was as lucky as the young Sigrid Björnsdatter. In the fall of 1407 an Icelandic ship on its way to Norway drifted off course to Greenland. The sailors spent the winter there—probably in order to trade. And that's how the sailor Torstein Olavsson met his bride. She promised to go with him when the ships left. They were solemnly wed in Hvalsöy Church on September 16, 1408, with many guests attending. We know this information, because what happened on that fall Sunday is described in the last written records about the Norse Greenlanders. This last communication indicated that everything was normal.[3]

But this was not the case.

Norway was nearly in chaos. An agreement dating to the 1200s that entitled Greenland to two ships calling every year, and Iceland to six visitations, was unheeded and forgotten. As a result the lands in the ocean became dependent upon the Norwegian fleet that was operating out of Bristol and Lynn in England. In 1412 the first English fish trader arrived on Iceland.[4] Others soon followed, and after that the provinces were no longer dependent upon Copenhagen and victims of Danish misrule. The tie between Norway and Greenland was never re-established.

In a letter dated July 1, 1419, the population of Iceland informed the king that the ships they were entitled to by law, had not come for many years. And therefore they did not intend to heed King Erik's edict of 1413 forbidding them to trade with foreigners. The same year Iceland's «hirds-tjore» (the island's highest chieftain) wrote that the wares they received from the English included cloth, canvas, malt, flour, «bjor» (strong beer), butter, wine, pitch, raw tar, iron, honey, codliver oil, copper vessels, footwear, blankets, planks, oars, salt, wax, horse shoes, hats, knives, etc.[5]

The ship traffic with England increased explosively, and England became Europe's primary supplier of dried fish. It says something about the extent of the trade that twenty-five English ships went down in a storm off Iceland in 1419.[6]

But in the wake of this fleet of ships, more pirates came.[7] They also were active in slave trade, kidnapping and buying children from destitute parents and carrying them to England as slaves. An Icelandic bishop— probably the Englishman John Craxton of Hole—found such youths both from Iceland and north Norway at Lynn, and ordered them sent home.

The same lawless conditions reigned in Greenland. Pope Nicolaus V wrote in 1448 that the pirate fleet came via «the heathen coasts»— meaning the coasts of America and Canada, where the trade in walrus tusks and polar bear skins must have been a veritable gold mine for the privateers. In Greenland too, churches were burned and young people carried off as slaves. Only the more isolated churches were left standing. The pope states that these slaves were also set free and taken back to their homeland, where they attempted to build new homes among the ruins.[8]

Transporting the Greenlanders was probably no problem—Bristol's shippers and traders were some years later spoken of as Greenland's primary trading partners.[9]

It is understandable that the Vatican was furious about the state of affairs in the far north, for among other things ivory was now ending up in French seaports and not in the Vatican's trading and financial centers in Europe.

1. Taranger (ed.), vol. III, 1915, p. 81.
2. Cortesáo, 1954.
3. Annales Islandi, vol. I, p. 268.
4. Taranger (ed.), vol. III, 1915, p. 265.
5. Ibid., p. 266.
6. Ibid., p. 267.
7. Magnussen, 1813, p. 112.
8. Diplomatarium Norwegicum, VI, no. 527.
9. Columbus, 1918, p. 20.

COLUMBUS MEETS «CHINESE» IN KAYAKS

In the 1460s, a young sailor named Christobal Colon, born in 1451, came to Portugal from Genoa. He was later to be known as Christopher Columbus. His brother, Bartolomeo, who had come to Lisbon before him, made a living as a cartographer and navigational consultant. Bartolomeo mysteriously bragged that his knowledge had not been gleaned from scholars. Christopher was bright, and well informed for his time, and very enterprising. Neither of the two brothers is known to have written or spoken Italian, between themselves or with others. Some researchers have suggested that they may have been Spanish-Jewish immigrants in Genoa.[1] The Norwegian genealogical researcher, Sven Grodys, believes that they were born in the Columba monastery on the island of Iona in the Hebrides, and that their last name hails from there, but that the family for some time lived in Genoa. During his active life, Columbus had contacts with Bristol in England and Galway in Ireland. Regardless of his roots, seafarers and traders from Genoa and Venice were accorded high status in all countries.

There are countless colorful, but unsubstantiated tales and fantastic stories about Columbus' voyage of 1492. He has also been lambasted as an irresponsible dreamer and religious fanatic, the latter because he wrote to the regents that he believed he was an instrument of God's will. (This was a common form of expression in the 1400s, and I have yet to see a letter addressed to sovereigns in which God's will was left out.) Columbus is touted as the inventor of the globe, and hailed as the discoverer of the round earth. There is no limit to the praise heaped upon him by history.

Despite all this, there have always been historians who knew that Columbus left very clear information about almost everything he did. There are few people from the 1400s that we know more about. The detailed agreement with the Spanish throne about his voyage and occupation of America («with God's help») is kept in the Spanish national archives, along with the Spanish license granting rights to occupy «Binini» (Vinini), Columbus' name for Florida-Georgia, which was his intended destination in 1492. Columbus' diaries are available in excellent translations. His notes and letters have been collected, and if we take all of this seriously, there is little left for speculation. The time is ripe for a re-evaluation of Columbus and his accomplishments.

With the help of experts I have consulted the original materials, and what follows is an attempt to reconstruct exactly what it was that he did.

He first sailed on several ships in the Mediterranean, visiting ports in Spain and Portugal. Later he sailed to the Portuguese colonies in Africa, as well as northward to England and Ireland. In between voyages he read much of the contemporary and ancient handwritten works available in Latin about geography and science. Portugal was then the center of world exploration, and many foreign geographers headed there to hear the latest news about the world outside of Europe.

Most of what we know about Columbus personally, was recorded by his youngest son, Fernando, who appears to have been closer to him than other family members, and who went with him on his fourth voyage to the West Indies. Fernando was a learned man with a large library and valuable archives. He carefully went through the papers his father left, and wrote honestly and dispassionately—for better or for worse a biography that still exists. Unfortunately it has been «edited» by some translators. Important information about Columbus' knowledge of the far north and the fact that he read Inventio Fortunatæ have been removed. So when in doubt, it is necessary to go back to the first edition of 1537.

As a young adult Columbus happened upon something that completely changed his life: A book about America. A sailor who went with him on the first three voyages to the New World and who later ended up in Turkish imprisonment, said that it was a coincidence that Columbus came upon the book—and that in it he found all the information he needed for his famous voyage to the West Indies.[2] «The Admiral's Book» is mentioned by Columbus himself in his diary—for instance during the voyage entries from September 25, October 3, and October 10 of 1492.

At this time there was only one book in existence about America, and that was Inventio Fortunatæ, published 110 years earlier. The printing press had not yet been invented, so there were just a few handwritten Latin copies in existence.

There was also only one map of America, or «Antilia»—and that was Pope Urban's map, of the same date as the book. In Columbus' diary entry of October 10, 1492, he says that the map he used was reproduced in the book.

97

Fernando Columbus writes about this: «What inspired my father's interest in discovering the New World, was the information he found in Portugal about the island Antilia, that lay 200 leagues [600 nautical miles] west of the Canary Islands and the Azores.»[3]

The 200 leagues mentioned by Fernando, can be found on all the 19 known copies of Pope Urban's map, where the east coast of the United States between Boston and Chesapeake Bay is called Antilia. Commmon to all the copies of the map in existence in Europe was the fact that they only went as far down as the Azores, and Chesapeake Bay in Virginia. Only the map in «The Admiral's Book» indicated that there was land further south.

The close friend and confidant of the Columbus family, the historian Las Casas, who made the copy of Columbus' diary that we know today, wrote the same thing as Fernando about the map of America in his work Historia de Las Indias.

And finally the «Director of Information» at the Spanish court at the time of Columbus, Pietro Martire, wrote that the land Columbus later went to find, was really a part of Antilia.[4]

By then the Portuguese had for many years sailed the 200 leagues west from the Azores, never finding any «mainland and some islands» out there in the sunset. The distance there remained the great mystery. No one considered the fact that the size of the paper on which the map had been drawn made it impossible to indicate the correct distance. After all, more than a century had passed since the map had been made, in another country.

But then along came Columbus, the clever lad who knew how to figure out the distance. Two hundred years after the birth of Christ the Greek mathematician and geographer Claudius Ptolemy had drawn and written the most important handbook of geography in all antiquity, in eight volumes. It incorporated the entire known world at that time, between the 10th and 60th latitude—between Guinea and the Hebrides—and from west to east between the Hebrides and Java/Sumatra. He had divided the round world into 360 lines between the north and south poles. These lines were farther and farther apart as they approached the mid section of the sphere. Ptolemy first became known in Europe when Jacob Angelus translated his astronomical work, Almagest, into Latin in 1409–10. But when we look closer, he had already been known for some time.[5] Since maps indicated that Antilia was located somewhere between the 36th and 42nd northern latitude, perhaps Ptolemy's system might provide the answer to how far away it was?

The twenty-three year old Columbus sent a letter to the Ptolemy-expert Paolo Toscanelli of Florence about the matter. The reply from the old scientist is dated June 24, 1474. He wrote:

«The distance from Portugal to Antilia, that you Portuguese call «The Island of the Seven Cities» (the 7 place names on the map of Antilia) is 624 leagues (1872 nautical miles.) Furthermore it is 625 leagues from Antilia to Japan, and 375 leagues from Japan to the Chinese coast that Marco Polo describes. A voyage west from Lisbon to China must therefore be divided into three stages.»

Toscanelli was really a mathematician, and the question of Antilia was a secondary matter to him. The letter indeed reveals that he based his estimates on the well-known copy of Pope Urban's map that was available everywhere, and that only went as far south as Chesapeake Bay. Therefore he suggested that the voyage go directly west from Portugal. Toscanelli's estimate of the circumference of the earth at 36°N was otherwise quite good, and he also included a map to support the figures. The map has disappeared.

The letter created no great stir. Young Columbus did not reveal any plans to follow Toscanelli's suggestion for an ocean crossing that far north. He had his own book with a map—and plans for quite a different way to cross the Atlantic.

Columbus came to Portugal at the same time that two shipowners sought help in Scandinavia to sail to North America.[6] The Portuguese and the Danish-Norwegian royal houses were related by marriage and had long exchanged maritime information. The Dane Vallarte, attached to the court of King Christopher (1440–48) for example, went on a Portuguese expedition to Guinea.[7]

King Christian in Copenhagen didn't have the slightest interest in such matters. He was the first of a number of kings who was interested in only one thing—himself. Christian had begun to «cash in» on the old Norse kingdom. He mortgaged the Norwegian Orkneys and Hebrides to a Scottish colleague in order to come up with a dowry for his daughter. The mortgage was never paid off. Royal misrule had the most dire consequences for Greenland. Thanks to the steady supply of ivory from Greenland, Bergen had become the ivory center of Europe. But Norway's foreign trade disintegrated under the most peculiar agreements between the king and the German Hanseatic League. Traders from as far away as Egypt waited in vain for Greenland falcons, narwhal spears, polar bear skins and ship ropes. The result was that sailors, traders and pirates from other countries took over the trade with Greenland. The sea ports of Dieppe and Rouen in France subsequently became the centers for the ivory trade of Europe.[8]

But King Christian solved the problem of the Portuguese request that the Danes accompany them by leaving the Scandinavian part of the expedition to two pirates: Didrik Pining, probably German, and Hans Pathorst from Helsingör in Denmark. They were not familiar with the northern waters, so they used the Norwegian Jon Skolp as pilot. He is mentioned both on Fricius' globe of 1536–37, and in Francesco Loped de Gomara's Historia de las Indias (Seville, 1553). From the Portuguese side the low ranked noblemen Alvaro Martins Homem and Joanno vas Corte Real participated—probably each with his own ship. Apart from Homem they were a plague on both the shipping and people of the small North Atlantic communities.

Even as the Portuguese now eyed the far north, it didn't mean that the lands in the south were less interesting. A letter dated January 12, 1473, from Portugal's king, Alfons, to the Infante de Brites (a prince without right of succession) grants rights to explore some islands or lands that are supposed to lie west of the Cape Verde islands. «They have long been sought, but they have still not been found,» wrote the king.[9] The information about these islands was available in the book Inventio Fortunatæ. But the king's son never reached this land, and the southern route never became popular. The European seafarers still had only the amputated copy of Pope Urban's map that ended at Chesapeake Bay.

According to both Norwegian and Portuguese sources, the Danish-Portuguese expedition called both in Iceland and Greenland.[10] This grim collection of pirates and thugs had to finance the trip themselves, and they knew no other way to support themselves than by a combination of trade and piracy.

For the isolated and defenseless Greenlanders the visit added new weight to their burden.

On the Faroe Islands a ledger has been found with an entry stating that Pining and Pathorst had been on Iceland for several years, and that from there they sailed a number of times to Greenland «to trade».[11] And Olaus Magnus says in his work about the peoples of Scandinavia that Pining and Pathorst fled to Greenland because they had been declared «outlaws».[12]

Most ominous of all was the fact that the slave trader Corte Real had made note of the isolated and defenseless polar community.

It appears that the expedition may have turned by the Labrador coast. Indications on old English maps may suggest that they headed south in the direction of the Hudson Bay—Ungava Bay area. The object was probably to buy, or steal, walrus tusks, falcons and polar bear skins.

It could not have been a voyage of exploration, because those required royal permission. On November 10, 1475, the king of Portugal wrote a letter granting Fernando Teles explici t rights to discover Antilia with the seven cities and other islands in the western Atlantic Ocean. Royal permission to discover America was never given to two persons at the same time, and Homem and Corte Real were very much alive. In the process, his majesty committed a political and historical dirty trick indicating that he had ulterior motives. The author of Inventio Fortunatæ stated that the legendary English King Arthur had discovered and claimed these lands as early as the year 530. Now the king rewrote history, stating that the land «Antilia» had been found and claimed by Spanish and Portuguese clergymen in the 700s. [13] Anyone who first found a «heathen» land, had the right to claim it.

The Portuguese version of the legend in Inventio Fortunatæ would hereafter accompany Pope Urban's map. This strengthens the supposition that the map and the book are one and the same thing.

In royal edicts found in the archives of the Agra castle on the Azores, dated February and April, 1474, Homem and Corte Real are appointed governors on some islands in the Azores. [14] In the letters of appointment we are only told that the two had returned home after a successful voyage to «Terra los Baccalaos» (dry fish land).

Three generations of Homems became noted cartographers. Maps from the Homem family show a correct coastline of the Gulf of Maine and Fundy Bay[15]—the heart of Norse territory in America. All other cartographers used the large triangle that we are familiar with from Pope Urban's map. The Homems also used place names that were otherwise unknown. Among other things we find «Grölandagno» between Boston and New York, which in Homem's language was a reference to Greenlanders. The Norse spelling was «Grönland».

The pirate Pining also made good use of his northern experiences.

In the winter of 1476–77 the Hanseatic League had forced the king in Copenhagen to stop all English trade in Norwegian countries. English ships were to be seized, unless they were storm driven and were seeking port in an emergency. In the winter of 1476–77 an unusual number of ships left Bristol headed for Iceland, according to the parchment documents that the customs officials kept.

Didrik Pining was therefore sent to Iceland as DenmarkNorway's top official. He promptly stopped all English trade in dried fish, and allowed the thugs on his ships to ravage the population—to plunder, kill and rape. For England, the dry fish situation became critical. There was only one country where the dry fish traders were not under attack: Greenland. There was only one thing for the skippers to do, and that was to go there.[16]

The colorful desperado Pining was later rumored to have been hanged from the rig by his own crew. But that was still a long way off.

Christobal Colon, Climate Observer

As all of this occurred, the sailor Christopher Columbus of Portugal was occupied with more scientific concerns, his son writes. He had read in Inventio Fortunatæ that west-southwest of the Cape Verde islands there were two floating islands held together by trees, branches and roots. The father had also read in a book, Naturales Questiones, by the Roman senator and philosopher Seneca, about floating islands in India made of pumice stone—and about reports of the half unreal island of St. Brendan, based on Irish saga-like legends.

The information in Inventio Fortunatæ about the islands is of particular interest because the floating islands referred to, really did exist—in Central America. The Indians made them from trees, branches, roots, underbrush, sticks and seaweed. On top of these «blankets» they put mud and dirt and half rotted plants from dams and lakes. This method of cultivation, called «chinampa», yielded excellent crops. In Mexico, where the method is best known, such an island would meet the needs of 100 large families for corn, pumpkins, and beans—the most important foods besides meat and fish. The information about the islands is so unusual that the author of Inventio Fortunatæ couldn't possibly have invented such a method of cultivation known nowhere else in the world, and even point out precisely where it was being used. Someone must have seen or described the artificial islands.

It is not clear why Colombus was so keenly interested in this phenomenon. Perhaps he was simply collecting interesting geographical information, because he was working on something else—a plan inspired by the same book.

102

By this time he had sailed extensively in the world which Ptolemy had divided into five climatic zones, from the torrid zone of the south to the icy north. Ptolemy's world map ended, as mentioned earlier, north and west of the Hebrides at 60°N. But now Homem and Corte Real and their crews returned to Lisbon after having sailed more than one thousand nautical miles further west than Ptolemy's western limit. Fernando says that his father objected to the learned opinion that offered such an erroneous presentation of the world. Las Casas writes: «Since the forefathers fell asleep, things had just continued as before.» Christobal Colon, as he was still called then, wanted to write his own book about the climate and conditions as they truly were in the five climatic zones and to do away with the scientists' claims that both the torrid south and the frozen north were uninhabitable for humans.[17] This was one of the most hotly debated issues of the day.

In addition to Inventio Fortunatæ, Columbus was particularly interested in Marco Polo's description of China, where the the author had lived as the first European for 24 years. Marco reported that east of China there were many islands rich in gold and spices, among them the large Japan. And to the northeast stretched a vast mainland in the direction of northern Europe—Tangut (now Siberia), which was also called «Bergi regio». Inventio Fortunatæ, the book about the Norwegian-Swedish-English expedition to America and the Northwest Passage in 1360, explained that the Asian land of «Bergi Regio» that Marco Polo referred to, stretched to «Grochlant»—in other words to 73–76 degrees just west of Greenland.[18] And here Columbus quickly drew a very important conclusion in his personal world description: People could live as far north as 70–80°N, because it said in Inventio Fortunatæ that the expedition had encountered «pygmees».

«Chinese» in the Desolate North

Columbus wanted to experience for himself the people of the northern outpost of the world, far north and west of the world's outer limits as established by the great Ptolemy: «Probandolo con la experiencia de la navegacion.»[19]

The only possible way to get there, that we are aware of—excluding the pirates—was to sign on with one of the English vessels that traded in the northern hunting areas. A name that figures in this context was the merchant John Jay of Bristol—a second generation immigrant whose father had the same name and who is thought to have been a Norwegian emigree, shipowner and merchant. In Bristol's customs ledgers John Jay Sr. first appears on the 20th of August of 1461 with a cargo of dried fish from Bergen. He is referred to as a «Denizen» meaning a foreigner who now lives in England. The ships belonging to Jay Jr. traveled between Spain-Portugal-Scandinavia-Ireland-England-Scotland and Iceland, with detours to America. According to the customs ledgers, Jay was an important importer of cloth from the Mediterranean countries. And as we shall see later, he was a very good and close friend of Christopher Columbus. He was a partner in a number of enterprises in the north and the west, and he was no doubt pleased to see a professional Italian seaman voluntarily sign on for one of these expeditions.

But Las Casas' Columbus biography and other sources imply that Galway in Ireland had something to do with the voyage that Columbus joined. Galway was the last stop before open ocean, and the first port that voyagers to America and Greenland reached when returning to Europe.

The ship sailed in February. Nothing is told of the journey out. But it is not unreasonable to assume that it followed the same course as the rest of the dried fish fleet which left for Iceland during the same month. They were risking running into Didrik Pining and his pirates, so they probably didn't tarry long after the water barrels had been filled.

In theory, the ship that Columbus talks about would have reached the hunting ground west of Greenland in the early summer. The latitude noted by Fernando Columbus is a little north of the North Cape in Norway, so they would have had midnight sun. The days were filled with sparkling clean air and a warm sun, and the nights were light, but cold. Ice would have been drifting from the fjords, and birds migrating from the south in a never ending stream. In this vicinity lay the magnetic north pole that could make the compass needle tremble and spin.

By 1477 there were Eskimos both in West Greenland and on the Canadian side. The description in Inventio Fortunatæ says that they had their homeland near there. And now Columbus made the discovery of his life—these people were Chinese. They had managed to reach Europe in their small boats, he wrote.[20] There must be a Northwest Passage between China and Europe. Christopher Columbus was the first man to state this fact.

Columbus wrote to Fernando about this voyage:

104

«In the month of February, 1477, I sailed one hundred leagues beyond the island of Thule, to an island that is in latitude 73°N—and not 63 degrees as some people believe. And Thule does not lie upon the meridian where Ptolemy says the west begins, but much farther west. And to this island, which is as big as England, the English come with their wares, especially from Bristol. In some places the difference between the tides was 26 bracios. When I was there, the sea was not frozen. The Thule of which Ptolemy speaks does in fact lie where he says it lies, but much farther to the west. And today it is called Frisland.»[21]

What Fernando here reports, is Columbus' geographical testament. If we study the map that Mercator made on the basis of the information in Inventio Fortunatæ, we can see that Columbus followed the exact same course as the Englishman who wrote the book in 1360, seventeen years earlier.

According to his own words, he sailed 100 leagues (300 nautical miles) past the place assumed to be «Frisland» on the southern tip of Greenland, which he named «Thule». The ship must have continued up to Kroksfjordheiene, or «Grochlant», as the Inventio Fortunatæ calls the Kroksfjords, with the trapping stations and Eskimo dwelling places at 73–76°N. The distance he cites from Greenland is correct. He also wrote that Thule, which Ptolemy wrote about in the year 200 (the Hebrides), was on the correct latitude, but that it was really «Frisland» which was at the tip of Greenland on maps for over 200 years. His «Thule» is assigned the same latitude as south Greenland. The French Laon globe from 1493 places Thule west of Iceland. Then Columbus provides some practical information—the ocean was not frozen when the ship reached 73 degrees. Normally the ice begins to break up in this region in May, or earlier.[22] The sea is not ice-bound for very long. In 1942, a ship unloaded its cargo here after the polar night had begun.[23] About the land he visited he reported that he observed a difference between high and low tides of 26 braccio (15.5 meters). This is correct. The world's greatest tidal difference, of precisely 26 braccio, could be found in the heart of the Norse area in Fundy Bay. It was an oddity that most seamen must have heard about, since it caused so many difficulties.

His information about the English ships that traded in «Thule», must refer to Greenland. In the summer of 1477, as mentioned, all the English ships were chased away from Iceland by Pining's fleet. His notes, in that case, would be the only account from the «scene of the crime» about the

Gerhardus Mercator copied this map from the book *Inventio Fortunatæ*, and it contains important historical information about a Norwegian-Swedish-English expedition that encountered Eskimos in 1360–64. A note on the island "Grochlant" at 73 degrees (the Canadian Devon Island) states that the inhabitants were Swedish.

Christoper Columbus, who also read *Inventio Fortunatæ*, writes that he sailed to an island (II) that was at 73 degrees north, 550 kilometers west of "Thule" (I). And that Thule, spoken of by Ptolemy in the second century A.D. (The Hebrides, III), really is "Frisland" (IV) at the southern tip of Greenland. Mercator did not correct the details, he said. The shape and location of Frisland and Iceland are therefore switched.

Some have interpreted Columbus to mean that he sailed 550 kilometers past Iceland to Greenland. In that case his ship must have followed the country's west coast up to the walrus hunting area of Upernavik at 73 degrees.

last days of the Greenlanders. It provides an explanation of the great mystery of all the «frozen» bodies in Herjulfsnes churchyard which the Danish archeologist Poul Nörlund uncovered in 1921. They wore clothes that were fashionable in Europe around the 1500s—almost a century after the connection with Norway had been severed.[24]

Columbus' voyage in the wake of the English geographer was to become the beginning of his great success and subsequent tragic fall. We can never forgive Fernando that he only quotes this excerpt from the letter. The world for 500 years has viewed what he wrote as more or less incomprehensible, in part because researchers could not understand what business a European ship could possibly have had in the Arctic. The traffic to the «ivory center» of Europe at 73°N is still a fairly unknown historical chapter outside Scandinavia. Some historians have thought that he simply presented a confused description of Iceland, although it is only at 63 degrees. Some of the blame for this rests with the Zeno map from the late Middle Ages, on which the position of Iceland and Frisland had been reversed.

Gerard Mercator also used the name «Thule» for south Iceland. This is such an important matter in Columbus' life that we must examine the possibility—that 300 nautical miles west of Iceland might also have denoted Greenland. Upernavik, the best hunting ground on Greenland, was located at 73°N as well. The inlet there was even marked by cairns. But this does not square with the information about the tidal difference of 15.5 meters between high and low tide—this is only the case on the American side. And it is completely at odds with what Columbus wrote; that «Frisland», on the south tip of Greenland, was «Thule».

107

It was important for Columbus to be specific about how far north he had been if he expected to be taken seriously as a climate observer. His writings had probably been misinterpreted before. Of all the notes that Columbus left, this is the clearest one. He specifies for all time that it is not the 63rd latitude that he had visited. Indeed, he had to go as far as the 73rd latitude and meet people there in order to correct the knowledge of the scholars about the climate, which indicated that the frozen north was uninhabitable because of the cold.

Regardless of whether Columbus was on the Greenland or Canadian side, he was in the «sound» that according to <u>Inventio Fortunatæ</u> was on the same latitude as «The 'Fortunate' Land»—meaning America.

Later unfounded speculation that he did not speak the truth, is akin to accusing Scott and Amundsen of having stayed on their ships in Antarctica, while claiming that they had reached the South Pole. By now Columbus was, though still unknown—a Livingstone, a Hillary, an Amundsen, a Heyerdahl, or a Peary of his generation—a man who had been both the farthest to the south and the farthest to the north. Fernando says in his biography about his father that before the voyage to the north Columbus had lived for a winter at 10°S—at that time the most southern known point in the world—in order to study the people and customs there for his book about the five climatic zones of the world. «I visited the fortress of Sao Jorge da Mina, which belongs to the Portuguese King and lies below the Equator; and I can testify that it is not uninhabitable, as some would have it,» Columbus wrote in the margin of the book <u>Aenas Sylvius</u>, in protest of the book's climate descriptions.[25]

Only once has Columbus been shown to have made a mistaken latitudinal observation, and he both admitted and regretted it. The reason for his error allegedly was a defect in the astrolabe he was using at a time when he was emotionally distraught, on November 2, 1492.

It may sound implausible that someone would head into the stormy North Atlantic during the month of February. But with the assistance of the British national archives I have been able to go through the parchment customs ledgers of Bristol harbor from 1477. And here it becomes apparent that most of the ships which traded in dried fish in the North Atlantic started in this month, and returned in late fall—the last ones around the end of the year and the beginning of the new year. The cargo is carefully catalogued. Unfortunately the ledgers from November have disappeared. Since trading in luxury items from Greenland was officially and strictly illegal in England, it is possible that the ship chose to unload in a less controlled harbor than Bristol—like Galway in Ireland, a city with which Columbus had had repeated contact.[26] Around half of all ships in the customs ledgers from the 1470s sailed to, from, or via Ireland.

But why would a ship from England go all the way up to 73 degrees on the Canadian side when they could have obtained walrus tusks on the Greenland side?

The reason is that a narwhal hunt took place on a grand scale every year in the bays around Bylot Island (as it still does). With the fabulous prices obtained in Europe, two narwhal tusks alone would finance the trip. If a captain managed to get his hands on 10 tusks from Greenland or Eskimo hunters, he would have a fortune. In addition he could trade in an occasional walrus tusk, falcons, and polar bear skins. He took a risk, but the payoff was that much greater if it turned out well.

The English seafarers obviously had no interest in letting anyone know about their secret trading partners in the north. The wares from there were supposed to be delivered as tithes to the Vatican, but nothing ended up going there anymore. The pope complained in letters—the last one in 1492—that the Greenlanders were nearly isolated and left to themselves.[27] However, things were not quite as bad as all that.

The Continent Without An Owner

Even if Columbus was now able to tell the world considerably more about the world than Europe's geographical idol, Ptolemy, we hear nothing more about Columbus as an observer of climates. That is because he discovered something far more important—America was in the peculiar situation of having no owner.

In the papers he left, his son Fernando found the next act in his father's life: He declared himself discoverer of America, and assumed the name «Columbus de Terra Rubra» («of the Red Land»). Fernando discovered a good deal of correspondence signed this way, and he writes in the biography:

«And because it will inform those who may note the phrase Columbus de Terra Rubra, I may remark that I have seen some signatures of the Admiral before he rose to that estate, in which he signed himself Columbus de Terra Rubra.»

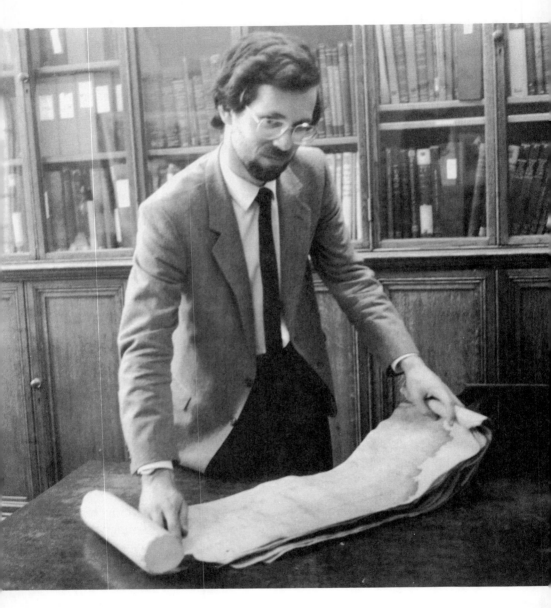

Chief archivist Andrew McDonald of The Public Records Office looking over the customs ledgers of Bristol harbor for the year 1477, when Columbus sailed up to 73 degrees north and made particular note of the ships from Bristol. Only the names of captains and owners are listed, and Columbus' name is nowhere to be found. But it is possible to make out which ships ventured to the far north on the basis of the cargo they brought back.

Columbus' brother Bartolomeo, who helped him in his efforts to find an interested occupying nation, likewise called himself «Bartolomeo Colon de Terra Rubra».[28]

Before his voyage in 1492, Columbus distorted almost all names of the lands he had heard about. This is understandable, considering the keen competition he was facing. Otherwise anyone with a ship could have sailed following his directions. In European shipping circles North America was consistently referrd to as Brazil in the 1400s. The name means «red tree». It is reasonable to suppose that Terra Rubra («Red Land») is a translation, or an allusion, to Terra Brazil.

As strange as it may sound, no one in Europe in the 1400s claimed to be the discoverer of America, even though navigators knew about the land. But knowledge did not become established fact in the Middle Ages until accepted by rulers and authorities. Not until the last century did Christopher Hansteen «discover» Vöringsfossen [a dramatic waterfall] in Norway, even though it had been known from times immemorial.[29]

Columbus now proposed to the city state of Genoa that he should go to America to formally claim the continent for Genoa. The matter was discussed in the city council, but they did not take his proposal seriously.[30] A common twenty-six year old seaman could not declare himself owner of a land. The land at the very least had to be discovered by a nobleman, and a governor had to be among the top representatives.

He had run up against a stone wall, and was apparently annoyed when he read a kind of «European journal» by Pope Pius II (1405–64), entitled «History of Notable Events That Have Happened in My Time».[31] In the margin he penned a reprimand to the author: «Men have come here from China. I have seen many extraordinary things. For instance in Galway, in Ireland, where two men and a woman of unusual appearance were adrift in two boats.» It was common for expeditions to catch Eskimos and bring them home as attractions and «entertainment slaves». (Among other things they demonstrated how birds were caught with Eskimo bird slings.) We don't know if the poor souls in Galway were taken back north by the ship that Colombus himself sailed on in 1477.

Meanwhile Columbus was collecting all the geographical information he could find about the north and the west. In Inventio Fortunatæ it is said that it was cold in the land of the «pygmees» (Eskimos) up at 73°N, but that in southwest America the soil was fertile and «healthy».[32] This agreed with Marco Polo's book, which stated that to the southwest of the Chinese polar land there was a fertile kingdom that was ruled by a Great Khan. Everything added up. And until his death Columbus believed that to the west of what is the United States, lay a rich and distant Chinese province—the land of the Great Khan. But he also felt that America itself, «Terra Firma and some islands in the ocean», was an ownerless land where he would become sole ruler and viceroy, titles that would be passed along to his heirs.

But Fernando also states in the biography that his father was preoccupied with another event. When a Portuguese ship reportedly had been on the American coast a little south of Antilia, some of the men were sent ashore to scrub their food kettles with sand. There they discovered a lot of gold in this sand—the story reports that a third of the sand was yellow.[33] Even if we allow for exaggeration, it seems that the Portuguese seafarers on the expedition in 1473 could find gold in the river sand, or on the sandy beaches, along the entire coast of Labrador, Newfoundland and Nova Scotia. In the 1800s the sand over large stretches of this coastline was hauled away for industrial extraction of the gold.[34]

Christopher Columbus had to shoulder his ambitions alone. An ordinary seaman had no chance of gaining access to the responsible authorities, and the noble title «de Terra Rubra» was home-made. He had no «letters of introduction» to present.

There are no sources to confirm the claim that he intentionally began to frequent a certain church favored by daughters of poor noblemen and widows of sea officers, but we can't dismiss the possibility that he may have done so—his options were limited. His position in society was established in 1479, when at age twenty-eight he married the high-born Felipa Môniz de Perestrello, whom he met in this church. She was the daughter of a deceased captain who had been in service to Henry the Navigator. At the time of his death her father was the governor of Porto Santo on the Azores.

Columbus didn't marry money, and the seafarer's income probably didn't give them much to live on. But as the husband of a noblewoman, he was suddenly able to see the king and the authorities about his fantastic plan.

In 1481 Portugal got a new king, John, a ruthless ruler intent on making Portugal the leading seafaring and colonizing nation of the world. The many foreigners in Portugal now came under scrutiny because they might be spies for Genoa, Florence or others; competitors that he intended to oust from the spice market of Europe. Foreign vessels encountered off the coast of the Portuguese colonies in Africa were to be seized, and the crew immediately thrown overboard and drowned.[35] The king was also very interested in finding Antilia with the seven cities, on Pope Urban's map. Fernando Teles, who had been given the right to discover America in 1475, had now been dead for four or five years.

Here Columbus saw his chance. He finally obtained an audience with the king, and offered to find and occupy America, in return for appointment as viceroy and governor of the land, and receipt of 10 percent of all trading income from this new province.

The king requested that he present a plan for his enterprise. This was a risky thing to do for a non-Portuguese, and it did indeed fail. A commission was appointed to review the plan, and of course it responded with a flat no—intending later to carry out the conquest with Portuguese nationals. Historians claim that Portugal sent an expedition west while the commission was still ostensibly studying Columbus' proposal.[36]

He received the rejection in 1484, and on March 3, 1485, the king gave shipowner Fernam Dulmo, a nobleman of Flemish descent, the right to discover America, together with the Portuguese sea captain and shipowner, Joham Alfomso de Estereito. The third partner in the deal was «a German who had the position of Antilia marked on his map», as it says in the royal letter of consent. This German was Martin Behaim from Nüremberg. He came to Lisbon together with several Flemish merchants, and became the king's geographical advisor when it became known that he had been a colleague of the advanced mathematician and Ptolemy-expert, Johan Müller (Regimontanus) in Nüremberg.[37]

He married a daughter of the nobleman Jobst van Huerter of the Azores. She, in turn, was the sister-in-law of the sister of Joanno vas Corte Real, who visited Iceland and Greenland/Labrador in 1473. The main players really, were few and conspicuous.

Martin Behaim was the expert in the commission that considered Columbus' material. And he and the two captains who «took over» the plan, would have become the discoverers of America if they hadn't become involved in a disagreement. According to their arrangement, Dulmo was to determine their course for the first 40 days. If America had not been found by that time, Estereito was to assume command and sail ahead of the others until America was found.

Estereito withdrew from the agreement fairly early, and on July 12 the king wrote a new letter of consent, in which Dulmo was given the sole right to discover «a large island, an island kingdom, or a continent that is assumed to be the Island of the Seven Cities».[38] He was granted the exact authority that Columbus had requested: The right to rule the land, supreme powers over the natives, the right to collect duties, etc.

The plan was for the expedition to get underway in 1487. But in June of that same year the expedition was still docked in the harbor of Terceira on the Azores. If Dulmo left at all, at least we know that he never returned.[39] No one any longer claimed that they wished to look for land south of 36 degrees. And here a question arises: Did Columbus tell anyone that his real destination was a coastline named Binini (Vinini), in modern Georgia/Florida?[40] Or did the commission not believe the country existed, because it was not included on any of the versions of Pope Urban's map that were circulating all over Europe?

Martin Behaim lived long and well for many years after these events. He made the world's first known globe, which he was honest enough to name the «Columbus' globe», and on which he wrote that the polar region was based on <u>Inventio Fortunatæ</u>. One of the pieces of information we find on the Canadian side by the 73rd latitude is: «Here white falcons are caught.» This is the latitude where Columbus was in 1477. But he made a grievous error, and reduced the earth's circumference to a fourth of its real size. Ptolemy had used Arabian miles; 1975.5 meters. Behaim assumed Italian miles, or 1477 meters. As a result, Japan ended up a little east of America. But Columbus states explicitly in his diary of October 6, 1492 that the information about Japan was incorrect. He knew from Toscanelli's letter that Japan was far west of America, or «The Land of the Seven Cities».

After the voyage in 1477, Columbus was never to see America again. But in Portugal they quickly made copies of the map he had presented to the commission. Over time it has become known as «The Admiral's Map», that is, Columbus' map. A version from 1501 (the Cantino map in Modena) shows a correct ice border between Iceland and Greenland, a correct coastline of Greenland up to the Davis Strait, and some of the American east coast. Greenland's name on the map is «Ponte de Asia»—in other words that this is how far Siberia stretched. It is clearly stated in the later editions by Martin Waldseemüller that this is the Admiral's (Columbus') map. There is nothing to make us believe otherwise.

The maps were now able to show a continuous American coastline all the way from Hamilton Inlet on the coast of Labrador to Chesapeake Bay in Virginia. But that's where it stopped. The commission had not been told of any land farther south. The maps, superimposed on Pope Urban's map, show a number of place names and information entered along the east coast. The historian Dr. Woodbury Lowery says that the language is poor Spanish and poor Portuguese,[41] and Professor Armando Cortesao says the text incorporates elements of Italian.[42] In 1974 I conducted an investigation of the names together with the leader of Biblioteka Estense in Modena in Italy, Nunzio Selmi. Later on I engaged language experts and linguists from several countries, and with different language backgrounds, in an effort to interpret the names Nunzio Selmi and I had gleaned from the map. The result is meager.

On the maps America was called «Terra de Cuba—Asie Partis» and «Terra Ultero Incognito», the same region that the cartographer Johannes de Stobnizca of Cracow called «Terra de Cuba: de Bona Ventura» (The Good, or Fortunate Land).

The island of Cuba was given this name because of a misunderstanding, as we shall see later.

Columbus' belief that there was a continent that far south was in complete agreement with what all seamen in England knew and talked about when America was mentioned.[43] Columbus' good friend John Jay, or anyone else that he may have met on his travels to England and Ireland, could have told him about it. So if he wanted to reach the land of the Grand Khan, he would have to go all the way down to Florida in order to get past the American continent. Columbus didn't need to be told this, for he had the book where it was written. And in his diary he repeats time after time that he had a map in his possession.

The Race for America Begins

Columbus had a competitor, Giovanni Caboto, who also stated that he was born in Genoa. He moved to Venice, married a woman in this seafaring metropolis, and had two sons. Caboto was a seafarer and merchant, and traded in spices that came by caravan to Mecca on the Red Sea from India and China.

In Venice he, too, became captivated by Marco Polo's account of his many years in China, and most of all by what Marco had said about the Asian land that stretched toward Europe in the north. He also studied a globe that showed Antilia, or America. But he had no idea about the existence of America's southern states. He thought it would be possible to follow the coast down to 36°N, where he assumed there would be open ocean in all directions, and thereafter to follow the coast west until America turned into Asia. Thereby the spice market would be laid wide open, and enormous profits realized, since the spices would no longer have to be hauled on the backs of camels.

He therefore severed ties with Venice and moved to Bristol—where Norwegian immigrants had the best connections to activities in the North Atlantic. Here he assumed the name John Cabot, and became a captain for John Jay, Columbus' good friend. According to the diary of his uncle, Wilhelm Botoner, Jay already had made an unsuccessful attempt to send a ship to America in 1480.[44] But in 1481 he had better luck. Both voyages apparently were intended as purely commercial ventures—perhaps to search for valuable types of timber.[45] John Cabot was therefore too late to get anyone interested in discovering America, and Bristol's merchants and shipowners wanted no part of the Italian's plans to reach Asia.

From 1483 we can follow Cabot month by month in Bristol's customs ledgers. He sailed to Spain and Portugal on the bark that the customs official called «Seint Spryte» (Spirito Santo?) from Fontarabia. The customs officials of Bristol were excellent writers, but in reading the faded parchment rolls, it is easy to become exasperated with their interpretation of place and person names. On October 15, 1485, Cabot became captain of the bark «Michael» of Bristol. He still shipped cargo from the Iberian peninsula for John Jay and Robert Thorne, such as textiles, that the two apparently bought from Italian and Spanish producers. At the same time wool and heavy woven wool fabrics were exported—England's economy was completely dependent upon the sale of woolens.[46] Thorne was also strongly interested in America and the trade in the northern territories. He visited America himself, as is evident from a letter in the British Museum.[47]

The bark «Michael» returned from Huelva to Bristol on March 14. The visit was a short one. By April 14 the ship returned to Andalusia. On this voyage it called at Lisbon, and didn't return home to Bristol until September 18th.[48] We know that Cabot went both to Spain and Portugal with a proposal for a voyage to America, but not when he did so. It doesn't matter. He was too late. After the voyage of Homen and Corte Real, the Portuguese apparently had already secured «their» land in the high north. And Columbus had been active for years. In 1488–89 Cabot had to endure the spectre of Bartolomeo Columbus showing up in England to convince the king to let his brother Christopher claim America.

116

Finally John Cabot gave up his dreams, and in 1490 he moved to Valencia. He decided to become an entrepreneur instead. But he never forgot the short-cut to Asia.

1. Bradford, 1973.
2. The sailor's account is reproduced in its entirety on the well known Turkish «Piri Reis' Map» from about 1500. See Aschehougs Verdenshistorie, vol. IX, p. 36.
3. Columbus, 1918, chapter 2.
4. Anghiera, 1912.
5. The Trier-Koblenz fragment from the early 1300s, found in the Klosterneuberg school, is the oldest known map divided into degrees.
6. Cortesáo, Jaime. Os decrubimentos Portugueses, no. 41, Lisbon.
7. Azuara, no. 94. See Cortesáo, 1954, p. 76.
8. Cappelens verdenshistorie, vol. X, 1984, p. 303.
9. Torre da Tombo.
10. Frucutuso, Gaspar 1590—see Larsen, 1926.
11. Purchas, 1906, vol. III.
12. Olaus Magnus, 1555, vol. I, pp. 94–95.
13. Cortesao, 1954.
14. Larsen, 1923.
15. Quinn, et.al., 1971.
16. Steensgaard in Aschehougs verdenshistorie, vol. VII.
17. Columbus, 1918, p. 19.
18. Norwegian translation available in the manuscript collection of the National Archives of Oslo, 150 fol.
19. Columbus, 1918, p. 33.
20. De Lollis, vol. II, pp. 291–523.
21. Columbus, 1918, p. 19.
22. Isachsen, G. and F., 1932.
23. Carson, 1952, p. 154.
24. Nörlund, 1924.
25. Bradford, 1973.
26. Norges gamle love, 2.R.1., No. 72.
27. Archivo Vaticana Diversorum, Alex. VI, Arm. 29. T 50 Fol. 23.
28. Translation from Fernando Colon, chapter 2, pp. 95–98, by Caddo, Milan, 1930.
29. Voksö (ed.), 1980, p. 139.

30. The translation of this account, on admiral Piri Reis' map of 1513, is by Dr. Yusuf Akcura, Society for Turkish Historical Research.
31. All of Columbus' shorter notations have been collected in De Lollis, 1892–94, pp. 291–523.
32. Beste, vol. I, pp. 34–35.
33. Columbus, 1918.
34. Henriksen, 1988, p. 355.
35. Grimberg, vol. XI, 1957, p. 11.
36. Bradford, 1973, p. 61.
37. Ravenstein, 1908.
38. Torre da Tombo.
39. Clissold, 1961, p. 26.
40. Anghiera, 1511. Decada 2. Libro 10, chap. 2.
41. Lowery, 1911.
42. Cortesao (ed.), 1960, vol. I, map no. 2.
43. Robert Thorne's letter.
44. Corpus Christi College, Cambridge, MS. 210.
45. Harrison, 1930, pp. 198–99.
46. Grimberg, vol. XIII, 1957, p. 168.
47. Robert Thorne's letter.
48. Extract from Williamson, 1962.

SPAIN STRIKES A BARGAIN—THEN BACKS OUT

Christopher Columbus was experiencing a difficult time during these years. He had become a widower, and after his defeat in Portugal he took his little son Diego and went across the border to Spain. Two wealthy patrons became interested in his plans, and introduced him at court. The monastery La Rabida, not far from the Portuguese court, assumed responsibility for his son while he was away, and this was to become Diego's home for the next seven years.

The introduction by the two gentlemen resulted in Columbus being granted an audience with the regents, King Ferdinand and Queen Isabella, and a half-hearted promise to accept his offer to occupy America. But not just yet—Spain was in the middle of a war with the Arab Moors, who were being driven out of Spain after years of occupation. He had to wait until that campaign was over. Once again a commission was appointed to look into the merits of his proposal. But this time he had learned his lesson, and he withheld certain geographical information from the commission, writes Las Casas. All he offered was a series of arguments in favor of colonization, among them the spreading of Christianity. Missionary work was a part of the time.

After the audience, he was granted a small amount of money as a stipend while he worked on his plans, and later a pension equal to the daily wage of the average Spanish laborer. It was just about enough to survive.

Then he had to wait and hope—for years. He had a pass that required all municipalities, judges, knights, lords, and bailiffs to provide him with free lodging, but he was expected to pay for his own food.

We know from descriptions that he was a handsome man, and that women liked him. But the road of love is full of thorns as well as roses. On August 15, 1488, the young and beautiful Beatriz Enrique bore a son, and Christopher Columbus was the father. Some historians believe the relationship had lasted for some time. The boy was given the name Fernando. Even though Columbus was now a widower and free to marry, it was out of the question for someone with plans to become viceroy of America to marry a common woman.[1] He had to choose between her and his life's work. She could in any case continue to be his mistress, since it was common for noblemen in arranged marriages to have a love relationship outside the home and the marriage. His letters show that he was genuinely fond of Beatriz, and the matter was to plague him throughout his life. Not until the end of his life did he ask himself the question, was it all worth it? His disconsolate answer was that there was no forgiveness for what he had done to Beatriz. In his testament he pleads with his heirs to look after her.[2]

This was a time during which the Spanish population was subjected to strict moral codes, and this child had been born out of wedlock, to a foreign father. An investigation into the matter was begun. There were also questions about a certain unsettled debt. The charges were so serious that Columbus prepared to leave the country. Someone warned the court about his impending departure.

At this point he received a reassuring letter from the king, who promised that no charges would be brought against him. On May 12, 1489, he received money from the Queen's coffers—on the condition that he not leave Spain.

In reading Columbus' letters, his thoughts and observations, we are left with the impression of a multifaceted and fine man, with extraordinary imagination and courage, considering the rigid confines of his society. He was also a man with gentle concern for his family. It therefore remains a mystery why neither he nor his brother ever mentioned the family back in Genoa. Did it not exist?

This author has made no attempt to try to glean the truth from all the versions that circulate about his long period of waiting in Spain. It is not possible, and perhaps not so significant in this context. Columbus himself wrote that the waiting period took a heavy toll. A full five years passed before he received a reply from the commission. It was a flat refusal.

Apparently it didn't come as a surprise. The commission had grown more and more doubtful about the arguments he presented whenever he was asked for clarification. He gave them no geographical information, fearing that it might be used by his rivals. Instead he expounded on matters other than what they wanted to know. The result was a lot of bible talk and theory. In addition, Columbus had no capital to contribute, and there was no royal fleet.

Time was of the essence, since the first Portuguese ship had already sailed around the southern tip of Africa en route to Asia. Bartolomeo went to London in an effort to get King Henry VII interested in the enterprise. Columbus already knew from personal experience that ships from Bristol were sailing to America.

But Bartolomeo was captured by pirates along the way and plundered to the bone.[3] He was eventually able to acquire new clothes and a new map, but it took a long time before he was able to get an audience with the king. Bartolomeo was a salesman of dubious ability. Fernando Columbus presents one of his reports from London, in which part of his sales pitch was written in verse. His nephew seemed embarrassed by the literary quality, since he points out that the «lyrics» are included for historical reasons only.

The English king responded with a firm rejection. No reason was given. But Bartolomeo must still have harbored hopes, for he did not return home.

Through the years Columbus had become familiar with the monastery La Rabida, and perhaps even more familiar with the monastery's library. He retreated there after the royal rejection while waiting for Bartolomeo to return. The region was celebrating, or mourning, the end of the war with the Moors. For Columbus, there was not much reason to celebrate the fact that Ferdinand and Isabella had become sole rulers in Spain.

And then a miracle happened: In the harbor of Huelva, not far from the monastery, Columbus was approached by the medieval merchant mariner, Martin Alonzo Pinzón. He originally came from Italy, where he had spoken with a geographer in the Vatican and had seen the map of the lands «that have not yet been discovered». The way the report is formulated indicates that they had spoken before, but that Pinzón had doubted Columbus' claim of a land farther south. However, after studying the map in the Vatican, he had come to the conclusion that the map Columbus had, was indeed correct. After having seen the original in Rome, he felt so reassured that he offered to be Columbus' partner in an ocean crossing and colonization of the southern part of North America. He and his two brothers owned the small caravels «Pinta» and «Niña», which were both partially open boats. Together they would be able to invest around half a million maravedis in the expedition.

121

At this point things began to take a different turn. Columbus had just about all he needed for the voyage, and therefore any country would be likely to agree to his proposal. He intended to offer France the New World, unless Bartolomeo had already received an affirmative response in London.

The prior of the monastery began to suspect something was in the offing. He had been Queen Isabella's father confessor, and he wrote her a letter asking her to intervene before it was too late.

Columbus shortly thereafter received a summons to immediately appear in court in Granada. Fifteen years after his journey to North Canada he was at last in control of the situation. But those who knew him, say his hair had turned gray.

The negotiations with the regents concerned formal occupation of «a large continent and a number of islands». Asia is nowhere mentioned in the negotiations, and there seems to have been no doubt, or discussion, about what America was. No war ships or arms were needed—the land was pristine and harmless. If he had intended to occupy India, as some imaginative writers have claimed, he would have needed a huge fleet and a well equipped army. For if there was one thing Marco Polo had seen a lot of, it was well armed soldiers.

The court did not intervene in the plan itself. The only thing discussed was the price Columbus demanded: To be appointed Admiral of the Atlantic Ocean, viceroy and governor of America, and the right to one tenth of all the lands he conquered—including gold, silver, pearls, diamonds, dyes, spices, fruits and other products. Furthermore he and his heirs were to have absolute ownership of one eighth of any lands and islands he would claim for Spain, a right that would pass to his heirs for all time. The Columbus family still holds this title, and the right to carry his coat of arms.

Several of the courtiers broke into laughter when he presented his demands. Talavera, who was the archbishop of Granada, and the head of the commission that had discussed the enterprise, became furious. The common sailor who had lived by the grace of the court for years, now demanded royal status! Queen Isabella, who for so long had championed Columbus and his cause, found herself in a difficult situation. She was also pressured by the archbishop, who felt the enterprise would bring ridicule upon the majesties if they let Columbus have what he wanted. Make a sailor the independent king of a continent, indeed!

Talavera gave Columbus short shrift and showed him the door.[4]

Experts who have studied Columbus' life—and there have been many throughout the years—are left with the impression of a man who yielded and endured. He closed his eyes to insults and absurdities and was always uncertain. Even during his glory days he was never petty, callous or unreasonable.

But on this occasion he didn't give an inch. According to legend, he was already on his way to see the king of France when he heard the thunder of hooves behind him. The court wished to speak to him again.

The capable and very level-headed Keeper of the Privy Purse, Santangel, had intervened and re-established contact between the parties. Later researchers have never been able to quite explain why the cool businessman and seasoned politician had become so enthusiastic. We know quite a bit about him—and he was not a man to entertain idle talk. Ernle Bradford thinks there is reason to believe that Talavera himself had indicated a willingness to invest in the enterprise if the majesties themselves were not.[5]

Columbus' stake in the expedition was his own idea. Pinzón was going to invest his entire family fortune. Of the participants Pinzón risked the most, and lost the most. The royal share amounted to one million maravedis—in reality a small sum—for provisions and rent for a «royal caravel». The king apparently was quite indifferent to the whole matter. He was occupied with other and more pressing domestic concerns. Santangel felt that the amount could be borrowed from the Aragon tax coffers and the king's personal fortune, and this was approved. Thus the voyage did not create an economic problem for anyone.

All of Columbus' demands had been met. He was appointed viceroy and head of all lands that he discovered, as well as Admiral of the Atlantic Ocean. The agreement between him and the regents was penned by Juan de Coloma, a skilled and precise scribe, who also composed another of history's most important decrees—the Spanish persecution of the Jews. The agreement with Columbus makes it very clear that it concerns a land that Columbus has already visited. Several historians, Louis Ulloa[6] and Cecil Jane[7] among them, point out that Columbus in his negotiations must surely have let it be known that he had already visited the land that he wished to colonize. When Fernando explains in his biography the reasons why his father became America's first ruler, he begins with the description of Columbus' voyage 500 kilometers past the island of «Thule» in 1477.

The agreement between Columbus and the majesties begins as follows: «The proposed demands and requests are hereby granted by Your Majesties. Don [Columbus was ennobled in accordance with the agreement] Christobal Colon is given these concessions as consideration for what he has discovered ['ha descubierto'] in the ocean, and for the voyage he is about to undertake in the name of the Lord and in the service of Your Majesties.» Both majesties signed the document as follows: «Signed and executed in the city of Santa Fe near Granada, April 17, 1492. I, the King. I, the Queen.»[8]

A caravel with a covered deck was chartered as the admiral's ship, and the owner, Juan de la Cosa, came along as her pilot. The original name of the ship was «La Gallega». Later La Cosa had christened her «Marigalante», which in modern parlance would be «Frisky Mary». Such a name obviously would not be appropriate for the ship of the viceroy of America, and so she was re-named «Santa Maria». The names of the two other ships were pretty raunchy too—Pinzón's open caravel was called «La Pinta»—«the painted», seamen's jargon for a prostitute. The third ship, owned by Juan Niño and his brother Peralonso, was the little open caravel «Niña»—the girl. These imaginative and vulgar ship names were not a phenomenon peculiar to the Spanish.[9]

Viceroy, admiral and captain Columbus brought along a royal butler, and a steward named Pedro Guliere. India was never mentioned during negotiations, but in the royal pass that Columbus carried, there was a clause stating that it was also valid for visits to «the Indies».[10]

The Indies were the assumed rich African or Oriental lands over which Portugal had been granted Vatican authority to attack and conquer in accordance with the papal bull DUM DIVERSAD of June 18, 1452. They were to subjugate «saracens, heathens and other non-believers, take from them their properties and territories, and enslave the population». This was confirmed in the bulls ROMANUS PONTIFEKS of January 8, 1455, and INTER CAETERA of March 13, 1456.[11] An expert in Arabic languages was also sent with Columbus, in case they came across Arabic-speaking provinces.

Among the top officials who prepared to leave for the new Spanish colony, was a royal controller—something like a state comptroller—and an expert in precious metals. Beatriz' nephew, Diego de Harana, was given an important role as second in command of the lands in the New World. A man named Gullielmo, an Irish citizen from Galway in Ireland with an Italian-sounding name, was also one of the members, along with one Tallarte or Alard from Lajes in England.[12]

The fifty-one year old Martin Alonzo Pinzón was the first in command on the «Pinta», with his brother Francisco Martin as pilot. Martin Alonzo Pinzón generally seems to have been the practical organizer of this fantastic enterprise. Without his skills as a seafarer and his solid, practical mind, it is unlikely that Columbus would have succeeded. The «Niña» was placed under the command of his brother, Captain Vincente Yanes Pinzón.

Each ship had a group of navigators, and its own barber/surgeon. The three small cannons they carried probably had more ceremonial than practical use. [Sea battles using cannons were not yet known.] As usual the crew was scraped together from the dregs of society. Some prisoners were granted a pardon in exchange for signing on. However, we must be careful not to stamp them all as criminals. A man could end up in a Spanish prison for a wide variety of reasons during the reign of Ferdinand and Isabella.

The most important passengers on board were Columbus' book and the map that contained everything he needed in order to sail to America—this according to a sailor who accompanied him on three voyages until he was captured by the Turks. This nameless sailor has given us the only account by a participant on Columbus' voyages. You can't get closer than that to what really happened.[13] Columbus' diary in the main confirms the sailor's account.

Early on the morning of August 4, 1492, the sails were hoisted on the three ships in the harbor of Palos. They had a bit of wind from the north in the course of the night, and in order to capture the morning breeze the ships headed out before dawn. They first headed south to the Canary Islands, 1000 kilometer south of Antilia's latitude as noted on Pope Urban's map. Here they stocked up on water and provisions before beginning the crossing.

The travel order was simple: The ships were to follow the 28th latitude along a westerly course, not veering off either to the south or the north. They would then expect to land on the American coast between present day Savannah in Georgia and San Augustine in Florida. As already mentioned, Columbus had named this area «Binini», and it was where he thought the American continent ended, according to his diary, and a statement by the Spanish court recorder, Pietro Martire.[14] Martire also drew an excellent map of the land of Binini on the Georgia-Florida coast, and noted that the distance from Haiti to Binini was 325 leagues, based on information from Columbus. It would be tempting to ask what the name means. It is pronounced «Bimini».

Columbus' book and map have disappeared, but according to the sailor's account the distance to America was no problem. The promised land was located where the compass needle pointed directly at the North Star, «with no arrangement» [no declination], the book said. This would be the latitude of Florida's east coast.

Therefore they constantly watched the compass and the North Star. The navigators on the three ships were quite skilled. On September 13 the sailors noticed that the relationship between the magnet needle and the North Star was not always constant. On September 17—far out in the Atlantic—Columbus reassured the crew, saying that it was normal for the North Star to have a slight variation in relationship to the compass every day. In 1492 the North Star moved around the north celestial pole in a circle of three and one half degrees, with the «gravity» on one side of the magnetic north pole. That's how detailed their observations were.

Life on board was simple and ordered, with six watches in a twenty-four hour period. The middle watch was split, so that there would be some variation. The three ships stayed together, and the captains had sealed orders as to what to do if they were to be separated. The two small ships were the fastest, and they had to slacken their sails so as not to leave the slower moving «Santa Maria» behind.

On the open ships, «Niña» and «Pinta», the men were always within view of one another, while there was more room on the «Santa Maria». Men slept on deck, on top of the cargo or under the aft toldilla, while the top officers had tiny cabins on the aft deck. The ships were loaded with firewood, because a hot meal was prepared every day. The reason the crossing cost no lives was in part due to the fact that the shipboard fare was fairly good—salt fish, salt meat, biscuits, olive oil, wine and ample supplies of dried fruits and vegetables. Peas and dried beans were the mainstays of the meals on Iberian vessels. But in a letter to court Columbus mentions almonds, raisins, and rice as well.[15] They also had brought along seed grain to the New World.

Columbus stayed awake a great deal, and in his diary he speculated a lot about the relationship between America and the Asian lands mentioned in Marco Polo's book and in Inventio Fortunatæ. It is apparent that he expected to be the Great Khan's neighboring regent. He spent a lot of time on deck during the nights. The sky was clear and the stars visible, according to the observations in his diary.

126

Around September 22 they were on the latitude of Antilia, 600 nautical miles west of the Azores according to Pope Urban's compressed map. Columbus reports that he and Pinzón had a long discussion as the ships sailed side by side, and that Pinzón also borrowed a detailed map.

Even if Pinzón knew how far they were going, he demanded to be on the safe side, and so they looked for land along the way, and held a little to the south. Columbus had consented to looking for «islands» at an early stage of the voyage. But at the same time he writes in his diary that they can't spend much time in this pursuit, since the mainland is still far away. And later, on October 14, he notes that his map shows no islands east of what we now know as the Bahamas.

Two log books were kept—one indicated distances less than actually sailed, so as not to make the crew anxious about how far from home they had actually come. The other indicated what Columbus thought was the true distance. Who tricked whom, is open to discussion, because Columbus' own estimates were far too optimistic.[16] The navigators did not agree with his figures.

As week after week passed without sighting land, the crew became afraid that they were being taken into an ocean that had no end. They had seen neither branches nor driftwood in the sea after September 17, and the wind constantly blew away from Europe. Columbus was confronted by a delegation demanding that they turn around. But he flatly refused. Nothing could make him go back on his decision. Some sailors contemplated throwing him overboard on a night when he was «intoxicated with the stars», making Martin Alonzo Pinzón their commander, and returning home.[17]

Martin Alonzo Pinzón took the brewing mutiny seriously, and said that he and his brother would hang the mutineers if Columbus didn't do it himself. For Christopher Columbus the idea of hanging anyone was unthinkable. But then a slight wind from the southwest came up, and that brightened everyone's mood. The serious situation passed. Each man did his job, accepted his pound of bread and his boiled fish or meat, a fistful of raisins and a drop of wine, before curling up on the deck or on the cargo barrels for the night, to the sound of the wake, the rubbing of the bone dry rigging and the mesmerizing slow rushing of water against the ship's hull.

During the morning watch on September 30 Columbus reports in his diary that southeast of Bermuda, the compass needle for the first time pointed directly to the North Star for a little while, as the star was in its westernmost position. On that day he calculated that they had come 2828 nautical miles west of the Canary Islands, and that it wouldn't be far to the mainland. His officer, Pedro Niño, revised the generous estimate to 2312 nautical miles. Columbus was now becoming excited, and ordered the ships to pay no heed to the islands (Bahamas) drawn in on the map in this area, but to head directly to the mainland. They could return later to explore these islands.

Now his geographical knowledge was being put to the big test. If they didn't find the mainland of Binini between present day Georgia and Florida, it meant they were in the great ocean that Toscanelli said went all the way to Japan and China.

On October 6 Martin Alonzo Pinzón no longer dared go directly west. Captains and navigators consulted and discussed. If the land they were headed toward did not lie where the ancient map in the Vatican and Columbus' book showed, they would end up in another ocean. And they didn't have nearly enough water and provisions to go all the way to Japan, said Pinzón. Columbus was sure he was right, and wanted to continue straight ahead to the mainland. But contrary to his expressed will, Pinzón gave orders, one hour before sunset, for the fleet to head down to the Bahama Islands. All the officers agreed with him. Columbus in his diary noted that Pinzón really didn't think that's where Japan was, as indicated on one of his maps, which we can assume was similar to Martin Behaim's globe.

What happened that night changed history. If Pinzón had listened to Columbus, they would have made landfall in the area of the Carolinas, in which case the United States would probably be a Spanish-speaking country today.

The next day they saw a large flock of birds heading from northeast to southwest. Columbus wrote in his diary that he thought these were birds that fled from the winter in the land from whence they came. «For the Admiral knew that the islands that the Portuguese hold, were discovered because of birds.» These «islands that the Portuguese hold» were Greenland, Newfoundland and Labrador, which Spain had never claimed.

They realized that they had reached their goal, and they reduced their speed during the night. The weather was calm and mild—the east wind rippled the waves and the rigging chattered. The next day they continued to follow the birds. On Thursday, October 11, the navigator, Pedro Niño, announced that according to «Columbus' book», it was 16 leagues, or at the most 20 (60 nautical miles) to the mainland. As we know, Columbus was a bit optimistic when it came to distance sailed. The navigator therefore asked that the fleet not sail at all that night, and everyone agreed. The moon came up in the evening, and the lookout on the «Pinta» spotted a white sandy beach. A shot from the cannon was fired to signal the event.

There is hardly a worse area in the world to sail than this, with shallows and reefs in every direction. Slowly and carefully the three ships were maneuvered throughout the afternoon, closer and closer to a landfall that was probably Watling Island. A group of people on shore was watching them. And Columbus was trying to figure out what this land really was.

Finally they arrived at what is today Long Bay. The anchors were dropped after 33 days of continuous sailing.

A boat from the «Santa Maria» was put in the water, with Columbus and the royal comptroller, de Escopedo, on board. Martin Alonzo Pinzón went on board the shore boat from the «Pinta» and Vincente Yanes Pinzón boarded the one from the «Niña». Then the small boats were rowed ashore. Here Columbus held up the royal Castilian flag, while the two captains held the expedition banner—a green cross on a white background, with the royal initials under separate crowns. Columbus then knelt, and asked everyone present to witness that he was taking the continent into possession on behalf of the king and queen of Castile.

The Indians didn't understand a thing of what was going on. But they assumed that the strangers in the canoes—who had made the sharp noise the night before—were gods, Columbus wrote in his diary.

Until now Columbus' map had been correct, but at this point nothing was correct anymore. For inexplicable reasons, some have claimed that Columbus rejoiced at having reached Asia. He did not. It would have been suicidal for the unarmed soldiers to have gone ashore in a kingdom that already had a ruler. It would have meant certain ruin for the Columbus and Pinzón families as well as for the owner of the «Santa Maria», Juan de la Cosa. It is true that Columbus toyed with the idea that these were distant Asian islands, and that he was in the vicinity of the land of the Great Khan that Marco Polo had so vividly described. On October 13 he also wrote in his diary that he thought the inhabitants of the American mainland rowed out to Watling Island. In reality it was another 300 nautical miles to the mainland.

The Bahama Islands were located exactly where Columbus' map said they were supposed to be. It was an enormous relief to know that they had found terra firma in the ocean. Pinzón therefore immediately wanted to continue the journey to the intended goal—the American mainland a little to the northwest. Columbus was more inclined to head to the land to the southwest, and insisted that they do so. Fernando has already told us of the floating islands that his father had read about in Inventio Fortunatæ, and the king of Portugal had written that a land had long been searched for west of the Cape Verde islands. The letters from the Zeno brothers—if we dare believe in their authenticity—indicate that the seamen had heard about the rich Mexican cities. The Indian groups that Columbus' expedition had met were Arawaks who had roots in South America. They probably tried to confirm his gestural questions about land in that direction. Still, neither understood the language of the other, even though both Columbus and Pinzón tried to rely on «their» Indian pilots, who had been taken by force on Watling Island.

Columbus wondered if the large and rich land to the southwest was the kingdom of the Great Khan that Marco Polo had written about. If so, he wanted to pay a visit to his neighboring regent. Who wouldn't have been interested in knowing what kinds of neighbors he had in such a situation? In the meantime the expedition visited several small islands. They had not yet decided upon a course when, on October 28, the fleet reached a northern coast that they had not anticipated. They followed it westward and after sailing for two days Columbus was convinced this was the target of his voyage: America, or «Terra Cuba», as he called the land.

The good friend of the Columbus family, Las Casas, who copied Columbus' diary, writes (diary of October 30): «The Admiral believed it was 42 degrees from the Equator to the northernmost point of this land—unless there is a mistake in the text I copied.»

No, there was no mistake. Antilia ends at 42 degrees (Boston-Cape Cod) on all the known versions of Pope Urban's map. Pinzón said he had understood Cuba to be the name of a city in this land. Thus he confirms that one of the seven place names, a little south of Boston, was «Choue», «Cua», etc., on the map with which he was familiar.

If it was not the mainland after all, Columbus speculated about whether this might be the north coast of a neighboring country or his own kingdom of Antilia. He discussed sending an expedition inland to look for cities, and taking along a letter that the inhabitants could forward to his fellow king. Pinzón warned against the plan to send a letter, saying that he had understood Marco Polo's account to mean that there was war

130

between the Great Khan and his neighbors. Columbus would have to proceed with caution if this turned out to be one of the neighboring countries. They certainly weren't equipped for war.

Was this still America, or wasn't it? Columbus said on November 1 that he thought the long coast seemed to make a northern turn and that the water became colder every day. The next day, on November 2, he sent an expedition into the interior to look for larger cities. He gives the impression of being fairly exhausted with overexertion and lack of sleep. They were constantly bombarded with new impressions, trading with Indians, chasing after gold, and trying to figure out where they were.

During the night Columbus went out on deck while the ship lay anchored off the present town of Garbarien on the northern coast of Cuba. He insisted that his quadrant showed that they had come up to 42° N, or in other words, Boston. In that case they were 1141 leagues west of Hierro on the Canary Islands. These two observations indicate that he had found the country he proposed to colonize, according to his contract with the royal house.

For Pinzón the situation was unacceptable. Three captains and six navigators knew that their boss was imagining, on this autumn night, that he was one thousand nautical miles farther north than was the case.

Columbus had a few nights of rest, and even ventured ashore to hunt birds. A peculiarity about this island world was that there were no animals at all, except a type of small, mute dog that the Indians bred for food. The dogs did not flee—if they did they would starve, because there were no other animals for them to eat, either.

Torvald Eiriksson's expedition had reported the same phenomenon half a thousand years before. It was still the only known island group in the world without animal life.

On November 5 something occurred that Columbus wrote he could not understand. Some of the people had begun to inhale the smoke from a plant, the way the Indians did. Columbus made it clear he didn't like it, and that they were to stop this nuisance. They were not to «drink» smoke anymore.

«We're unable to stop,» they answered.

After six days the inland expedition returned and reported that they had seen nothing except small, poor and peaceful villages. There was no sign of gold.

All at once Columbus snapped back into reality. He christened the island they had sailed along «Isabella», in honor of the queen. Long afterwards the name Cuba was moved here from the mainland by confused geographers.

1. Bradford, 1973.
2. Wassermann, 1955.
3. Columbus, 1918.
4. Wassermann, 1955.
5. Bradford, 1973.
6. Ulloa, 1928.
7. Jane, 1930.
8. The unabridged document is included in Libro Registro de la Corona de Aragon XCIX.
9. Nansen, 1911.
10. Jane, 1930, Vol. I, s.ciii.
11. De Witte, 1958. See also Boxer, 1969.
12. Navarrete, 1825.
13. Bradford, 1973.
14. Anghirea, 1511. Decades del nuevo Mundo, 2. Libro 10, chapter 2.
15. Bradford, 1973.
16. Morrison, 1940.
17. Columbus, 1918.

TRIUMPH AND TRAGEDY IN THE WEST

One of Columbus' first official duties was to put an end to escape attempts among the Indian prisoners they had taken. In his diary he wrote that he intended to take the Indians to Europe, teach them Spanish and then bring them back as his trusted representatives in the name of Spain. He sent ashore an expedition that captured some women and children, in the belief that the prisoners would settle down and be easier to handle if they had women. In the evening the husband of one of the women came, crying and begging to be allowed to be with his family. Columbus finally consented, even though he writes that the man was about 40 years old, and therefore not worth very much.

For the women this became a terrible existence. Columbus writes that in addition to being language teachers, they were also «souvenirs» for the crew.

What else happened while they were anchored in this harbor on the north coast of Cuba we will never know, because Martin Alonzo Pinzón died before he had a chance to tell his version. Columbus wrote a letter to the king and queen in which he said he had come to realize that this was not a mainland, but an island that he had planned to name «Johanna», after the regents' daughter, but he ended up changing his mind and gave it the queen's name—«Isabella».[1] Furthermore he told them they had decided to head back in an easterly direction, without having seen the western part of the island.

The fleet then sailed in a northeastern direction. When it approached present day Inagua, Columbus wrote that this was where the most eastern island on his map was located.[2] This is in complete agreement with the location of the Bahama Islands in relationship to the American mainland. In his log book he called these islands «Babeque». But the historian Herrera, a contemporary of Columbus, writes in his <u>Historia general del mundo</u> that «on his first voyage, Columbus named this island group

«Biminis [Vininis] Islands» because of a large 'island' [Florida-Georgia] that lay ahead of them and among them.»[3] On Herrera's map in the same book, and in the royal archives, the islands are named «Binini»—the same name that Columbus used for Florida-Georgia.

The discrepancy between the letter n and m may be philological. Herrera and others used the spelling «Binuni» and «Binvni» interchangeably. In Spanish an n before v is pronounced as 'm'. Therefore it was natural to say Bimini.

The relationship between Columbus and Martin Alonzo Pinzón had become increasingly strained as they approached the new world. And when they found no gold-strewn beaches around Inagua, things came to a head. Together with his brother, Pinzón left the expedition and headed east with the «Pinta». Columbus wrote in his diary that Pinzón had gone looking for gold, and he threatened to hang Pinzón from the doorway of the forecastle. But then he admits that they had disagreed about their location, and offers an excuse. It was a mistake on his part to have claimed on November 2 that they were all the way up at 42 degrees north, he says, but he didn't do it by design. His astrolabe, which had malfunctioned, showed them to be at the same sun altitude as at home in Castile. Nor had it been cold, as he had noted in his diary that day. He offers assurances that the instrument will be repaired as soon as they reach land.

The expedition then headed in the same direction as Pinzón. Soon they found a new and very large island, which, like Isabella (Cuba), was not on any of their maps. It was Haiti, which they named «Española». Columbus then dropped his plan to visit mainland North America. They were all very thrilled about the new paradise. But here too, they found no gold.

The land was systematically explored with survival in mind. All unknown plants and roots were imaginatively tested and utilized—a new type of bean, a nutritious root they had heard was grown in India. This is the only time the country of India is mentioned in Columbus' diary. They made note of new types of fish. And Columbus wrote that he believed the sweet potato to be a nutritious food. In the beginning they did not have support for this view, but today a world without potatoes is unthinkable.

Since Columbus already had a map of the Bahamas, others must have been there before him. Columbus never recorded any thoughts he might have had about who had first discovered the mainland coast and the islands. And he showed no surprise that white blood had reached that far.

On October 17 they met a native who had a gold coin nose ornament. On December 13 he met two women who «were as light skinned as anyone found in Spain», and on December 16 they encountered people who were «exceedingly white».

The Spaniards were well established in the New World when a calamity befell them on Christmas Eve. They had anchored in a good harbor in Haiti. Columbus had gone for 48 hours without sleep. He took a last look at the ships and moorings before going into his cramped cabin to rest. The owner of the «Santa Maria», Juan de la Cosa, was on watch when a terrible storm struck. The «Santa Maria» began to drift, and went aground on one of the sharp reefs. There is reason to believe that the lookouts had taken an early taste of the Christmas wine. Attempts to save the ship were futile and they were unable to get the ship clear before several bottom planks were crushed. The local Indian chief mobilized his subjects for a large scale rescue action and thus most of the belongings on board were brought ashore in canoes. Not a pin disappeared in the process.

Christopher Columbus emerges as an impressive and dynamic man during this Christmas of 1492. The only ship he had left, was the small, leaky coastal vessel «Niña». He had not found Antilia with the seven cities. His family would have trouble claiming their rights if anything were to happen to him. It was becoming urgent to get started on the long way back to Europe.

Columbus began by establishing a friendly relationship with the local Indian chief. An Indian messenger network was mobilized in an effort to locate Pinzón somewhere along the coast, but to no avail. He got the crew started on the construction of a fort from the planks from the «Santa Maria». He made Beatriz' nephew his representative and deputy, and left fifty men at the fort. The king's controller stayed, and apparently the Irishman and the Englishman as well. The two of them must somehow have been close to Columbus.[4] The men left behind had a surgeon, enough provisions and wine for one year, seed grain for two crops and plenty of fishing gear. The cannon from the «Santa Maria» was installed for use in the fort. The gun powder was kept dry in small barrels.

Why build a fort when the population had no weapons, and had shown no evidence of hostile intentions?

They had already taken several prisoners and claimed Indian women in more or less permanent relationships. The shipwreck had taught the Indians an important lesson—the foreigners were not gods. When they left Columbus made sure the chief understood that they would not be gone for long. As a last farewell—or perhaps as a warning—they fired the cannon on board the «Niña».

They headed east along the coast, and almost immediately ran into Pinzón. Once again he had been disappointed. There was no gold to be found where he had come from. They had done a bit of charting, and had christened the mouth of a river «Pinzón's River». Columbus immediately renamed it, and was furious at his next in command. Pinzón didn't take it too hard—it was a much more serious matter that the family fortune had been squandered.

All who were close to Columbus say he was an excellent navigator and a master when it came to making important decisions. This may explain why he chose not to go home by tacking back along the east wind on the 30th parallel. Farther north there were currents and winds heading toward Europe, and he wanted to take advantage of them. The Russian Columbus expert, David Tsukernik, thinks this was one of the most important decisions Columbus made, and that he had heard about this current and wind from Scandinavians who had been there previously.[5]

A collective protest and threats of mutiny had no effect. They would go north to the latitude of Cape Hatteras. From January 16th to February 2nd they headed northward, battling the prevailing westerly winds and the Gulf Stream.

And then they began a record sail. In the course of 13 days they sailed 1619 nautical miles by day and 1896 by night.[6]

This was the first time during the expedition that Columbus did not live in fear of a possible mutiny by his crew. Instead he was overcome by depression and a strong fear of death. He enclosed a report of his voyage in a bottle, in the event they did not reach home alive. The wind grew into a gale force storm. The men had to bail around the clock. Little «Niña» was built for coastal sailing, where it was easy to make landfall during a storm. Columbus closed himself up in his little cabin and wrote a letter to the sovereigns—a resumé of what had happened during the voyage. It was a calm and dispassionate document, and tells us most of what we now know. This is the letter that has come to be known as the appendix to his diary.

It was painful for him to accept that there was no gold in West India, as he had assured everyone there would be. The only thing he was able to report, was having seen natives with gold rings in their noses. On the other hand he gave an enraptured description of bird songs, and of the trees, which he was certain contained dyes and medicines. Dyes at that time were nearly as valuable as gold. He assured the regents that the Indians had no religion, so claiming their souls would be an easy matter. And finally, perhaps to pique the interest of potential investors, he notes that most of the natives he had seen were young men, who would be excellently suited as «servants»—meaning slaves.

To criticize Columbus because he considered slaves to be one of the commodities of the lands he had discovered, is to ignore the historical context of that era. All of his contemporaries, perhaps with the exception of the Greenlanders who had emigrated to America, believed that Indians, Negroes and Eskimoes were not «humans». Portugal had been bringing boatloads of slaves from Africa. Trading in slaves was quite legal as long as Christians were not taken. In Muslim countries Christians were kept as slaves, and were there regarded as heathens.

The Ruler of the Atlantic Ocean

The returning ships were separated during the crossing—Pinzón's ship disappeared to the south.

As if by a miracle, the little «Niña» drifted to the Azores. Columbus quickly went ashore—in a hurry to tell the Portuguese that they would have to cease all activity in the western Atlantic. The promised land had been found.

Thereafter he went directly to Portugal. Off the coast the seafarer Nines, aboard the world's largest war ship, came alongside to take a closer look at the storm driven little caravel.

Columbus stood tall and told the Portuguese admiral to get lost. For here was the discoverer of the lands that Portugal had been unable to find, and he warned the admiral not to do anything rash—lest he bring the wrath of Castile down on his head. He happened to be talking to the viceroy of Castile and the admiral of the Atlantic Ocean and he wished to see the king of Portugal.

Permission to do so was granted immediately. The two had met before. At that time Columbus had appealed in vain for the king's support. Now he wanted to take the opportunity to tell the king that he wished him to cease all activity in the Atlantic Ocean, where Columbus was now king.

King John protested, and referred Columbus to the papal bull «Romanus Pontifax» of January 8, 1454, which gave Portugal the sole right to discover «The Indies». He threatened to send a large fleet west to Antilia, or the land of the seven cities, which had not yet been visited by Columbus.

Portuguese historians claim that an anticlimax occurred when King John saw the exhausted and frightened Indian prisoners. They were not white, as the people of «the Indies» were said to be.[7]

Columbus was apparently uncertain about what the next Portuguese move would be, and was in a hurry to stop them. As soon as he returned to Spain, an envoy was dispatched to the Spanish-born pope, Alexander VI, in one of history's grand diplomatic tricks. By May 3 the pope signed a bull that acknowledged Spanish dominion over the western Atlantic Ocean and the lands that lay there. The bull denied the Portuguese any right to continue the search for Antilia on Pope Urban's map.

Meanwhile Columbus was cheered as the grandest of heroes. A triumphant march toward the capital began. The king and queen stood, and asked him to be seated when he arrived—something they had never done before—for anyone.

Six of the Indians were alive when Columbus reached Spain, and the sight of such strange creatures caused quite a sensation. They were baptized, and given as presents to the regents. Prince John received one as a servant, but he didn't live long. «Our fear of God leads us to believe that he was the first Indian to be admitted to heaven,» wrote Las Casas in Historia de las Indias.

The other poor souls soon followed him.

Martin Alonzo Pinzón also survived the storm in the Atlantic. He made landfall just south of Gibraltar. When he returned home to Palo, Columbus' triumphant march had already ended. Pinzón had written his own version of what happened on the voyage, but who cared about his rebuke? He broke down completely and died a few days later. The family was ruined. A lawyer made an attempt to claim for them some small profit from the new land, as the informal agreement had specified, but it was in vain. His brother, Vincente Yanes Pinzón, went on to become a wellknown seafarer, and later discovered Brazil.

Hope Dies For Greenland

Something important had happened while Columbus was realizing his ambitions. The Vatican initiated a rescue action for Greenland when it became evident that the king in Copenhagen was neither inclined nor able to help the country. The Danish monk Mathias Knutsön, in Vår Frue monastery in Århus, declared himself willing to travel there as a missionary and bishop. The matter was taken under discussion by the Spanish cardinal Rodrigo Borgia, and finally the decision was taken to re-establish the connection between the rich polar region and the mother church. During these negotiations the pope died. And on August 11, 1492, a week after Columbus' departure from Spain, the cardinal was elected pope under the name Alexander VI.

He did not forget his plans for Greenland, and confirms in a detailed letter of October 23 the appointment of Mathias as missionary and bishop. In the letter he also notes that he has had recent news of Greenland. The king in Copenhagen, who had let Greenland fall into such a state of decline, was indirectly criticized. There has not been a bishop on Greenland for a hundred years, wrote the pope. The miserable population is heathen and has given up the Catholic faith. They have no wine for communion, no bread, no oil for the dying. An old altar cloth is the object of worship. Ships call there only sporadically, and people in this land at the edge of the world live only on milk and dry fish.[8]

True to form, Denmark did not take part in these preparations. On November 21 the pope wrote directly to Mathias indicating that relics would be made available from Rome or a nearby location and that he would be able to take them to his new cathedral on Greenland.[9]

It was still winter, however, so the Greenlanders would have to wait a few more months before they would be able to re-enter the European Christian fellowship.

But it was not to be.

Portugal protested vigorously against Pope Alexander's decision granting Spain exclusive rights to America. After all, they had been to North America with John Skolp as pilot nineteen years before Columbus' voyage. According to their reckoning, Newfoundland/Labrador was 370 leagues (about 1110 nautical miles) west of the Azores and Cape Verde islands. It was therefore their land and their Atlantic Ocean. Very difficult and protracted negotiations about this matter ensued. Portugal was then the world's foremost sea power, so the country could not be simply dismissed without consequences. One year after Columbus' return a treaty was signed in Tordesillas, in which the pope gave Portugal right to the area east of a north-south line drawn 370 leagues west of the Azores and the Cape Verde islands. All land west of this line was to be considered Spanish.[10] Greenland thus fell within the Portuguese sphere of interest, and in the end did not get a Danish bishop. What was even worse—the populace was seen as half heathen and therefore subject to being enslaved.

For the Mediterranean states of Venice and Genoa, and for the seafaring nations of France, Holland and England, the agreement was a catastrophe. Portuguese war ships now brutally and effectively blocked the ocean route around Africa to the East. In the west, all would henceforth have to pass through Spanish or Portuguese territory in order to find an ocean route to Asia.

They were trapped within Europe.

Greenland, and hence the Greenlanders in America and Canada, had for 350 years been under the administration of Norway's bishop in Nidaros. Why were these lands «taken» from Norway and transfered to Portugal?

A brief retrospective may in part help to explain Pope Alexander's decision:

When King Christian I in May of 1481 lay dying in his castle in Copenhagen, he summoned the queen, his young son Hans, the successor to the throne, and a trusted scribe from the chancellery. The dying king then summarized an agreement he had made with some of the regents of Northern Europe, which he expected his son to honor. It was in essence an agreement designed to deprive the church, the nobility and elected governments of any and all power. Resistance to the inherited absolute monarchy was to be drowned in blood.[11]

These guidelines were later described in detail in Machiavelli's famous and infamous book The Prince—the bible of oppressors.

The last will and testament of the dying king was to fall hardest on the church. No bishops would be allowed to live in fortified castles or keep more than 4–5 horses, while the archbishop was to be allowed 12–14 riders. Brothers of the cross in the cathedrals were to eat together and from the same pot, and not keep more than one servant each. All profits from churches and monasteries would come to the king. In practice this meant that the pope was to be stripped of all influence and power in Denmark and her dependencies.

In order to muzzle any Swedish resistance to these ideas, the plan presumed that the male population of Dalarna in Sweden would be exterminated and replaced by «wild Scots» that the king of Scotland had promised to make available. The entire population of Stockholm was to be killed and replaced with compliant immigrants. This dictum, which is called Christian I's political testament, was sent to the Swedish governor Sten Sture, who also fought the church and against the Swedish system of elected national officials. Sten Sture sent copies to several north German towns, and before long it became known everywhere.[12]

Norway's powerless archbishop Gaute was placed in office by the Danish-Norwegian king's attorney in the Vatican, the Cardinal of Mantua. Thus the pope was kept well informed about the Scandinavian revolt.

Hunting falcons, walrus ivory, narwhal tusks, ship ropes and seal tar, which had previously come to the church in a steady stream from the land beneath the North Star, were now bartered and sold directly to Europe via Bristol. Almost the entire Norwegian fleet had moved there. Basque and French merchants were also involved in this trade with Greenland. The pope received nothing.

The fall of the Norse Greenland society has spawned theories that the Eskimos destroyed the community, that the climate grew colder, with more ice and less precipitation—or even that swarms of insects ruined their grazing land. These may have been minor contributing factors, but in reality it was the Treaty of Tordesillas that finally laid waste to Greenland.

It would be interesting to know whether the pope was threatened, enticed or bribed by Portugal, when he suddenly betrayed Greenland during the negotiations. We can not exclude this latter possibility. Both catholic and other historians have viewed him as the most unworthy person ever to fill The Holy See. His greed and criminality elicited disgust and horror among his contemporaries. In any case he killed two birds with one stone with the Tordesillas treaty. Portugal quieted down, and at the same time he was able to clip the wings of his majesty in Copenhagen.

Christian's successor, King Hans, and his chancellors, obviously knew about the Treaty of Tordesillas, but they had their hands full with their Scandinavian chaos—the endless quarrels with the Hanseatic merchants and the Dutch skippers about rights to the most important Norwegian resources—dried fish, lumber and boiled sea salt. And there was constant friction between the garrison commanders and the dying Norwegian nobility, who demanded that some of the collected taxes be allowed to stay in the country.

The pope was unable to establish meaningful contact with Norwegian authorities, because the Danish kings viewed Norway as their private property, separate from the Danish state. The king's personal friends and favorites were given posts where they were free to exploit the Norwegian population in return for a fee to the king. Lawlessness, seizure of property, rape and brutality were overlooked.[13]

«The people were kept hostage within their own borders,» wrote the German historian Albert Kranz in a retrospective in 1517. And the Danish King Fredrik I called the country a «safe haven for desperate people» from Denmark.

The inhabitants were regarded almost as children. Whenever the situation became unbearable, a delegation of Norwegian farmers would be allowed to speak to the king. Danish farmers on a similar errand would have been killed long before reaching their destination. But even if the king jovially humored the farmers clad in coarse homespun, upon their return home they would at best be ruined, at worst killed as rebels. Eventually all such initiatives were squelched. It got to the point where all waterfalls that could support a sawmill were confiscated by Danes in the name of the king. Anyone able to hew a few planks to take down to the harbors where the Dutch buyers were waiting, had to bring a third plank for every two, for the «occupiers».

In this natural prison, North America and Greenland became something distant and unreal to the Norwegian population.

From Paradise to Hell

Initially the Treaty of Tordesillas was of meager benefit to Portugal. But during a voyage to the south, Vincente Yanez Pinzón discovered a foreign coast that extended into the Portuguese part of the Atlantic Ocean. On April 22, 1500, Pedro Alvares Cabral concluded that this had to be a very large land. The following year the Italian merchant Amerigo Vespucci offered to explore the entire coast on behalf of Portugal. They called the vast land «Ihla da Vera Cruz»—all American land was still referred to as «islands».

It was not until 1533 that King John III saw to it that the land came under formal Portuguese administration. The old Norse country in North America had been called «Brazil» since the 1400s—the land of the red trees. It is assumed that the name refers to the Norway Pine (Pinus resinosa) and red spruce (Picea rubens), because Portuguese accounts make a point of the ships' masts that grew there. This was now partly Portuguese land, and it may have seemed natural for the name of Brazil to include their new southern province in America also. The geographer Lopo Homem, on his beautiful and famous map from about 1516–1519, called the land in the south «Nova Brazil».[14] Later it was called only «Brazil».

Today the name Brazil is no longer found in the north.

The overwhelming reception Columbus received after having rediscovered and discovered his islands in the west, led to a second expedition of 17 ships and 1500 men. Fantastic rumors circulated that anyone could become fabulously rich in the new land in the west, without the slightest effort. Lumps of gold were lying on the ground, just waiting to be picked up.

During this voyage Columbus' geographical world view was still intact. He firmly believed that Florida-Georgia existed and was called Binini. One of the participants on the expedition, Juan Ponce de León, made note of the information. Other than that, no one was particularly interested. Pietro Martire at the Spanish court wrote that no one believed this claim.[15]

This was the last occasion that Columbus had time to think about North America. From then on he was helplessly drawn into a headlong search for gold that at times brought him to the edge of collapse. He found himself in the middle of intrigues which, given his character, he was bound to lose to sharp hucksters, and he had assumed a governorship for which he was unqualified.

The second expedition stopped at several Caribbean islands where a wave of systematic plunder and rape was initiated, transforming a paradise into hell. The conquerors noted cannibalism on some islands, which presumably justified their own licentiousness. Reluctant Caribbean girls were flogged with ropes with great merriment until they were willing.

The floating migration eventually reached the fort that Columbus had constructed on the north side of Haiti before he went home. A cannon was fired, but there was no reply from the cannon on shore. No people appeared. When they reached the fort, the entire crew had disappeared or been killed, and the fort had been destroyed.

Very possibly it started when the men of the garrison had a fall out with one of the chiefs of an inland valley. He was a Caribe, and not as compliant as his colleague on the coast. After a battle in the interior, where both Beatriz' nephew and the king's precious metal expert and controller

143

were killed, the fort was next. The crew who were staying there with a group of native women were slaughtered.

The Spaniards visited a cruel and unnecessary revenge on the innocent community. Most of the Indians would subsequently die anyway, in a series of «harmless» epidemics that became catastrophic for a population whose immunological defenses were inadequate after living for generations on these isolated islands.

At the same time that the islands in the Caribbean were being discovered, the disease syphilis appeared in Europe. An epidemic ran rampant from country to country, hitting Italy especially hard. It was said that it was brought there from the Indians in America, and the most grotesque explanations for its appearance have survived to this day—including that it was caused by crimen bestialitatis—sexual relations with llamas. No reliable sources to support the theory exist. Medical research, however, suggests that syphilis reached Europe from the East in a more distant past. Skeletal and mummified remains found in Middle Eastern graves show definite signs of syphilis. The wave of infection may have been dormant for a long, long time—when no trade, cultural or other communication existed between Europe and the Middle East. Ptolemy's revolutionary map, for instance, took 1200 years to reach Germany from Alexandria. Dr. P.M. Ashburn claims in A Medical History of the Conquest of America that the re-emergence of syphilis in the 1500s was caused by spirochete parasites spread by the European men to Indian women, who already carried an indigenous North American strain. It is the union of these two parasites which may have resulted in the disastrous epidemic that the Spaniards unleashed in Europe.

The syphilis epidemic was felt in Norway as well. The syphilitic outbreak was the main reason why Norway in 1788 was given county doctors, similar to contemporary district physicians.[16]

Pinzón had had no map in his possession—he had only seen one in the Vatican. And now he was dead. Columbus had had a book and a map, but «The Admiral's Book» had disappeared. Nor did any other maps exist that showed the continent and the islands that Columbus had headed for in 1492.

When «The Admiral's Map» was presented by Martin Waldseemüller in Strasbourg some years later, «Isabella» (the present Cuba) had been extended east of Florida-Georgia up to Chesapeake Bay in Virginia. This was to be the cause of countless and often strange theories about Columbus' destination in 1492. Recall that America was referred to as «Cuba» on

144

the oldest maps. A geographer took it upon himself to move the name «Cuba» down to the large island the expedition reached, and to remove Columbus' name «Isabella». Subsequently everyone followed suit.

Soon the general idea arose that Columbus had really been on his way to India. Only those few who knew the content of his diary knew for a fact that this was not so. But they didn't quite know what to believe either, because no map was found that agreed with the diary. And so the «Columbus Riddle» arose.

1. See appendix of Columbus' diary.
2. Columbus' diary, November 13.
3. Herrera y Tordesillas, 1612.
4. Harrisse, 1882.
5. Doctoral disseration, Leningrad University, 1950. English summary in Tornöe, 1965, pp. 94–102.
6. Tornöe, 1965, p. 100.
7. Grimberg, vol. XI, 1957.
8. Diplomatarium Norwegicum, XVII, no. 759.
9. Ibid., XII, no. 761.
10. Morison, 1940. The full wording of the agreement on pp. 60–62.
11. Taranger (ed.), 1915–17, vol. III, p. 174.
12. Ibid., p. 171.
13. Ibid., p. 204.
14. Cortesao (ed.), 1960, vol.I, map no. 24.
15. Anghiera, 1511.
16. Bache, Torchel. Manuscript in progress about the history of physicians' county service in Norway.

THE VINLAND VOYAGES BECOME A EUROPEAN POLITICAL ISSUE

While Columbus' first little fleet sailed on a gentle breeze along the 28th parallel across a glittering ocean, the Venetian John Cabot lived a greyer life in Valencia in Spain, sitting at his drawing board. On September 27— when the caravels were about half way to their destination—the general governor in Valencia, Don Diego do Torre, wrote a letter to King Ferdinand. He had received a sketch from Cabot for a proposed new harbor in Valencia. The old one was hopeless, and he thought Cabot's colorful proposal seemed «realistic and attractive».[1] The king accepted without hesitation. By October 25 the matter had already progressed to the point where the governor general asked the king for money for ships and stone for Cabot's harbor project. Columbus was then sailing among the lush Bahama Islands.

A few months later, in the middle of his hard work with stone and dirt, Cabot received the news that Columbus had returned. The promised land had been found, and an elated population celebrated the discoverer.

To the experienced seaman and map expert Cabot, the news was joyous indeed. Columbus had not claimed Antilia, nor the forested land Brazil. Cabot immediately departed and a few months later was back in Bristol with his family. He arrived in the nick of time. His old employer Robert Thorne and the experienced captain Hugh Elliot were ready to ship out to America, more specifically «Brazil». They arrived in North America in the spring of 1494. Their voyage nearly changed history.

Thorne's son, Robert, wrote in a subsequent letter to the English embassy in Madrid that it had been generally accepted in Bristol that America was a continuous continent, and that they had planned to travel south along the coast to Florida. But the crew mutinied, and they had to return home. «If the men had obeyed their master, all this would have been ours,» was his bitter conclusion.[2]

On the back of the map of the North Atlantic that John Dee drew in 1580, it is written that both Robert Thorne Jr. and Sr. took part in the expedition, so the letter can be considered first hand information.[3]

146

The Spanish ambassador in London immediately reported the matter to Seville, and added that more ships from Bristol in recent years had «attempted to find Brazil». The Spanish regents sent an embittered protest to King Henry VII of England, in which they pointed out that according to the Treaty of Tordesillas, these would be considered hostile actions against Spain and Portugal.

At this point an interesting figure appeared on the scene—Charles VIII, the king of France. He pronounced that the Tordesillas treaty concerned only those islands and lands discovered by Spain and Portugal at the time the treaty went into effect in September of 1493, and that the rest of North America would have to be excluded—in particular «Antilia», the land of the seven cities. This set off a diplomatic flurry of activity across the channel. An important plan was about to see the light of day.

The keeper of the Canadian archives, Dr. Biggar, has come across an indignant letter that the Spanish regents wrote to their ambassador in London, Gonzales de Puebla, on March 28, 1496. The majesties ask him to take the English king to task and warn him against his plans to occupy the west. They are fully aware that Charles VIII of France is the moving force behind attempts to get Henry VII of England to send «someone like Columbus» on an expedition similar to the one Columbus made for Spain. But the king is mistaken if he thinks he can interpret the treaty (Tordesillas) to mean that he can interfere in Atlantic Ocean matters without harming and offending Spain and Portugal.[4]

King Henry still chose to follow the advice of his French colleague. Cabot was commissioned to find the land «Norumbega» in North America. R.A. Skelton, former head of The Map Room in the British Museum, writes that he has no explanation for this name other than that it first arose in connection with Cabot's journey, and subsequently on his map.[5] It is possible that France and England used the name «Norumbega» in order to underscore the fact that the Norwegians had been in America long before the Treaty of Tordesillas ever saw the light of day. The Spanish and Portuguese also began using the name «Norumbega» and «Noruega». But America's past in no way changed their agreement about dividing the western world between them. Nor were there any Norwegian or Greenland administrators in America.

Cabot thought that North America was the northeastern Asian province of Tangut, described by Marco Polo. The Bristol merchants and the king had more realistic opinions, but this was less important than the political game that was being played out.

On March 5, 1496, Cabot was granted the same rights by the English as Columbus had received from the Spaniards. He was to become governor and English viceroy of North America, and the titles would be inherited by his sons, and he and his heirs were to be knighted. All Englishmen were required to offer him and his heirs and descendants the rights to which nobility were entitled.[6]

As far as Norway was concerned, the occupation was a legally questionable one. But France and England were apparenly confident that Denmark and Norway would not awaken from their slumber. The Danish king simply couldn't have cared less about America. Norway, which he controlled, was itself still a wilderness, with rich codfish banks and enormous forests with an abundance of trees so sought after for ships' masts.

Cabot's orders were to formally occupy and claim «all heathen lands, islands and provinces in the north, east and west». The seafarers of Bristol cared little about such things. Nevertheless the city of Bristol was still granted sole right and duty free access to all goods shipped to and from America. The king did not forget himself, of course. He planned to collect a generous toll on all merchandise to be imported from the new possessions.

The little ship «Matthew» with a crew of 18, plus Cabot and his son, «crown prince» Sebastian, sailed west on May 11, 1497. The weather was good, but they were caught in a storm the last few days before they reached Newfoundland or the south coast of Cape Breton on June 23.

Three accounts of this journey are available, and they agree for the most part. On December 18, 1497, the Duke of Milan's envoy in London, Richmondo de Soncino, wrote to his lord that he had spoken to Cabot and seen the map of the voyage.[7] Based on Marco Polo's geographical data, Cabot thought he had sailed along the distant Asian province of «Tanais».

In the Gulf of Maine they apparently turned around and headed back. On the way they stopped for the first and last time during the voyage. The English flag and a flag from Cabot's home town, Venice (where he was a registered resident), were planted. The land was re-christend «Terra Igleterra», «England's Land». Twice on their journey they saw creatures on shore that they took to be people. Both parties were apparently frightened by the other. After replenishing their water supply and finding some man made items on land, they started their home journey on a brisk wind. The return voyage across the ocean took 20 days—they frittered away some time because they disagreed about the course. The king's account book indicates that they were back home before August 10.

148

On September 1 the Venetian Lorenzo Pasqualgio wrote a letter from London to his brothers home in Venice:[8]

«Our fellow citizen, who sailed from Bristol to find new "islands", has returned. He reports that he discovered mainland China, 700 leagues from Ireland. And that he sailed 300 leagues along the coast and went ashore. He saw no people, but brought the king some snares for catching game and a needle used to make fishing nets. He also saw some trees with notches in them, which made him conclude that there were inhabitants there. But he felt it safer to return to his ship. .....The king has promised him ten ships next time, and has given him a crew of prisoners, except men jailed for high treason. Now he is with his Venetian wife and sons in Bristol. He calls himself Grand Admiral and dresses in silk. The Englishmen pursue him like mad, but he wants nothing to do with them.»

The seafarers of Bristol considered him a silly fool and were irritated that he was called the discoverer of a land they already knew very well. The diplomats sent triumphant messages to their homelands, included with the map—Asia's coast had been reached by the Venetian captain, who was now the viceroy of North America.

Columbus Asks For Details

One of the persons most interested, of course, was the other viceroy of the western world, Christopher Columbus. He was having major problems in his colony. Barely any income was collected for the motherland. Colonists who had sold all they owned in Spain in order to move to the West Indies felt cheated. The first adventurers had already begun to return home, completely ruined. There was absolutely no gold on Española and Isabella and the other islands. The regents kept a protective hand over Columbus while he defended himself against jealous foes. But it would be safe to say that even the court's enthusiasm had cooled somewhat.

He was naturally quite preoccupied with the rumors about Cabot and his «neighboring» kingdom. And by a coincidence his reaction has become known to us. In 1956 the American historian, Dr. Vigneras, was doing research in the Archivo General de Simancas Estado de Castilla, when another researcher alerted him to an old document about an English voyage. At first glance Dr. Vigneras didn't think it was of any particular interest. But three weeks later he re-examined one of the letters. Slowly it dawned on him that he was holding a document of immeasurable historical value.

In the fall of 1497, when Columbus was home in Spain, he had written to the Bristol merchant John «Day», who was then in Andalusia. He asked for information about what really happened to Cabot. What Vigneras held in his hand, was the reply letter.

Thanks to English stone houses that prevented fires, a diligent bureaucracy and the English Channel that stopped plundering armies, the British archives of the 1400s are the best in Europe. But there is no John Day in the conscientiously kept customs and trade records. On the other hand, the shipowner and merchant John Jay is constantly referred to. He was, as we know, Cabot's employer when he was carrying cargo to Portugal and Spain. Jay himself sent a ship to North America in 1480 and 1481.

The reply letter was dictated to a Spanish scribe. The scribe must have taken the name to be Day—possibly because of the English pronunciation «Dzay». Still, to be on the safe side, let us summarize what John Day and John Jay have in common. They are both merchants with extensive trading business in Andalusia. They are very well informed about what merchants and seafarers in Bristol had been doing up until that fall. They both knew the land «Brazil» in America and the journeys of Bristol merchants to the abandoned land in the west. It is obvious that we are talking about John Jay. And it is just as obvious that this is a man Columbus already knew.

Columbus had asked Jay for a resumé on the Cabot matter, and to borrow his copy of the book Inventio Fortunatæ as well as Marco Polo's book. His home was now in the West Indies, and that's probably where he kept his own books, unless they had gone down with the «Santa Maria» or had been destroyed by Indians in the winter of 1493. Finally he had asked Jay to get him a map of Cabot's voyage.

Jay's reply letter, which is still in excellent condition, says that Jay can't find his copy of Inventio Fortunatæ, even though he thought he had brought it to Spain. But he includes the book about Marco Polo's journeys and Cabot's map, which he regrets he has not been able to put more work into. Regrettably the map has been lost, but in his letter Jay fortunately summarizes its main features:

The land Cabot first sighted, was 1800 nautical miles west of Dursey Head in Ireland. And this peninsula, which Cabot claims to have been

150

the first to discover, is the same one discovered by men from Bristol earlier, when they sailed to «Brazil». And here Jay adds: «...which your Highness is well acquainted with.» The peninsula was actually called «Brazil's Island» and was thought to be connected to the mainland of «Brazil» which men from Bristol had also visited.

As far as «the land with the seven cities» is concerned, Jay explains that the enclosed map showed that it was on the latitude of the river Bordeaux in France. This latitude is the same as the southern tip of Nova Scotia, which is a bit incorrect. Farther into the letter we get the explanation for this. Cabot was aware of the compass declination here, but he thought that the needle was only two notches «too low» in relation ship to true north. It was far too little—the magnetic north pole at that time lay near Resolute Bay in the Northwest Passage, and an error of 10–12 notches would have been more correct. This hidden error caused Cabot to believe that the American east coast continued westward and ended in the land of the Great Khan.

John Jay's letter is quite long, and his account in the main repeats what we know from the other reports about Cabot's journey. Cabot and his crew had been frightened for their lives. The one time they went ashore they had followed a path and seen evidence of camp fires. They had also seen places where plants were being cultivated and the land farmed. They also found a pole, about half a yard long, with both ends carved and decorated with «brazil» [red color]. This made them believe that people lived in the region, and therefore they decided not to push on any farther.

Jay confirmed that an expedition from Bristol (obviously Thorne and Elliot in 1494) had had difficulties with the crew, low supplies of food and bad weather, and therefore had to return home.[9]

The king of England gave Cabot an annual pension of 20 pounds. All that remained now, was to annex the land between Cape Cod and Chesapeake Bay—the true Vinland, or «Antilia» with the seven cities. The king was willing to chance this venture as well, but not to be the official occupier. When Cabot was ready to leave the following year, Henry VII informed him that he would not be issued prisoners as crewmen, that he would have to leave without royal support, and that he could not have more than six ships totalling 200 tons. The merchants of Bristol then stepped in, and from the kings' account books we see that he advanced a bit of money to encourage their investments.

In early summer of 1498 five ships headed west out of Bristol.

The Spanish ambassador in London, Ruy Gonzales de Puebla, apparently wrote in July to the Spanish regents that he had had a conversation with Henry VII, but that he was not satisfied with the information he had been given about the destination of the expedition: «The king of England sent five armed vessels with another Genoan, like Columbus, to search for Brazil and «Vicinidades» (the seven cities—the letter is written in code). Judging from the direction in which they are headed, the expedition is going to the lands in the possession of Your Highnesses.»[10]

On July 25, the Spanish envoy, Pedro de Ayala, wrote to Spain: «The land belongs to Your Highnesses in accordance with the treaty with Portugal. I have the map here, but it seems to me they are attempting to show they are different "islands" than the aforementioned.»[11]

There is a theory that Cabot died near Nova Scotia, where a sword of Venetian manufacture was later found. This is not very likely, since Cabot was paid his annual pension on September 29 that same year. His son, Sebastian, later told the Spanish court scribe Pietro Martire that the ships had gone all the way up to 60°N (Labrador), and that they thereafter followed the American coast.[12] Medieval cartographer Rasmusio writes that they reached the border of «Florida» at 36°N—the southern tip of Vinland and «Antilia» at the inlet of Chesapeake Bay. That is the same latitude as the Strait of Gibraltar, Martire adds for good measure. More recent research, by L.H. Vigneras among others, confirms Sebastian's account.[13] But Cabot probably died shortly afterwards, because he then disappears from history. The somewhat cautious Henry VII bided his time.

Cabot's original map is gone, but there are several accounts that describe it. He wrote that there was «Brazilwood» (Norway Pine?) where he traveled, and that silk possibly could be grown there. And from now on, «Norumbega» became the destination for English colonists in America.[14]

The French name was «Norumbegue» and the French sphere of interest was to become today's Canada. Now Norumbega's long coast was christened «Terra de France» in the Gulf of St. Lawrence, and «Terra Ingelterra» along the Gulf of Maine and further south along the Atlantic coast. The most famous map was the one made by Juan de la Cosas (not Columbus' navigator of the same name), a world map from 1500 kept in Museo Naval in Madrid. It includes the island of Frisland earlier noted by the Zeno brothers, right next to Greenland. But the new English and French colonial names were soon forgotten, and on the maps the land

152

was simply called «Norumbega» from the Gulf of St. Lawrence down to New York—a name that was not changed on any of the thousands of maps that were drawn, says R.A. Skelton.[15]

Greenland Becomes the «Slave Land»

When England showed no indication that she intended to respect the Treaty of Tordesillas regarding the division of the Atlantic Ocean, Portugal's King Manuel took action:

On October 28, 1499, he commissioned Joâo Fernandez, a «labrador» from Terceira on the Azores, to «discover some islands in the northwest» and become governor there. He was to have the same rights as the governors on the Azores, regardless of whether the countries were populated or not, writes the king in the document, which is kept in Portugal's state archives at Torre do Tombo.[16]

It undeniably seems strange that the king would assign such a commission to a «labrador», which means an ordinary laborer. Historians have speculated that he may have been a small land owner. I have consulted experts in Spain, Portugal and the Azores about the matter. They all agree with the American linguist Dr. Mario Pei, who in a letter of July 5, 1977 confirms that a «lavrador» is a laborer, a farm hand.

Portugal in this period secured a work force for farming by bringing home slaves, especially from Africa. Slave trading was a respected profession, and there is reason to believe that Fernandez' title may not be an indication of his own status, but rather of the goods in which he traded— that he was a slave trader and supplied workers to Portuguese estates. Nansen claims that he visited Greenland in 1500 and gave it the somber name «Terra Laboratoris».

But the ink on the royal letter was barely dry before the family Corte Real appeared. The general attitude in those days was that the first nobleman to visit a land had the right to be its discoverer. The saying, «The land on which the sultan's horse puts its hooves, is the sultan's land» was a truism in the Christian world as well. And the land in the northwest had been visited by Joanno vâs Corte Real during the Danish-Norwegian-Portuguese expedition in 1473. Portuguese historians also claim that the son, Gaspar Corte Real, made another visit to the north in 1488. Therefore the land belonged to them, a claim Columbus seems to have agreed with, because in his diary of October 7, 1492, he said that Portugal «possesses» these lands. The king of Portugal apparently agreed as well. On May 12, 1500, he already issued a new decree, in which the rights to the land are transferred to Gaspar Corte Real and his heirs—who were to have a quarter of all the income they squeezed out of the «colony» in the high north. All signs indicate that Gaspar left for the north immediately. Fridtjof Nansen, who investigated this matter quite thoroughly, says that the land Corte Real visited in 1500, based on all available information, could only have been Greenland. Gaspar's contemporaries all agreed that he was on Greenland. Some maps use the name «Terra Verde» («The Green Land») as the name of the country.

On the Cantino map (to be discussed later) it is stated that King Manuel gave Gaspar Real the task of «discovering»—i.e. annexing—Greenland.

Daniam de Goes writes in Cronica do Fellisimo Rey dom Emanuel (Lisbon, 1566) that in 1500 Gaspar Corte Real was in a land where the inhabitants were white when they were young, but that they became weather beaten and darker of skin with age. He further reports that the people of this land practiced marriage, and that the men were very jealous. This probably describes the desperation among the men when they were bound hand and foot and their women made available to the sailors. The story of piracy during this era can be compared in malice to any other debasement and terror to which man has subjected his fellow beings throughout history. It is impossible to verify the information about skin color, because it was only the young who were taken as slaves. It may have been a kind of insurance, because theologically the Greenlanders could be considered Christian, and therefore protected against slavery. Gaspar Vopell's world map of 1541, based on older Spanish sources produced by King Philip personally, says that the Greenlanders were known for their heathendom. The only copy of the original map can be found at Harvard University. It also notes that the volcano on Vestmannaeyar was thought to be a branch of hell—an addendum to Pope Gregor's earlier statement that «hell proper» was the Etna volcano on Sicily.

About Corte Real's next voyage, during the summer of 1501, we have considerable documentation.

Venice's envoy in Lisbon, Pietro Pasqellagio, wrote in the spring of 1501 to the bureau in Venice that the king of Portugal had sent ships to the land that borders on Antilia to gather tall trees (ships' masts) and male slaves.[17] The king supported the expedition. On April 15 King Manuel wrote to the baker of the city gate La Cruz that he was to provide ships bisquits to Gaspar Corte Real at the king's expense. The supply of bisquits was delivered April 21.[18]

Near Newfoundland, where they apparently had a land base for their activities, the three captains agreed that Miguel Corte Real would stop, while the other two ships would head in different directions to hunt for slaves. They were to meet on Newfoundland on August 20 and return home to Portugal together. The direction referred to must have been toward the Labrador coast and Ungava Bay, and eastward to Greenland—since they had come from the south.

One ship, whose name and captain we don't know, arrived at the agreed time and had 50 male slaves onboard. But Gaspar, who had probably gone to Greenland, did not arrive. Manuel headed south after waiting for a few days, while the third ship stayed behind and waited. Fall was coming.

On October 18 Venice's envoy again writes that two ships arrived on October 9, with 7 captured men, women and children, from a land that lies 1800 nautical miles to the northwest. Other sources say that the number of slaves was far greater on Miguel's ship. But the third ship, with Gaspar Corte Real on board, had not arrived.

The slaves were well built and looked like gypsies, the envoy writes. The land they had visited that summer was thought to be a mainland, but he believes there is a connection between it and the land they visited the previous summer (Greenland), and it borders Antilia and Brazil. This must mean that they visited Labrador/Ungava Bay. The description of the slaves also indicates that they were talking about a mixed population.

The envoy finally writes that more ships will now be made available to bring back greater numbers of slaves and lumber from the north.

Because of England's activities, it was important for the king to announce his acquisitions in the north. Immediately after his arrival he let Miguel be introduced to all of Lisbon's diplomats while His Majesty was present. The king declared that Portugal now had all the big and strong work slaves it needed, and that never before had such fine slaves been brought to Portugal. King Manuel's dream of finding male superslaves to work the farmland had become a reality.

One of the diplomats present, Alberto Cantino, the envoy of the Duke of Ferrara, wrote on October 17, 1501 to his lord that one or more of the ships had sailed so far north they were at the edge of the ice cap. Here they gave up on «a certain purpose» and turned to sail a more westerly course for a long time.[19]

«...on the first day of the fourth month they found a very large land, where many fresh water rivers flowed into the ocean. One of them they followed one league [ca. 5.5 kilometers] inland. And when they went ashore, they found a lot of delicious and varied fruits, and trees and needle trees so high they would have been too tall for masts for the largest ships that sail the ocean. The people here live from fishing, and from hunting the animals that are plentiful in the land. Here are many deer with long hair, and whose skin they use for clothing, and for boats and houses. There are also wolves and foxes and tigers [lynx?] and sables here. They assert—and I find this difficult to believe—that there are just as many falcons here as there are sparrows in our land. I have seen them, and they are very beautiful.»

This last statement indicates that their assault was against a trapping camp where the birds had been collected for shipment to Europe. And therefore that it must have been people with connection to Greenland.

Cantino continues:

«Of the men and women in this place they took about 50 by force, and brought them back to the king. I have seen them, touched them and watched them. To begin with their size, they are a little taller than we, with well proportioned and well formed limbs. Their hair is long from our point of view, and hangs in «loose curls», and their faces are painted with large figures, similar to Indians. Their eyes tend to the green, and when they look at me, I get an impression of considerable wildness. Their language is incomprehensible, but not coarse—rather quite human. Their behavior and manners are very mild. They laugh a good deal, and show a lot of spirit. The woman has small breasts and a very lovely body. She has an attractive face. The color could just as well be said to be white, but the males are much darker. All in all, if it hadn't been for the wild eyes of the males, it would seem to me that they are completely like us in all other things.»

Finally he says that the third ship was to follow the coast and find out whether this was an island or a mainland, and that the king was impatiently awaiting their return.

Gaspar never came back.

The next year his brother Miguel again went north with two ships. They planned to look for their brother, and to finance the voyage by taking slaves, of course.

Both ships disappeared without a trace.

The different historical sources disagree as to whether the king sent any more expeditions north. He probably did. But he denied the third Corte Real brother, Vasquanes, permission to go. He held several important posts both in Lisbon and on the Azores.

Among the few pieces of information we have about the colony in the north, we know that Portugal in 1506 established a duty on all fish caught near Newfoundland. The colony continued in the hands of the Corte Real family for the rest of the century, until the last male of the line, Manuel Corte Real II, died at the king's side in the battle of Kasrel-Kebir in 1578.[20]

The Duke of Ferrera became very interested in the lands that Portugal had occupied, and asked his envoy to send him a map of the Portuguese possessions in the north. It was not easy, because Portugal had instituted the death penalty as punishment for divulging geographical secrets. But by paying the dizzying sum of 12 gold ducats he was able to have a cartographer make him a secret copy. From a letter dated November 19, 1502, it becomes evident that the map was sent home to Italy. Today this map is called the Cantino map, and is kept in the Biblioteca Estense in Modena in Italy in a climate controlled room.

As mentioned before, America on this map is identical to what the Admiral himself (Columbus) described. In addition we have, for the first time, an excellent map of Greenland and Greenland's western coastline. It has a correct ice border between Iceland and Greenland. At Greenland it says that Gaspar Corte Real discovered (conquered) the land, but that it was first seen by an earlier expedition that did not go ashore, since they saw nothing but steep cliffs.

West of Greenland, Newfoundland and Labrador are shown as Portuguese all the way down to the Gulf of St. Lawrence. Two Portuguese flags are positioned on Greenland.[21]

An anonymous map from 1506 or later, which historians refer to as «Kunstmann II», has seven Portuguese names on Greenland and the surrounding area.[22]

On an Italian map drawn the same year, from a Portuguese source, Greenland is called «Terra laboratoris». The same name is used on a host of others, among them the famous Italian map from 1503 that was found in the Oliveriano library in Pesaro. Many of the maps confirm that «Terra Labrador» simply means land of laborers. A good example is reproduced in the latest edition of Dictionario de Historia de Portugal. Here the chapter about the Corte Real family is illustrated with Fernâo vas Dourados' map of the Labrador coast. The illustration shows several farm slaves plowing with oxen. There is reason to fear that the last Norse Greenlanders and the mixed population on the Labrador coast, the Ungava peninsula and other inhabited places in the north, ended their lives behind the oxen ploughs on Portuguese estates, after a last journey bound hand and foot and beaten in the cargo holds of the pirate caravels.

From the period 1516–19 we have a very beautiful map, drawn after the first Spanish landfall in North America in 1513.[23] It shows a Portuguese flag on Greenland, and calls Labrador «Corte Realis Noruega» in the text. The masterful geographer Ribeiro's epoch making map of America from 1529 (in the Vatican) has an inscription stating that the Portuguese finally lost interest in Greenland, but that the English then went ashore there.

It appears that this was the case:

Don Joâo Fernandez from the Azores who had to relinquish his right of discovery and the governorship to Gaspar Corte Real in 1500, immigrated to England. In the winter of 1500–1501 he is present in the Norwegian-dominated marine environement in Bristol. Already in Archivo dos Acores, XIII (1494) it says that he was a «llavrador» (slavehunter?) who operated at sea with one Bero de Barcellos.

On March 19, 1501, King Henry dispatched a letter to Richard Warde, Thomas Ashehurst and John Thomas. Together with three Portuguese, John [Joâo] Fernandez, Francis Fernandez and John Gonsalves, they were granted the right to discover and take possession, on behalf of England, of all islands and lands that had been previously unknown to Christians in the east, west, north and south—in other words in the entire world. The right to exploit the land was valid for ten years, and at the same time the king cancelled the permission granted to «another foreigner». That foreigner, of course, was Cabot.

This company went on expeditions to «the newfound land» both in 1501 and 1502. Robert Fabian's Chronicle reports that in 1502 they brought back three white men who were given to the king—apparently as house slaves.[24] They seemed quite wild upon arrival. But when the author two years later saw them in Westminster Palace, it was not possible to distinguish them from native Englishmen. There can be little doubt that he was talking about Greenlanders from Greenland or North America.

One of the veterans from Bristol, Hugh Elliot, who had been in North America in 1494, participated in an expedition in 1503. That fall they brought back «hawks» (Greenland hunting falcons) to the king.[25] This indicates that there were still people catching falcons north of the Norse Greenland communities.

When King Henry died in 1509, it meant the end of all the activity in the northwest. His successor, Henry VIII, was to become better known for his extraordinary home environment and married life.

Once again North America was owner-less. The well informed map maker Ruysh notes, in the inscription on his world map of 1508, that he draws his source material from Inventio Fortunatæ—and that «Antilia» has not yet been found.

Eskimos Confirm the Slave Hunt

The only Greenland account in existence about the demise of the Greenland settlements, is what an Eskimo told Niels Egede, son of «Greenland's Apostle», Hans Egede, in the 1700s. The account was written down and preserved.[26]

The Eskimo reported that his people had migrated to the south of Greenland and reached the Norwegian communities. The relationship between the two peoples was somewhat strained—the Greenlanders wanted nothing to do with the Eskimos, except for trading. And the Eskimos, who were still migratory, were a little frightened. But after a while they came to trust each other somewhat, as the Eskimos became more numerous and a few family groups appeared.

This had not been going on for very long when three pirate ships arrived. Fighting ensued and plundering took place. The Norsemen managed to overcome the crew on one of the ships, while the other two fled.

The following year «a whole fleet» arrived, that plundered, pillaged and killed with abandon. Some of the survivors fled in boats, apparently over to America. But some stayed behind. The tragic events brought the Eskimos and the Greenlanders closer together, and the Eskimos promised to help if more pirates appeared.

But when the slave traders arrived the next summer, the Eskimos became frightened and fled inland with five white women and some children. When they felt it safe to return, everything in the Eastern Settlement, to which this account refers, was razed. Eskimo youths took the five women in and married them.

For a few years things were quiet. The Eskimos increased in number, he reported. Occasionally a ship arrived that traded with the local population.

The Eskimo says without hesitation that the ships were the same ones that ravaged the American side. That agrees with the Portuguese accounts, which state that they had their main base on Newfoundland where the ships would gather after rounding up slaves. The Eskimo also said that the English ships later acted threateningly. It would not be surprising for the Eskimos to know this, since the women who joined the Eskimo families were probably well aware of what was going on.

Egede said that if the Eskimo's account was to be printed, perhaps the form would need to be polished a bit. It's a good thing he didn't, because an Eskimo account of this kind is just as reliable as a printed book. Stories such as this were repeated word for word from generation to generation.

But the five women and «some children» in the Eastern Settlement, where the Eskimos also lived, were not the only survivors.

Bishop Ogmund of Iceland and a crew of eleven men, left Bergen on June 13, 1522, with a crew of 11, and were storm driven all the way to the southern tip of Greenland. They spotted people and sheep at Herjulfsnes, but were afraid to go ashore.[27] They were probably afraid they had come upon a «pirate's nest».

A man who was called John Greenlander because he had drifted to Greenland three times on his way to Iceland, told about one of his trips when he was sailing on a ship from Hamburg. They entered a still and deep fjord, with many islands with houses that were still standing. They didn't see anyone, and went ashore on a little island where there were stalls and stone houses for drying fish—just like on Iceland. They found a dead man lying flat on his face. On his head he was wearing a well made hood. His clothing was partly woolen and partly seal skin. Next to him they found a curved knife that was very worn after much use. They took the knife along as a souvenir. This account dates from 1530–40.[28]

When the German captain Gert Mestermacher sailed along the coast of Greenland in 1542, there was no sign of life.[29]

An unusually good map made in 1558 by Diogo Homem [the grandson of Homem from the expedition of 1473] has the following legend for

Greenland: «Desertibusoz Terra Agricule.» Homem is not easy to understand because of his stilted Latin, but the inscription seems to mean «the deserted farm laborer land».

The «Greenland Mystery» probably cannot be explained more simply than this. There were no more slaves left to be captured.

1. All documents pertaining to this matter are kept in Archivo Regional de Valencia, Archivo de Real. Epistolarum, Vol. 496. English summary: Williamson, 1962.
2. British Museum, Cotton MS, Vit. C VII, pp. 329–45.
3. British Museum, Cotton MS, Aug. I. i.
4. Archivo General de Simancas, Estado Tratados con Ingleterra, leg. 2, fol. 16. English summary: Williamson, 1962, p. 203.
5. Quinn, et.al., 1971.
6. Nansen, 1911.
7. Harrisse, 1882, p. 324.
8. Ibid., p. 322.
9. Canadian Historical Review, Vol. XXXVIII, 1957. Original document in Archivo General de Simancas, Estado de Castilla, leg. 2, fol. 6.
10. Harrisse, 1882, p. 328.
11. Ibid., p. 329.
12. Anghiera, 1511.
13. Canadian Historical Review, Vol. XXXVIII, 1957, p. 219.
14. McManis, 1972.
15. Quinn, et.al., 1972.
16. Cf. Harrisse, 1883, p. 244.
17. Ibid., p. 209.
18. Ibid., Supplement Post Scriptum, p. 6.
19. Ibid., p. 204.
20. Nansen, 1911, p. 571.
21. See Aschehougs Verdenshistorie, Vol. VII, p. 230.
22. Williamson, 1962, p. 141.
23. Cortesâo (ed.) 1960, Vol. I, map no. 24.
24. Hakluyt, 1850, p. 23.
25. Harrisse, 1883, p. 270.
26. Osterman, 1939.
27. Annales Islandi, 1922, Vol. I, pp. 94–95. See also Diplomatorium Islandicum, Vol. IX, pp. 97–99 and 110–111.
28. Grönlands historiske minnesmerker, Vol. III, p. 513.
29. Hansische Geschichtsblätter, 1940–41.

THE BLUE EYED GUEST IN MEXICO

The most incredible experience reported during the great discoveries was the one that happened to the 34 year old Spaniard Hernando Cortéz:

An expedition from Haiti encountered a peaceful group of Indians on the west coast of the Yucatan peninsula, and Cortéz went there in the spring of 1519 to exploit their hospitality and take the opportunity to conquer the entire area. Rumors were circulating that Mexico was a land of enormous wealth.

This voyage is described in Cortéz' detailed reports to King Carlos of Spain and in an excellent book by the foot soldier, Bernal Diaz. What follows is a summary of these two accounts, supplemented by details from Maurite Collis' Cortéz and Montezuma, and oral information given by Indians in Mexico.[1]

First the ships went to the present vacation paradise of Cozumel, where they found a Spaniard who had been enslaved by the Indians. They brought him along so he could act as an interpreter. The other survivor from the same shipwreck, however, had become a local chieftain for the Mayas, had married a Mayan woman and had three children. He categorically refused to go back to his old and belligerent countrymen. The Indian wife raged at Cortéz. The conquerors thereafter followed the coast to Tabasco, where the Yucatan peninsula and the Mexican mainland meet. Here the population was Aztec.

This time several thousand Indian warriors mounted a devastating attack. Grimberg writes, based on Spanish sources: «The battle raged, and the Spaniards would not have been able to resist the Indians who greatly outnumbered them, if it hadn't been for the cavalry that came thundering into the arena. It was a sight that filled the natives with panic and fear. Such strange creatures had never before been seen. They thought the horse and the rider were one and the same, and dared not stand up against them. The entire force dispersed in desperate retreat.»

When the battle was over, Cortéz hit his sword three times against a tree, with a Spanish scribe as witness. Thereby the land became Spanish.

162

After the battle the Indian chiefs began to behave oddly—with humility and subservience. They requested a meeting with Cortéz. To this meeting they brought gifts, and twenty young girls from prominent families.

A Spanish diary offers this explanation:

«The chieftains said they had been told by their forefathers that a god had once said that men would arrive from a distant land in the east, to conquer their land and become their rulers. They now thought we were those men. That is why they negotiated with us and gave us their daughters.»

Cortéz had never heard this story, and did not put much faith in it. He suspected it might be a ruse.

The twenty girls were promptly baptized by Padre Fray Bartholomé. Thereafter they were distributed among the officers as mistresses. One intelligent and beautiful girl, who they baptized Marina, was first given to a captain. But when he disappeared, Cortéz himself took her over. She spoke both Mayan and Aztec. The Spanish interpreter spoke Mayan, so she was very useful during their journey through the land of the Aztecs.

In order to understand one of the most peculiar events in history, we need to take a closer look at the Aztec kingdom.

During the previous 150 years this warrior people had conquered Mexico from the Pacific to the Gulf of Mexico and made the neighboring peoples slaves and vassals. Thanks to an abundance of free slave labor, they transformed a small village into one of the world's most magnificent and richest capitals, Tenochtitlân—today's Mexico City. Gold and silver, necessities and luxuries, came there in an endless stream from the oppressed population.

The king of the land, Montezuma, had been an accomplished warrior who had fulfilled his forefathers' dream of subjugating the neighboring people. The Aztecs were at the pinnacle of their power and glory. A ruling class was able to reap the fruits of the labor of their subjects. There was nothing more to conquer.

As a result the culture began showing signs of malaise. The religion that they had inherited from the Toltecs dictated that the gods were to be offered human sacrifices on special occasions. This had developed into near mass murder, and it is estimated that 15–20,000 youths, mostly women and children, were sacrificed every year by the ghastly «priests» who slashed their victims' chests open with stone knives.[2] The smallest journey, negotiation or decision, required killings and the spilling of blood

163

in order to assure the consent of the gods. Their godly houses were stinking slaughterhouses, and ritual cannibalism was part of the scenario. Their entertainment was another symptom of cultural crisis. Prisoners had to fight to the death against armed soldiers, just like the Romans let prisoners fight wild animals for the entertainment of a decadent upper class, during the waning days of their empire.

All Mexican religions included elements of fatalism. Fortune tellers and prophets of doom had their heyday as things began to come apart, as happens during such cultural crises.

Fortune tellers and astrologers reminded people that a white man who had once visited Mexico left during a «reed year». And they knew, or believed, that he would also return during a «reed year». The year 1519, when Cortéz began his conquest, was also a «reed year». The foreigner who had once visited the Indians was not an ordinary man, but an invincible god! He was the mighty god Quetzalcoatl. The ruler, Montezuma, and his viceroys became very frightened.

The following is a summary based on Grimberg's Menneskenes liv og historie [«The Life and History of Man»] and conversations I have had with Indians about the legend of this white man.

In legends he was described as a strong man with light skin, blue eyes, and a big beard. This last part is particularly startling, because the Indians themselves have insignificant growth of beard. He also wore a big and special hat. Furthermore this white man was said to have lived among the Aztecs for a while and had taught them new ways of farming and building, as well as how to work with metals. He had also told them that there was only one god, the god of compassion and love, and he had ordered the Indians to stop all human sacrifices. He left in a long boat, that looked like a snake, and with a stem formed as a falcon's head. It was built «like the feathers of a bird», with boards overlapping. It seems to be an accurate description of the characteristic clinker-built Norse long ship. Even the name is reminiscent—the most famous of all Norwegian long ships was called «Ormen Lange» [The Long Snake] and was owned by Olav Trygvasson.

When he left the land headed east, he said he would be back. And that he, or his god, would be their master. The words are reminiscent of those often heard during the time when Scandinavia was christened, three–four hundred years earlier.

The first Aztec king ascended the throne around 1370, about the time metal work first began to appear in Mexico.[3] It is striking that the stranger also taught them a new way to cultivate crops. In the 1300s the Aztecs began using «floating fields» that multiplied their yields in the tropical climate.

Researchers believe that the stranger visited several lands in Central America.[4] This new method of cultivation—which is probably none other than the floating islands—was in use in other central American countries before it reached Mexico. The stranger may have learned it there before he encountered the Aztecs.

The «reed year» when this happened, was 1363. It could not have been the next «reed year», 1467, because Montezuma said that several generations had passed since the visit took place.

Later in his voyage Cortéz encountered a group of Indians of rank who waved them ashore and showered them with gifts. They were scouts from the mighty ruler, King Montezuma. Cortéz suspected as much, and put on a frightening show of armored riders and horses, furious dogs and the firing of cannons at close range.

The scouts were now fairly certain that Cortéz was the «god» that once had visited the land. They knew him by his hat, among other things, and were astonished by the divine powers he unleashed in their presence.

They were in a hurry to return to the capital. At home Montezuma was waiting, restless, anxious, sleepless and depressed. The vigorous warrior was obsessed with the dismal prophecies.

Two prisoners were sacrificed, and their blood sprinkled on the scouts before they delivered their unpleasant report. An Aztec legend summarizes their initial impression of Cortéz:[5]

«Their fireweapons go off on order. It sounds like thunder, it is overwhelming and your ears go deaf. And when they are fired, a stone ball comes from the belly of the weapon, flaming and bursting with sparks. It smells of sulphur, and makes your head hurt. If it hits mountains, they break into little pieces. If it hits a tree, it is ground into dust—as if a wind took it away.

They dress in iron and cover their heads with iron. Their swords are made of iron, their bows are iron, their shields iron. And they have deer that carry them on their backs, so they can reach as high as a rooftop. Their bodies are covered, only their faces are visible, white as chalk. They are brownhaired, but some have black hair. The beard is brown, wavy and curled. [...] And their dogs are very large, with droopy ears, eyes like fire, with yellow eyes and a thin, lean belly. They are big, wild and hungry. They sniff around while breathing heavily. They always walk with their tongues hanging out...»

«I have the fear of death in my heart,» said the mighty ruler, who now was certain that Cortéz had to be the strange god. «Who can advise me?»

A serious question was whether his soldiers should fight or not, if the stranger approached the capital. If they were invincible gods, that would be futile in any event.

Additional bad omens followed. A comet was seen in the sky, an earthquake shook the country, and a subterranean volcano made water boil somewhere in the Gulf of Mexico.[6] With all this, the astrologers did not become less hysterical.

For two months Cortéz waited on the coast. For the elite Aztec soldiers it would be an easy matter to obliterate the Spaniards. Cortéz may have been aware of that. But he had also found out that there was a people unwilling to be subjugated by the Aztecs in the state of Tlaxcola. These were people he would be able to use, and so the expedition headed there.

After a brutal encounter, the state joined him as an ally against the Aztecs. The pact was sealed when Cortéz was given the highborn and beautiful Doña Lucia. He passed her on to his next in command, Pedro de Alvarado. Their daughter later married into the highest nobility in Spain.

Meanwhile the ruler in the capital continued to send gifts to Cortéz, who didn't care one iota about Indian holy garments or fragile feather mosaic. He was a great deal more interested in large gold ornaments, among them the Quetzalcoatl mask that today can be seen in the British Museum. In truth he was a bit suspicious of all the generosity.

His new ally gave Cortéz 6000 soldiers to take along with him on a fall march toward Mexico's capital. A unit of Aztec soldiers who arrived to accompany the Spaniards, were cut down by mistake.

On November 8, 1519, the invading army reached the beautiful capital, which reminded them of Venice, with its canals, wide moats and bridges. They described it as a vision. And the largest attraction was the Indians' immense floating islands, where they harvested several crops each year. The inhabitants were said to number half a million, but it is believed there were no more than 300,000.

166

The ruler, Montezuma, came to meet them, carried on his gold adorned litter. He stepped out, so that he and Cortéz could meet on foot. The ruler of the Aztecs hung a flower wreath around Cortéz' neck. And on the ground in front of the Spanish conqueror he placed gold necklaces and chains with jewels.

Then he gave a speech:

«Sit down on your mat, your throne, which I have guarded for you while you were gone,» he said. «Your vassals, the old kings, my forefathers, who are now long gone, protected your throne before me. I wish that one of them could arise from the dead and see with his own eyes what my own eyes now behold...»

The miracle had happened—Cortéz had been given one of the richest lands in the world by a misunderstanding—and the world's best trained and best organized army without lifting a sword.

Missionary Church In A Heathen Land?

Mexican researchers and Indians from different tribes agree that the white man who once visited Mexico, really did exist. All relevant materials, including oral legends, are now being gathered for a collection at UNAM University in Mexico city.

The visit may be confirmed by yet another source.

In an original document from 1566 the Spanish missionary, monk and later bishop, Diego de Landa, notes the following in his report Relacion de las Cosas de Yucatan:

«...besides all this, I must tell what was told me by the chiefs of the Indians—a man of high intelligence who had the respect of all [the inhabitants]. One day I was speaking with him, I asked if he had ever heard about Christ, our Lord, or about the cross. He said that from his forefathers he had not heard of either Christ or the cross—except for one time when some of his people tore down a little house all the way out on the coast. Inside the house there were some graves, and on the bodies or bones of the dead there were small metal crosses. Since then they have seen no crosses until the day they were christened and saw the cross worshipped and adored. They therefore thought that those dead men had also worshipped the cross. If this was so, it is most likely that the little group had come from our land of Spain, and had thereafter disappeared without a trace.»

167

The place referred to, is Cap Catoche on the northern tip of the Yucatan, the point closest to Florida. And the small house must have been a house of worship—perhaps a little missionary church? The possibility that it had anything to do with the 1500s was dismissed by Diego de Landa—it had to do with events that had taken place much farther back in time.

Some researchers have suggested that the white man may have been Bishop Eirik, who in 1118 went from Greenland to America to search for «more» of Vinland. But that was almost two hundred years before the Aztecs arrived on the scene. A more obvious connection can be made to the book <u>Inventio Fortunatæ</u>, which in the 1360s described lands and «floating islands» at this latitude.[7] Christopher Columbus knew before his first voyage that the islands were not imaginary ones, writes Fernando Columbus in describing his father's preparations.

In all likelihood there was a missionary, geographical and treasure hunting expedition in America in the «reed year» 1363, but if it traveled that far south, there would most likely have been a map. If we dare believe Antonio Zeno's letter from around 1390, we have a believable account of the Greenland fishing expert who was in Mexico for 13 years, and about a small group that had established a colony far to the south some years later. The latter is of great interest, because they were described as having boats that could be rowed, in contrast to the heavier pirate caravels.

The white blood apparently did not disappear from Central America with the white stranger. On December 13 and 16 of 1492, Columbus and his companions met white people on Haiti—«as white as anyone seen in Spain». And on October 14 they had met an Indian who wore a coin as a nose ornament.

On his second voyage Columbus found an iron pot on one of the Caribbean islands and the keel of a ship built in the usual European way. A ship with white men had shipwrecked there. That is all we know for certain. But at that time, white men had for four hundred years been on the American coast a short sailing distance to the north. It would be incredible if the Greenlanders, who went as far as the Polar basin, would not also have ventured to the south.

Ponce de Léon Completes Columbus' Voyage

Columbus died in the old royal residence town of Valladolid north of Madrid in 1506, just as spring was coming to the high meadows, while the mountains in the distance were still white with snow. He couldn't have been farther removed from his element. He was bitter and lonely, after having been pushed aside both in the West Indies and at the court. His dream was ridiculed—his planned «peaceful kingdom» in the West Indies was an impossibility in such ruthless times. Among other things he had wanted to turn the cannibals away from cannibalism by letting them have livestock and become peaceful farmers.[8]

The discovery of fabulous South America also meant that he never saw more of North America than he had seen during his summer journey to 73°N in 1477. But he had one consolation before he died: His son Diego, whose mother was of noble birth, became his successor in the West Indies. Beatriz' son, Fernando, did not have the right of inheritance. But Fernando was an accompliished writer, with a prominent circle of friends in Spain.

The courtiers laughed at Columbus' claim that the land «Binini» lay on the coast of Georgia and Florida, «325 leagues northwest of Espanola» (Haiti). Someone added that there was also a well there that gave eternal youth, vitality and potency. The court scribe Pietro Martire wrote a caustic note to the king about this. He didn't think God gave Mother Nature such powers, but that he personally reserved the right to any such wonder.[9]

Over time the claim about the well has been given much more weight than the facetious superstition really warranted. The Spanish administration actually was quite realistic during this time of spiritual oppression.[10]

Columbus' diary lay unattended, and thus his critics had no knowledge of where he had truly been headed in 1492. All the well known copies of Pope Urban's map showed an open ocean in the West Indies-Florida region. And eventually a belief arose that has survived to the present: Columbus had no idea where he was going. He was just issued a dozen criminal prisoners and haphazardly headed west. The Spanish copy of the diary was not known abroad, where Columbus increasingly came to be viewed as «a mystery».

Meanwhile, one of viceroy Diego Columbus' problems was his father's old colleague Ponce de Léon—the governor of Puerto Rico. He had instituted a veritable reign of terror there. According to Herrera, he was especially well known for his war dog «Bercerillo», who had the marvellous ability to distinguish the «bad» Indians from the good ones. «The Indians were more afraid of 10 Spaniards with that dog than of 100 Spaniards without it,» it is written. And because of its unique abilities and thirst for blood, de Léon demanded that the dog be given one fourth of everything they took—the game felled by Indians who dared carry a bow and arrows, or of gold that was found and slaves that their master «acquired» and sold. The latter resulted in a lack of slaves in Puerto Rico. Finally de Léon was fired.

Diego Columbus had to institute slave rationing in all of New Spain, in order to ensure that every estate owner would have between 30 and 60 Indians. In 1510 the first shipload of Negroes was shipped to the West Indies from Guinea in Africa. They endured the slavery better, and it was estimated that one Negro equalled four Indians in work value.[11]

But the freight across the Atlantic Ocean was expensive and the losses heavy during the inhuman transport, and the crown demanded a fee of two ducats per head delivered in West India. The church warned against this practice, because it was feared that the slave traders would smuggle in loads of Jews or Muslims from North Africa.[12]

All efforts to economize on the Indians were in vain. When outlaws and criminals in Spain were pardoned and sent to the new colony, they did not establish themselves as laborers, but as independent slave-dependent landowners. They also lived with Indian women, without marrying them or having them baptized. The church in this regard was in a real bind. Nor did things improve when the slave traders were asked by the authorities to bring poor or criminal white women from Europe to sell them to the colonists. This merchandise came up short compared to the undemanding Indian girls. «White ivory» was such a poor investment for the slave traders that the traffic stopped by itself.

The situation, simply put, was that more Indian slaves had to be found. And that could be combined with solving another serious problem. Spain had not yet discovered a single square foot of North America, and England and France were becoming more and more aggressive in their attempts to prevent them from getting a foothold there.

The dismissed Juan Ponce de Léon then offered to search out «the island of Binini» (Vinini) in Florida-Georgia. The king of Spain was well informed about this land. In a very extensive letter, dated December 12, 1512, de Léon was granted permission to «discover and colonize "our island Benini" free of duties for 10 years» and to find slaves for the colony Espanola.[13] The discovery seems to have been the main object.

On March 3, 1513, de Léon sailed from San German on Puerto Rico with three small ships. They took their time in the Bahama Islands—spring was in full bloom, and in the quiet lagoons the subtropical vegetation was lush. They sailed up to the latitude that Columbus' ships had followed on their voyage west in 1492—and now completed the journey that Martin Alonzo Pinzón had interrupted when he changed course toward the Bahamas on the evening of October 7, 1492.

Columbus' information turned out to be correct. On April 2 they found the mainland. Herrera says that it happened at 30°8'N. Spanish historians agree that the landfall happened closer to present day St. Augustine.[14]

The slave hunt was not going well, but they discovered something very important. The land stretched further south. Another surprise was their encounter with the strong Gulf Stream. At one point the ships were completely still in the water, even though they had a northeasterly tailwind. They christened the cape there «Cap Canaveral», which is said to be the oldest place name in America. This is not correct—that name was and is «Norumbega» in New England.

Things were not all well there. During a stay where Miami is now located, they concluded that this was an area where human beings should not settle.

Apart from this, they were amazed at the warlike Indians who gathered in large armies and mounted well planned mass attacks with deafening screams and noise. One Indian chief had amassed 80 canoes that suddenly attacked. It was a replay of what Torvald Eiriksson and his companions had experienced a little farther north five hundred years earlier.

Ponce de Léon, or rather his crew, was preoccupied with the story about the island with the well that guaranteed youth and potency. They discussed whether it was on the Bahama Islands, «Binini's islands» east of the mainland. The sailors took special notice of the inaccessible and large Andros Island.

Ponce de Léon was sick and tired of the unsuccessful slave hunt, and went straight home to Puerto Rico with his heavy ship which drew too much water. Their entire slave harvest consisted of one male and four female Indians. He ordered the lightest boat to stay behind to look for «Binini's islands». The experienced pilot, Anton de Alaminos, together with the captain, Juan Peres de Ortubia, and two Indians, navigated across the shallows of the Great Bahama Bank. It was a real achievement in these dangerous waters with dark coral reefs sticking up everywhere, and even more that couldn't be seen. They chose to approach Andros from the east, maneuvered across one of the world's longest coral reefs, and

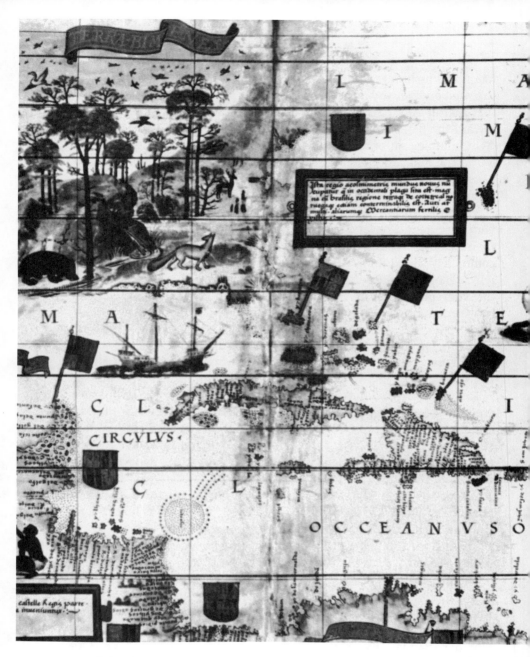

Columbus' voyage in 1492 was interrupted before the ships reached the American mainland. After Columbus died, admiral Ponce de Léon completed the voyage and found the coast of Georgia-Florida. The text in the frame starts out as follows: «This region of unknown size is called the new world...It borders the large land Brazil and Corte Realis' Noruega.» There is a Portuguese flag on Greenland.

172

reached shore unscathed. But they left disappointed. There was no spring here that ensured eternal youth. It wasn't an enticing place at all.[15] The island has so many swamps and primeval forests that it actually was not properly mapped until the 1980s.

Everyone now realized that the expedition had found the mainland Columbus was prevented by Pinzón from discovering in 1492. It was a sad thing that Columbus was not alive to experience this triumph. Several maps were subsequently drawn of «Binini», as the coastline was still called. At the same time we are told that they re-named the land Florida, «because it was discovered during Easter»—the festival of flowers.

The most beautiful and best map was drawn by the Portuguese geographer Lopo Homem in 1516–19, apparently at the request of the king of France. The map is now in the Bibliotheque Nationale in Paris.[16] Here we read in Latin about Florida, which he calls «Terra Bimenes»: «This region of unknown size, that lies on the coast in the west, is called the New World. It is bordered by the large country of Brazil and Corte Real's Noruega, and is rich in gold and commodities.»[17]

The «Brazil» mentioned here, is the northeastern part of the United States, where the trees with red wood grew. (What is now Brazil was at that time still called «Ihla de Santa Cruz».) «Corte Real's Noruega» was Labrador/Newfoundland—thus the neighboring country of the original «Brazil».

In Archivo General de Indias in Seville there is a map from about 1520, where the discoverer Pineda, after having seen Florida, called the land «Florida—earlier Bimini.»

People were preoccupied with «The Binini Islands» for a long time to come, and they finally became the name of today's Bimini, off the coast of Florida, where Hemingway had a home.

Slaves had to be found, and the traders went on to conduct a relentless slave hunt on the Bahama islands, while the crew from regular ships rowed ashore and grabbed any Indian girls they came across. Some they kept for themselves, while others were placed on board the ships as «cleaning girls» and in time sold on shore. Soon the islands were empty of people. Diego Columbus then prohibited Indians from being taken on the American mainland.

The discovery of Florida created no great stir. More sensational was the fact that the 38 year old Vasco Nunez in September of the same year sighted an ocean to the west from a hill on the Panama isthmus. He hurried there, and clad in full armor he waded into the water. Standing in water up to his crotch, he claimed the entire Pacific Ocean, «with islands and coasts from pole to pole» for the Spanish throne.

Some now began calling Central America «Antilia», and the islands east of there the Antilles. After all, that's where Columbus had gone to find them. To this day Cuba, Haiti and Puerto Rico are called «The Greater Antilles», while the smaller islands in the West Indies are called «The Lesser Antilles».

The meticulous geographer Martin Waldseemüller from Strasbourg was the cause of another name problem. He published «The Admiral's Map» (Columbus' map) of North America a number of times. He suggested the name «Ab Amerigo Inventore» for South America in honor of the modest captain Amerigo Vespucci, who had charted the coast of present day Brazil on behalf of Portugal.

When Columbus was lonely, critically ill and neglected, he wrote in a letter to Fernando that he and Vespucci had had a long conversation in 1502. There is nothing to indicate that they were either rivals or enemies.[18] Not until 1522 did a map appear that carried the name «America Prouinci» for North America. But another century would pass before the name came into use.

The Strait Between Noruega and China

In the meantime the European assault on the Treaty of Tordesillas and the Spanish/Portuguese monopoly on the new world continued. In 1515 the spineles King Francis I ascended to the throne of France and threw himself into the race to reach Asia directly, without waiting for the Tordesillas treaty to be put aside. He did as Portugal had done in Brazil and engaged an Italian sailor to undertake a voyage directly to China. The Italian was named Girolamo de Verrazzano, and he headed west on the latitude of what is now North Carolina. According to Pope Urban's map this should have been open ocean. But the expedition found terra firma instead. Verrazzano then changed his course to the south—enough so that he reached Georgia-Florida, which Ponce de Léon had found. After that he headed north again. When he sailed along the outer bank off the coast of North Carolina, he believed it to be a narrow spit of land that divided the Atlantic Ocean from an Asian ocean. His «Pacific» was in reality Pamlico Sound.[19]

The expedition continued further north—all the time looking for a waterway that would lead directly to China. In the course of the summer Verrazzano undertook the first known European close investigation of the coast of North America, all the way up to the Gulf of St. Lawrence. Discussion about whether he entered the harbor of New York will never end conclusively, even if the striking Verrazzano Bridge reflects how the New Yorkers themselves feel about the matter. Verrazzano's handwritten account in Italian about the journey, «Cellere Codex», is kept in the Pierpont Morgan Library in New York.

Verrazzano gives the impression of being generally well oriented. He placed the name «...orambega» (Norumbega) by Rhode Island-Boston. And his account reports that the Indians living in that area were the most civilized on the entire American coast. Verrazzano told a contemporary French scribe, Pierre Gringon, that the natives had told him the land was called Norumbega. But the name was well known in France before this voyage—as countless maps can attest.

Black Slaves in Vinland

For Diego Columbus it was of vital importance to establish a Spanish presence north of Florida ahead of the threatening European rivals. A lawyer, Luckas Vasquerde de Ayllon, took on the responsibility for founding the colony «Binini» and to lead the new community.

Francisco Gordillo, a well-known captain, headed northwest from Haiti to find a suitable location for the first Spanish colony in North America. But along the way he met the slave trader Pedro de Qexos, who was catching natives on the Bahama Islands.[20] And then things went wrong. They forgot that the Indians on the mainland were protected, and together they traveled inland from the coasts of Georgia and South Carolina. When the two slave ships with 150 Indians arrived in Haiti they were found out, and the sentence required that they bring the prisoners back. Only one was kept to give information to the new colonists.

Gordillo, who was poorly prepared, sent the colonists north of Savannah—past the well-organized and warlike Indian societies with their huge mounds. When de Ayllon arrived with three ships and 600 colonists, they went ashore near the present-day Santee River in South Carolina. But the mouth of the river was so sandy that they could only pass during high tide. The soil was swampy and difficult. They hurried on to the inlet of Pee Dee River, because the winter of 1526–27 was approaching.

They had brought what they needed to survive, and in order to spare the Indians and establish relatively normal relations with them, they brought along negro slaves.[21] It was the first time that whips came lashing down across black backs on the American continent. Forests had to be cleared, houses built, and fields cultivated. Women and children helped, and de Ayllon himself was possessed by the pioneering spirit. But in spite of the fine climate, the colony was too poorly organized to establish a self sufficient society in «Winyah Bay» in such a short time.[22]

There was a shortage of food from the very beginning, and in the fall many people fell sick. In October the enthusiastic de Ayllon died of a fever. The slaves immediately revolted once the master was gone. The Indians in the area soon realized that something was amiss and kept attacking the colonists throughout the winter. The result was several bloodbaths, and many of the colonists and negro slaves were led away to torture and death. When spring came, 450 of the colonists had died or disappeared. The 150 survivors went on board the ship «Catalina» and set course for Haiti. But only 143 of them made it back alive.[23]

For King Carlos V this was a serious set back in the battle for a Spanish North America. At the same time rumors were circulating that Antilia and its seven cities really were in the interior of the country. It was called both «Cibola» and «Quivira», and was supposed to be located by a river or waterway that was called «The Strait of Anian» or «The Waterway between Noruega and China».

Rumors had it that both England, France and Portugal had «the key» to this secret. It was therefore of the essence to «discover» both the waterway and most of the country in a hurry.

Charles V chartered Magellan's navigator, Estevan Gomez, who in 1526 sailed all the way from Newfoundland to Florida. Now the Spaniards claimed that they had discovered the entire east coast of America. Verrazzano had done so without authorization, according to the Treaty of Tordesillas. But Goméz was disappointed and angry at not having found the river that was supposed to come from China. In order to off-set his expenses, he brought back 48 Indians that he had captured along the way. But Diego Columbus was adamant, and Goméz was ordered to take them back to the mainland.

The resistance to the Tordesillas treaty became more and more defiant, and there was no longer a corrupt and debauched Pope Alexander to hold a protective hand over the Spanish and the Portuguese. In 1526 the French king, Francis I—an incorrigible boozer and art lover—entered into a «holy alliance» with Pope Clemens and the somewhat doubtful Henry VIII of England. The agreement was directed against Spain's powerful ruler, Carlos. He reciprocated the following year by storming Rome and taking the pope prisoner. But the holy father was the stronger of the two, and he was set free.

The Map of America Gets A Face-Lift

At this point Spain chose a new tactic. In 1526 King Carlos V commissioned the Portuguese geographer Diego Ribero to convince the pope and the world that Spain and Portugal owned all of North America. He made a map—a «padron general»—which can now be seen in Biblioteca Apostolica Vaticana. It is a masterpiece of political craftsmanship that was to set the standard for all maps of America for the next hundred years.

If we place Pope Urban's map over it, we see that he also had used the well-known amputated version that ends in the south at Chesapeake Bay. Ribero stretched the map in a north-south direction, ending up with the inlet of Chesapeake Bay far down on the Florida coast.

In the north the Gulf of Maine was made so wide that Cape Cod near Boston became Cape Hatteras in North Carolina. The old name of «Kjølneset» (Keel Point) from the time of the Vinland voyages was adopted—or perhaps the point was coincidentally given the same name by Goméz. On the Spanish versions of the map we find outside Cape Hatteras «Carenas» (ship's keel, or a place where ships are careened). When the map was copied, we get the Italian «Carinas», the French «Carénes», and the Portuguese «C[osta] de Sarinas». The French geographer Gutierés called the promontory «C[osta] de las Arenas». He illustrated it with a sinking ship with the keel sticking out of the water.

From this headland Ribero drew a coast northward that is an enlarged version of the Gulf of Maine. Both this map and the many hundreds to follow, had a deep bay, or a river in the area of Maine. Ribero did not give it a name. Labrador was named «Tiera nova de Corte Real», and was thus Portuguese land. America's coast down to Chesapeake Bay was given the name «Tiera de Estevá Goméz». All land south of Chesapeake Bay is named «Tiera de Ayllón», after the leader of the tragic attempt at colonization.

When the copies began to appear, the river or the bay up in Maine had the name «Rio de Noruega» or «Rio de Norumbega». The cartographers unanimously assumed that it referred to the Penobscot River in Maine. The city «Norumbega» is drawn in approximately where the city of Bangor now lies—where the tidewater stops. Later discussions have indicated that the river Rio de Norumbega really is the Charles River in Boston. It may have been displaced during Ribero's enlargement.

Spain Accepts Norumbega As A Neighbor

Ribero's map still wasn't convincing enough. In 1533 Pope Clemens announced his revolutionary decision. Spain and Portugal had interpreted the Treaty of Tordesillas incorrectly in 1493. Their rights to the new territory only pertained to lands that had not already been discovered by others. Portugal was allowed to keep the rights to Labrador and Newfoundland—where Corte Real and Homem had visited with a Norwegian pilot in 1473. But this is not made entirely clear in the decision.

Spain soon made a complete about-face. The Spaniards had aquitted themselves poorly in saying that the land «Binini» was located in Florida before they had been there themselves. Others necessarily must therefore have discovered it. But when they undertook a «colonial inventory», the situation was not all that bleak; Ponce de León had discovered the land south of «Binini» on the Florida peninsula, and de Ayllón had discovered «Winyah Bay» up in South Carolina. None of the two areas were on Pope Urban's map. A discreet and clever diplomat therefore placed the northern border of Florida near the inlet of Chesapeake Bay. The bordering land to the north became «Norumbega», which Spain accepted both orally and in writing without protest. Whether this would hold up, remained to be seen. France felt that Spain didn't own any part of America at all.

In April the following year King Francis sent an expedition to «Norumbega» in the north. Jaques Cartier claimed a strip of land south of the Gulf of St. Lawrence, and called it «Terra Francia». This was a veritable wonderland for trappers. Francis had to keep his hands off the Gulf of Maine and Nova Scotia, for the Bristol seamen had been there on behalf of England. But King Henry VIII kept a very low profile in this matter, so the French sent trappers to Massachusetts-Maine as well.

178

Cartier had hoped that the headwaters of the St. Lawrence River were in the distant provinces of China. He traveled the river inland and on October 5, 1534, reached a lovely elevation that he called Mont Royal, where Montreal lies today. But after making four journeys there, he realized that this would not be a short cut to the gold and spices of the East. Exasperated, he wrote a letter to the king: «This must be the land God gave to Cain.»[24] The French occupation continued, however, and the French were also the first to send missionaries to the area. Their reports indicate that «civilized» people had been there before they arrived.

The French scribe Charlevoix reports that in the eastern regions the population had a very European appearance, with big beards and blond hair. The Catholic church historian, Dr. Jelic, announced at the Congrés Scientifique International des Catoliques in 1891, that the population of «Gaspesien» (New Brunswick) were called cross bearers (portecroix) by the missionaries, because the cross was their religious symbol. European-style Christian mass was celebrated in this region in 1530. The Christian influence, with the cross as their symbol, was widespread over a large area.

French trappers and colonists had no problems associating with either the local mixed population or the pure Indians. All were hunters and had the same needs when it came to survival in the wilderness. An Indian custom that the Europeans thought splendid, was the fact that the women in most tribes had the right to choose their own mates. The French-Indian population today numbers in the millions.[25] The French colonists made occasional references to finding evidence that other white men had been in the area before them, but this didn't seem to strike them as extraordinary. After all, they were in «Norembegue».[26]

Near Quebec they came across stones with mystical inscriptions that the Jesuit priests were unable to understand. At least one of them was sent to the Minister of Culture in Paris, but no reply was ever received.

The Swedish scientist and professor, Peter Kalm, visited Quebec in 1749, where a captain La Verendrye told him about an expedition the French had sent west in order to investigate a possible connecting route to the Pacific Ocean. In several locations far to the west they came across large rocks placed on top of each other, as in a wall. They discovered one large rock and one smaller, which had inscriptions on both sides. It was about one foot long, and four-five inches thick.

The stone was brought back to Canada. They were unable to agree on what sort of letters they were. The priest thought it could be letters from the alphabet of the Tartars. The Indians in the area had offered no explanation except that the stones were very old. The stone with the inscription was sent to Paris where it became part of a collection that belonged to the foreign minister, the Count of Maurepas. It cannot be found today. The description of the stone is reminiscent of the disputed Kensington Stone that was found in the same general area two centuries later.

The head pilot of the big Roberval expedition of 1542, Jean Allefonse, explained the following to the geographer Raulin Secleart—in a manuscript now kept in the French national library. Fifteen leagues up a river with many islands at 45°N they came across a village called Norombegue. The Indians there were friendly, and they kept all kinds of birds and animals. He thought the river originated somewhere around the St. Lawrence, because the inhabitants explained to him that the saltwater went 40 leagues up the river at high tide. It is said that this is reminiscent of the Charles River in the Boston area. But it is more similar to the Penobscot River in Maine. «Leagues» must here be confused with French miles.

Coronado's Company Scribe Makes An Important Discovery

All this time Spain was engaged in a frantic effort to consolidate her part of America, south of 36 degrees, and to prevent others from discovering «the land with the seven cities» and «the river between China and Noruega». Rumors about the land with the seven cities gained strength when the Indians in the Gulf of Mexico told the Spanish adventurers that they knew about a group of cities to the north and northwest.

In 1540 a large military expedition under the leadership of Francisco Vasquez Coronado went to the interior of New Mexico to look for the land and its magnificent cities. The expedition started with 300 cavalrymen and 1000 Indians as porters and servants. True to tradition they raped and pillaged wherever they went.[27]

As their pathfinder they used an Indian who had heard about the waterway. It was 12 kilometer wide, and there were fish as big as horses. Large canoes with as many as 20 oars on each side had been observed. They also had sails, which the Indians rarely or never used. The stem was adorned with an eagle, and on a throne in the middle of the ship sat a king under a canopy. It was suggested that this was a Japanese ship, and consequently there was a good possibility that it was the waterway to Asia.

Instead of cities they found endless plains with bisons, and a couple of nomad Indian tribes—Apaches and Tejas. When they finally reached the cities that the Indian had talked about, they were the ancient and peculiar pueblo cities of Kansas. Coronado became so disappointed and enraged that the Indian was strangled by garrotting—a slow strangulation applying pressure against the throat.[28]

Meanwhile de Soto's expedition became the first Europeans to explore the eastern inland regions. By Ogeechee Creek in Georgia they encountered the tribe that would later be called Creek Indians and who were descendants of the Indians who probably killed Torvald Eiriksson half a thousand years earlier. Just as the Norsemen had done, the Spaniards took note of the huge mounds they found in their camps. Later they found a very large river—the Mississippi.[29]

In the far west the Spanish admiral Mendoza was on his way up the Pacific Coast. In 1543 a Spanish ship reached 44°N—between San Francisco and Seattle—without having seen Asia.

The old picture of the new land was now coming apart. The company scribe in Coronado's expedition, Pedro de Castaneda, came to a fairly revolutionary conclusion in his diary. North America was not a part of Asia, but a very wide and different continent. He does not exclude the possibility that the continents may be connected, but he wrote that «...the mainland between Noruega and China is much farther north than previously assumed.»

The diary, which reveals a clear head, continues:

«I believe, from what we now know of the southern ocean [the Gulf of Mexico], and what is known from ships that have sailed along the western part of the continent [the Pacific Ocean], and what is known of the northern ocean toward Noruega, the coast of which begins at Florida, that "Cibola" [the new name of the place with the seven cities] is inside this area. But only God in his wisdom will decide when this land is to be discovered, and who will be so fortunate.»

Although the Spanish had not achieved much by their expeditions, they slowly came to be tacitly accepted as the owners of America south of Chesapeake Bay.

Nevertheless, a group of protestants in France decided to leave their homeland and go to Florida, where they founded the colony of St. Augustine at 30 degrees north. Spain protested, but the French knew very well that this land had not been discovered by the Spaniards and was thus excluded from the Treaty of Tordesillas. Besides, the Spanish fleet was overextended to the point of bursting and spread all over the western world.

But the Frenchmen had their hands full just staying alive, without making enemies. One day a Spanish fleet appeared that wiped out the colony in a terrible blood bath. Those who got away either became victims of Indian arrows, or were taken as slaves.

The Spanish nobleman Juan Rodrigues de Noriega, who was responsible for the destruction of the colony, asked in a letter to the king dated Seville, March 29, 1565, that the French prisoners be thoroughly interrogated about the explorations the French had undertaken along the St. John River. He suspected that it originated in the land of the seven cities.[30]

The Spanish continued to hold St. Augustine together with a few French survivors. This became the first Spanish city and garrison in North America, under the command of Pedro Mendéres.[31]

A New Generation in the Greenland Sea

The re-discovery of America had begun when the book Inventio Fortunatæ in 1364 pointed out that there was a wide strait around the world south of the North Pole, and with Columbus' claim that the Eskimos were Chinese who were heading for Europe through the Northwest Passage in their small boats.

In the 1570s English merchants and shipowners decided to send an expedition to Asia through the Northwest Passage, which had not been in focus for a very long time. The leader of the project was the naval officer Martin Frobisher.

They collected an amazing amount of material beforehand, but were unable to find a copy of Inventio Fortunatæ, which contained the only known description of the land near the Northwest Passage, and nearly seventy years had passed since the last Greenlander had disappeared. Their voyages to the trapping stations by the entrance to the Northwest Passage had been forgotten. Even the English seafarers who had traveled north and bought their tusks were long since dead. Martin Frobisher had no one he could ask in London. He gives the impression of being as ignorant as he was enthusiastic. During preparations expectations were high about gold mines and spice fields and other riches.

In the summer of 1576 he went north with the 20 ton vessel «Gabriele». He headed toward Ungava Bay, to the same location that the Danish-Portuguese expedition with the Norwegian pilot John Skolp had gone 103 years earlier, and where, according to the accounts of the Zeno brothers in the 1300s, there were towns and communities. Had Frobisher followed the Norse Greenlanders' old ocean path along West Greenland, he probably would have reached the Northwest Passage without problems. Instead he ended up in pack ice near Baffin Island. Eventually he found an opening to the west and headed there, believing it to be the path to China. It was later to become known as Frobisher Bay. In one place they came across a dark rock formation that they thought might be a jewel. They also caught an Eskimo, and displayed him as an attraction when they returned to London in October.[32]

The following year three vessels shipped out under the command of Frobisher. This time the Eskimos were prepared. A bloody battle ensued when the Englishmen went ashore, but the English captured and brought back a woman, a man and a child.

The Eskimo «main course» was the fresh innards of fish and animals. They mostly avoided the rest, and it was precisely this «refuse» which the English considered food—thighs and shoulders that were even salted and dried. Not to mention dry fish, and the ship's biscuits that were usually mouldy because they lacked preservative agents. All of this was a shock to unaccustomed stomachs. It is also a known fact that Eskimos came down with something that Russian scientists call «psychic cramps» in new, and for them unpleasant, surroundings. Their world was an icy infinity, and not a dirty and ill-smelling London with continual epidemics.

The three miserable creatures lived for about four weeks—just long enough for the talented reported John White to be able to sketch them.

Meanwhile the expedition organizers had been in touch with the contemporary great geographer Gerhardus Mercator, who in his world map of 1569 had drawn the North Pole area according to the information found in <u>Inventio Fortunatæ</u>. He sent his copy of the book to the investor Dr. John Dee in London on June 8, 1577.[33] It indicated, as we already know, that the North Pole was surrounded by a mountain range at around 78 degrees north. Between it and the north coast of the large continents there was open ocean around the world. This was illustrated on the Mercator map, which today is kept in the Maritiem Museum Prins Hendrik, in Rotterdam.

The next year the Asian expedition headed out, with 15 smaller vessels and the best winter equipment known at that time. For inexplicable reasons they once more headed to the Hudson Strait, and followed the north coast westward. They soon had occasion to use the winter gear in storms, cold, fog and snow. Despondency followed in their wake. They finally realized that this was not the place to find gold mines, or ice free water clear to the Asian spice markets.

George Beste, the next in command during the expedition in 1578, described the voyage in detail. He reports, among other things, that they met Eskimos who understood writing.[34]

By this time the investors in the enterprise were bankrupt. But at least one of them kept the faith—Michael Look. In 1582 his map, which showed a large strait between Grochlant (Devon Island) and the Canadian mainland, was made public. It also showed a smaller strait named Frobisher. The land of Norumbega included all lands between the Gulf of Maine and the Gulf of St. Lawrence.

In many ways this was the sum of two generations of misunderstanding. Unless something radical happened, they would simply have to accept the fact that the strait between Noruega and China could not be located.

The coast had been scrutinized for fifty-five years, and there were hundreds of maps of America from many countries. They may vary a great deal, but if we superimpose Pope Urban's map on them, they have one thing in common. All have precisely the same coastline as Pope Urban's map, the one Ribero enlarged in 1529.[35]

The old Norse hunting grounds Greipar in North Greenland and Kroksfjordheiene were not completely forgotten. With the backing of a group of English investors, Captain John Davis from Dartmouth in England in 1586 followed the old route along western Greenland with four ships. The purpose was to hunt and to find the Northwest Passage, and to be especially alert to the existence of any metals in the mountain regions.

The first year apparently was promising, because they returned the two following years and christened the ocean northwest of the Western Settlement «Davis Strait». Davis reached 72°12′N, just as easily as the Greenlanders had, almost as far as the Inventio Fortunatæ geographer had gone in 1360 and Columbus in 1477. The last voyage was simply intended as a hunting expedition. The ships returned with dry and salted fish, whale oil, seal and bear pelts, and narwhal spears. Walrus tusks are not mentioned, possibly an oversight on the part of the writer, because there was suddenly once more a very good European market for walrus

184

tusks after 1550.[36] If the Norse Greenlanders had managed to survive a few more decades, the land would probably have experienced a real rejuvenation.

At first the animals were as unperturbed as when the Greenland hunters first arrived six hundred years earlier. But just as before, the hunters soon had to move farther and farther north in pursuit of their quarry. On July 10, 1616, William Baffin discovered the northernmost sound that the Greenlanders called Kroksfjordene, and that the author of Inventio Fortunatæ reported was located at «Grochlant», on the same latitude as «The Fortunate Land» (America). It now received the name Jones Sound.

The English did not initiate any substantial hunting, even though there was great demand for blubber and whalebone. Basque merchants, lacking Greenland trappers, established their own trapping stations in the high north. The Dutch whaling and walrus tusk boom that ensued in both the Greenland and Svalbard area was to last for several hundred years.

1. Collis, 1955.
2. Aschehougs Verdenshistorie, Vol. VII.
3. Ibid.
4. (Grimberg, Vol. XI.
5. Abbreviated from Collis, 1955.
6. Ibid.
7. Columbus, 1918, p. 33.
8. Navarrete, 1825, Vol. II, p. 149.
9. Anghiera, 1511.
10. See Lowery, 1911, from p. 131, about the assumed Binini.
11. Ibid.
12. Ibid.
13. Documentos Inéditos del Archivo de Indias, Vol. XXII, Ano de 1512, p. 26.
14. Scisco, 1913, pp. 721–27.
15. This account of the journey is described in the royal cedula of July 22, 1515, by King Carlos. Documentos Inéditos del Archivo de Indias, Vol. XI, p. 295.
16. See Cortesao (ed.), 1960, Vol. I, map no. 24.

17. From a Norwegian translation by Ludolf Krohn.
18. Wassermann, 1955.
19. See Hagmann Hall, 1910.
20. Lowery, 1911.
21. Anghiera, 1912, p. 267.
22. Quattlebaum, 1956, pp. 126–29.
23. Quinn, et.al., 1971.
24. Biggar, 1930.
25. Linderholm, 1988.
26. Thwaites (ed.), 1896–1901.
27. Diary from the journey is kept in Archivo General de Indias in Seville. See Winship, G.D.: Facsimile and translation to modern Spanish and English in The 14th Annual Report of the American Bureau of Ethnology and Archaeology.
28. Ibid.
29. Hodge, et.al., 1907, 173–362.
30. Biggar, 1917, pp. 253–70.
31. de Meras, 1923.
32. Collinson (ed.), 1867.
33. Dee, 1842, p. 4.
34. Beste, 1938.
35. Prytz, 1977, pp. 57–67.
36. Janes & Davis, 1589, pp. 776–92.

ENGLAND «INHERITS» VINLAND

The controversy between England and Spain about the Tordesillas agreement would turn out to be most costly for England. They were Europe's largest exporter of wool and wovens, and now their main customers Spain and the Spanish-dominated Netherlands stopped this trade. It lead to a crisis that was amplified by the fact that England was ardently Protestant, while Spain was just as ardently Catholic.

In the course of a few decades England was brought to her knees economically. Portuguese ships continued blocking her route to new and distant markets. In desperation the English merchants started a company which was granted trade privileges with the northern regions of Russia, by Ivan the Terrible. But it wasn't enough.

The situation was grave when Henry VIII's daughter, Elizabeth I, came to the throne in 1559. When it came to difficult matters, she always lived by the rule of «wait and see». In truth she sympathized with the Catholics, but in her official capacity had to permit a few hundred of them to be hanged. She was also against the decapitation of Mary Stuart of Scotland, but after 16 years of hesitation she had to consent when the Protestant activists presented accusations that made the death sentence unavoidable.

Elizabeth actually was interested in a reconciliation with Spain. But instead of attempting a diplomatic rapprochement, she decided to finance the slave trader John Hawkins after he had broken the Spanish trade boycott against England by selling slaves in West India. In general, she did very little unless she deemed it absolutely necessary. Foreign affairs advisor Francis Walsingham, for instance, did not get her support when he suggested that England should take colonies from Spain by force.

Enterprising men, especially younger ones, had the opportunity for greater freedom of action. They made unabashed overtures to their ambivalent and indecisive queen. Shameless flattery was only the beginning— they wrote glowing and bold love letters to her, and made sure to send the most passionate looks her way when she was near. It worked. That the game stopped short of Her Majesty's bedchamber was understood by both parties.

«The suitors» in this tragic comedy of manners had different objectives. They wanted to get their country out of the corner that it had been forced into and make England a world power. They demanded action and aggressive new thinking, but at the same time they had to keep their queen happy in order to get her blessing for their ideas. William Shakespeare later summarized the English view—the world was a pearl oyster, but only a sword could open it.

The young suitors had long since figured this out. The slave trader Hawkins thought the Spanish ships would be easy prey for the English, if they built relatively small and easily maneuverable ships and fitted them with cannons that could hit a target from far away. Naval battles had thus far mainly involved either ramming or boarding the opponent's ship, killing or capturing the crew, and claiming the spoils. Hawkins had several small ships built just for the purpose of waging war, and he thereby became the father of the modern naval battle. Doubters were soon won over when the light English cannon ships in 1588 wreaked havoc on the once invincible transport fleet of the Spanish armada. From then on England ruled the seas.

The daring captain Francis Drake agreed with Walsingham that they ought to take the Spanish colonies by force. When he completed the world's second circumnavigation of the globe in 1577–80, he thoroughly plundered the South American Spanish colonies. He also went all the way up to California and occupied the land on behalf of England. But it was not feasible to maintain contact, via Cape Horn, with a land on the «backside» of the New World. «Drake Bay» eventually became «San Francisco Bay». The queen criticized the looting, but was one of Drake's financial backers nonetheless.[1]

The hottest suitor in the queen's entourage in the 1580s was the arrogant artist and officer, Walter Raleigh. Elizabeth did not stand in his way in 1580, when he sent John Walker and Simon Fernandéz, a pilot of Portuguese descent, from Bristol to America to prepare for the occupation of the old Norse lands. They started from Chesapeake Bay in Virginia— Leiv Eiriksson's Vinland on the 36th parallel, and the southern point on Pope Urban's map. The coast was charted up to the Penobscot River in Maine—then called «Rio de Norumbega» or «Rio de Noruega».[2] Surrounded by her young studs, Drake among them, Queen Elizabeth the following year gave her approval of «Operation Norumbega».

Walter Raleigh's half brother, admiral Henry Gilbert, was given a simple and direct order. He was to go to America and formally occupy Norumbega.[3]

188

In the summer of 1583 a fleet went north, with Simon Fernandéz as pilot. They first occupied Corte Real's Newfoundland, since the last male heir to that region had died in Portugal. Thereafter the ships continued to the mouth of the Penobscot River in the Gulf of Maine. Here the «Norumbega» region was declared English territory.

On the voyage home the expedition met with a storm that wrecked the admiral's ship. Gilbert died, but the occupation remained in force.

We have very little information about this journey, because the occupation was virtually a private enterprise and the admiral's ship «Delight» sank. Of the few documents that remain, there is an account of the loss of the ship. The title of the document is «....Going to the Discovery of Norumbega, with Sir Humphrey Gilbert».[4]

The Spanish ambassador in London, Bernandino de Mendoza, immediately reported to Spain that Gilbert had sailed the northern route to «Norumbega»—to the part that was near «New France», or Canada.[5]

He had established a fairly efficient network of spies in England, but showed too keen an interest in the project. The following year he was expelled. He moved his headquarters to Paris instead, and from there he kept Seville informed about what was happening. And things now began happening in quick succession.

Among the English explorers, the land between Chesapeake Bay at 36 degrees and New England was called «Wingan de coe», variously spelled with a 'v' or a 'w'. The occupation of the territory was left to the queen's favorite, Walter Raleigh, but he himself was not allowed to leave his amour in the castle. Instead he sent two barks, in the spring of 1584, with Arthur Barlove and Philip Amadas as captains, and Simon Fernandéz as pilot.

This time they followed Columbus' route along the 30th parallel and turned north when they approached Florida. Fernandéz and the captains made a blunder on June 13th, when they reached 36°—they made a turn straight west and went ashore on Roanoke Island. Thereafter they found a passage between the outer sand banks into Albemarle Sound and the mainland. On Pope Urban's map the inlet to Chesapeake Bay was at «thirty-six and one half degree». The exact latitude was 36°54'. That is where they were supposedly going.

The expedition stayed for six weeks. The participants used the time for extensive examination of flora and fauna, and were thrilled with the land. Then, after no more than a couple of days, they encountered Indians. Two of them were taken back to England, to be trained as interpreters. The colonists would be prepared when the large influx began the next year.

A Danish midshipman, Morten Lauritzen, participated in the expedition. The chief archivist of the state archives in Copenhagen, Vello Helk, has studied this matter, and has found no evidence of any political motives behind Lauritzen's participation. There is a copy of an application to Queen Elizabeth—forwarded through the royal Danish representative —for Morten Lauritzen to come to England and learn naval warfare. The rumors about Hawkins' new war ships probably stirred considerable interest in many countries.

On December 7 that same year the British House of Lords discussed an application from Walter Raleigh to have the occupation approved.[6] The application had been one of three matters on the agenda the previous day, but was held over. There may have been a bit of resistance to Raleigh, and there was certainly potential for diplomatic fireworks if for instance Denmark—Vinland's «owner»—were to wake up from its political slumber. The Danes controlled Öresund, the inlet to the Baltic and Russia, and they knew how to make use of it.

The next day the application was postponed until the afternoon session. On this grey day before Christmas the notary seems to have had some trouble with the protocol. He started out by saying: «At the behest of Walter Raleigh a new land, Wyngandacoia, has been found—never beinge heretofore.» But then the writer seems to have had second thoughts—or it may have been done later. The last part of the sentence, «never beinge heretofore», has been crossed out. And then the protocol continues: «...which is not in the hands of any Christian prince or Christian men. Some of the men born in these regions have been brought to our kingdom of England. They intend to immediately become subjects of our Majesty, to be returned by said Walter Raleigh.»

The protocol further states that the land is uncommonly rich in resources, and that «diverse other persons» had tried to find the land earlier, but no one had succeeded until now.

The colonists made no effort to hide the land's name «Wingan de coa», from anyone. All reports from the journey use this name, spelled somewhat differently. Drake called it «Wingan de coy».

The great geographer—and perfectionist—Abraham Ortelius, wrote to England and asked for confirmation of the correct name of the region. In the reply letter, which still exists, the name is given as «Wingan de coa»,

190

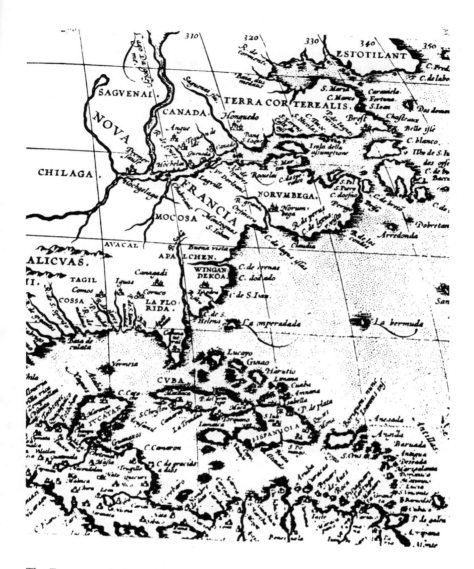

The European rivalry over "Norse America" is over. Spain was allowed to keep Columbus' "Binini" in the south, and they renamed it Florida. England got "Vingan de coe" (Vinland det gode) and christened it Virginia. They also got the southern part of "Norumbega", which they named New England, while the French christened their part "Nova Francia" or Canada. The Portuguese kept "Noruega", and named it "Terra Corte Realis", later Labrador. Baffin Island became an English possession, and was called "Estitoland". This is Abraham Ortelius' map from the late 1500s.

in three words.[7] The two prominent geographers, Ortelius[8] and Mercator[9] included it on their world maps. But they both wrote that the name of all of North America, Norumbega, could be explained by the fact that «there were some Norwegian colonies here earlier».

Professor D.B. Quinn writes that the name «Wingan de coa» does not seem to have its origin in any of the Algonquin Indian dialects.[10] It would also be somewhat of a linguistic miracle if the Norse and Indian names of the land should differ by only two or three phonemes. What has happened, is that when the scribes wrote «Vinland det gode», it resulted in «Wingan de coe» and «Wingan de coa». It is a very decent result, compared to the efforts of other scribes from this period, in which fanciful spelling was fashionable.

Walter Raleigh, who organized the whole thing, still had a close— perhaps even intense—relationship to his queen. The next winter she had him knighted, and charged him with the task of finding a name for the new colony. Overstating things a bit, he gave the land the name Virginia, in honor of the alleged virgin queen. By March his new coat of arms was completed, with the inscription: «Propria Thnsigna [insignia] Walteri Ralegh milits Domini & Gubernaritos Virginiae» (Virginia's military leader and governor).

But even if the re-christening of the land happened with admirable speed, Drake and everyone else continued to use the land's original name. Raleigh was bitter about this—it reduced the significance of his honor as discoverer. Many years later, when he sat jailed in the Tower of London, after having «forsaken» the queen for one of her attendants, he wrote that history had repeated itself. When the Spaniards came to South America, they knew no Indian language. Therefore they mistakenly named the land along the Pacific Ocean «Peru», which Raleigh claimed was simply a common Indian term for rivers, creeks and water. Then he added that the men he sent to America, were not a hair better. Some «saluage» (native) had tricked the English leaders into believing that the land was called «Wingandacon», which he claimed meant good or interesting clothes. The fault for the «blunder» he placed with the expedition's leader, Greenville.

English researchers have rejected all of this as pure nonsense, including the reference to Peru. The name Peru comes from the little river «Biru» where the conqueror of the Inca kingdom, Pizarro, went ashore in 1526. Raleigh's outburst was a reflection of the imagination and self aggrandizement of a bitter man awaiting execution. He never was a discoverer in the real sense of the word, and the British statues of him are rather small.

But after Virginia had been given a name, no one was really sure where it was supposed to be when the colony was established in earnest in 1585. It was referred to as «Virginia, which lies in Wingan de coe». The prominent natural scientist and governor, John White—a total unknown who entered history via a back door and disappeared the same way—explained that the colony lay in «Norumbega». He wrote about a silk plant, for instance: «There grows in that part of Virginia, or Norumbega, where our English men stayed, an enormous plant which the Indians call wisanek...» Later he twice referred to this plant, for which they had great hopes: «It grows, as previously mentioned, in the land Norumbega, which has now been named Virginia by the noble Walter Raleigh. He has used great sums to discover it, and it is now visited by Englishmen.» The third reference is when he discusses the important issue of naming the plant. Should it be called «English swallow herb» or «the silk herb from Norumbega»? The first name was chosen, but no one used it. On the contrary, this «Vinlandian» raw material was named «vini silk» or «silke vinerovns». «Vinisilk» became a common term used in the silk business, and is still the name of silk from Virginia.[11]

Virginia was to be settled as soon as possible, and be the base for a major attack on all Spanish activity on the American mainland. On February 22, 1585, Ambassador Mendoza reported to Seville:

«The Queen of England is preparing to have Sir Francis Drake attack our forces in the West Indies. She has given Drake 20,000 pounds to outfit a fleet of 24 ships. These will be ready to sail to Norumbega at the beginning of next month. Drake will sail with 2000 men, and hopes to meet Your Majesty's fleet before it [the Spanish fleet] gathers in Havana.»[12]

But this ominous report was followed by a brighter message during the last days of April:

«Drake's ships, which have left for Norumbega, have been separated in a storm. The largest of them, which belongs to the queen, attacked a Spanish ship en route to Newfoundland. They killed everyone on board and returned to Ireland [with their bounty]. Drake has been reoutfitted, but is considerably weakened.»

This did not mean that Spain would be able to operate freely in North

America. An English colony was established at 36°N at Roanoke in North Carolina. There is quite a lot of material about this colonization, and the name «Wingan de coe» is consistently used throughout. They found both China spices and medicinal plants. But the strangest piece of information about the land we hear in the book De Herba Panacea, which was published in Antwerp in 1587:

«In Wingandecaow, which is now called Virginia and is a province in the New World and is 36 degrees from Equator toward the North Pole, they found inhabitants who used some pipes made of clay. From the pipes they pulled smoke from tobacco that they had lit. It grew all around in great quantities, and they drank it directly to maintain good health. When the English returned home, they used such pipes themselves and drank the smoke of the tobacco. Afterward this drinking of smoke has become very common in all of England—especially among courtiers who have acquired several such pipes to drink smoke from.»

But the Englishmen were not used to wilderness, and the colony was abandoned after a short time. Later, when all of Europe had learned to «drink smoke», Virginia became a profitable colony. The only reminder of the first attempt at colonization was the name «Wingan de coe», which was used on maps into the 1600s.

North America had by now lost much of its allure. There was no road to Asia, no fabulous gold mines. At the turn of the century England once again made an attempt at colonizing Virginia, but it failed.

More interesting at this time, is the French scientist Samuel Champlain, who made several exploratory voyages up to Norumbega between the Gulf of St. Lawrence and the Gulf of Maine. Among other things he sailed up Rio de Noruega (the Penobscot River), but didn't find the city that was drawn on the maps in the location where Bangor or Old Town now lies. If there was ever a community of wooden houses there, it had been abandoned at least a hundred years before. The only thing Champlain reported of interest, was a single wooden cross.[13]

In the summer of 1609 he set off on a journey through the wilderness from Canada to the southwest. Lake Champlain is a reminder of this trip. Two white men and a group of Indians followed him. Along the way they fought Iroquois warriors and killed two chiefs. Because of their fire arms they commanded great respect. Champlain wrote a very interesting and detailed description, and was pleased to see grape vines, chestnuts, and lime rocks, white as snow. To their great joy they also found a big river, that they were able to canoe on for two whole days. He reports that it flowed into the ocean «on the coast of Norumbega, near the coast of Florida.»[14]

Precisely one month later the English sea captain Henry Hudson, who was in Dutch service, came to the mouth of this river with his ship «The Half Moon». He immediately thought of the possible waterway to Chinese territory, and headed up the mighty river. They had a good wind, and did some good business trading otter and beaver pelts from the Indians, in exchange for pearls, knives and small axes. The natives were friendly, used tobacco pipes of yellow copper and boiled their food in clay pots, he wrote in his diary. He christened the river Hudson River.[15]

On September 22 he had reached the area of Albany, and at this point the river became less navigable. He gave up the idea of sailing to Asia, headed back down, and anchored by a green and friendly island that the Indians called Manahatta. Terrible weather ensued, but Hudson determined that this was an excellent harbor—protected from all sides. A Dutch representative later bought the island of Manahatta from the Indians for a few small trinkets and a supply of firewater. A Norwegian, Cornelius Sand, was interpreter during the transaction. No one knows where he came from, and how he came to speak Indian. The Indian island name was changed to Manhattan.

Hudson's life came to a sad end. The next year he sailed north to find the Northwest Passage for his English sponsors. He made the same mistake as Frobisher and went directly across the Davis Strait instead of following the old course of the Greenlanders. He also went past Ungava Bay. He spent the winter of 1610–11 in the «inland polar sea», Hudson Bay. In the spring a mutiny broke out. There were strong and ruthless wills on both sides of the conflict, and it ended when Henry Hudson, his son and seven others were put in a small boat and left to their fate, while the ships turned back.[16]

No one ever heard from them again.

The English protested vigorously against the Dutch activities in the New York area, but the Dutch did not relent.

A Danish-Norwegian King With Polar Dreams

The first Danish king to show any real interest in Norway, was Christian IV (1577–1648). He visited the dependency in the north 26 times and secured Finnmark for Norway by fighting the two-year long war of Kalmar, against Sweden. The Swedes not only had to give up the churches and houses of East Finnmark and the right to collect taxes. They also had to pay a million «riksdaler» in war reparations. The peace was a humiliating one for Sweden. But the newly appointed chancellor, Axel Oxenstierna, considered it a necessity in order to avoid a catastrophic military defeat. From that point on he was preoccupied with clipping the wings of Norway-Denmark, while at the same time organizing a modern Swedish military force.

Christian IV meanwhile built the city of Christiansand in Norway, as well as the new Christiania after old Oslo burned. He let Danish-German investors begin mining in Norway, and requisitioned great forest regions for trees to be used in the mines.

He had mining plans for the distant and forgotten Greenland as well. In 1605, at the age of 28, he organized an expedition under the leadership of William Cunningham of Scotland to search for the old Norse colonies in the polar region and bring home some settlers so he could talk to them.

One of the expedition's ships went directly to Greenland. The two others, with John Hall of Hull as pilot, sailed the other old route to the trapping grounds up in North Greenland. They reached 66°38', which was roughly the location of the Greenlanders' popular hunting ground of Lysefjord. Here they stayed for about a month. James Hall drew a number of sketches and maps and reported about salmon, seals and whales in great numbers. In return for their commission they named a cape «Cape Christian». Their search for metals was fruitless, of course, nor were there any Greenlanders to be found one hundred years after the last Norsemen had disappeared from the land.[17]

The high flying, peripatetic and dissolute majesty also decided to conquer the Northwest Passage. He sent one of the captains from the Kalmar War, Jens Munk, off with two boats in the spring of 1619. Munk had been in foreign service and obviously had a European orientation to the current geographical theories, because he entered Hudson Bay instead of going up to the Kroksfjords at 73°N, where the Northwest Passage began. By fall he had come as far west as the present town of Churchill. Here most of the expedition's 65 members died of scurvy.

196

Munk described the whole voyage in a diary, which is both a revealing historical document, a gripping human drama and a study in ignorance and foolishness.[18]

Munk and two others performed a singular feat of seamanship when they were able to sail one of the boats, the sloop «Lamperenen», back to Bergen.

The Norwegian Coast in the Sunset Becomes English

On April 10, 1606, England took a definitive step and issued a declaration that America was to be considered English land from 34 degrees north (North Carolina) to 45 degrees north (the border of Canada and «the town» Norumbega). This was not accepted by Holland, but England didn't care.

Unfortunately we have only a few scattered glimpses of what New England was like in the early 1600s. Bristol's merchants and shipowners made several expeditions there to find or buy medicinal plants that were highly valued in Europe. It was also established during these voyages that there were ample supplies of grapes, for example in Maine, where modern Augusta lies.

Odd pieces of information from those years indicate that the Indians in New England had «an upper class», or a ruling class, who dressed in European clothes and used regular wooden boats with sails, European cooking utensils and iron weapons. Conversely, the tribe's subordinate members went naked in the summer and covered themselves with animal skins against the winter cold. The lowlier Indians used only log boats or canoes.[19]

Most of the world had by now become «colonized». The major players, England and the Netherlands, had early on learned to use negotiation in dealing with colonial matters. Colonial conferences were held on a regular basis, and the discussions were later published in book form.[20]

The head of the Dutch delegation was Hugo Grotius, who is considered the father of both international naval law and human rights. He was probably the best informed man of his era. In the book De origine gentium Americanarum—which we will return to shortly—he wrote that legally speaking, North America was Norwegian land from Mexico up to the far north:

«The Mexicans and their neighbors came before the Spanish. They say that they were not natives, but had moved from a northern land. The area that they lived in first, after Estotiland [Labrador], is also named for its sources. It is called Norimbega, which is nothing other than Norwega, where the sound [W] is softened by the Spanish, who used to write B for W.»[21]

In 1616 the Englishman John Smith made a thorough survey of the coast from Virginia to the north and drew the first correct map of the east coast of North America. He called his geographical description My first voyage to Norumbega now called New England.[22]

In 1617 a tragedy occurred that prevented us from ever finding out for certain about the alleged mixture of «European» chiefs and regular Indians. A pestilence broke out that killed nearly the entire population of the coastal region of present day New England. This calamity is described only in passing, because there were no known Europeans in the area while the epidemic raged.

1. Krarup Nielsen, 1930.
2. de Costa, 1890.
3. McManis, 1972.
4. Ibid.
5. Translation made from code. Summary in Archivo de Simancas, Estado de Castilla, K. 1563, no. 22–25. See also Quinn, 1955.
6. House of Lords MS. Microfilm in State Papers, Domestic. Elizabeth S.P. 12, 169 and 36.
7. Quinn, 1955.
8. Ortelius, 1590.
9. Mercator, 1595.
10. Quinn, 1955.
11. Webster's English Dictionary.
12. Calendar State Paper.
13. Champlain, 1613.
14. Ibid.
15. Purchas, 1906, III, pp. 817–820.
16. Ibid.
17. Ibid. Notes and sketches from the voyage in British Museum, Royal MS, 17 A XLVIII, fos. 7–10.
18. Munk, 1960.

19. Bereton, 1906.
20. <u>The Colonial Conferences Between Britain and the Netherlands</u>.
21.° Grotius, 1714, p. 40.
22. Arber, 1910.

ONE HUNDRED COLONISTS ON A WINE SCHOONER

In 1606 a resolution was passed which made it possible for a group of English dissenters to begin colonizing North America. The group received permission from an English trading company to settle on the islands of Manhattan and Long Island at the mouth of the Hudson River at 41°N. The Dutch settlers had not yet arrived there—they were to come in 1626.

One hundred people—men, women and children—headed west in late summer of 1620 on the 12 year old schooner «Mayflower». The ship previously had been carrying wine from Bordeaux and La Rochelle. Because of the popular cargo (and leaky barrels) it was considered a «sweet ship» among sailors. [1] But the wine ship was not at all suitable for passenger transport.

On the other hand, it appears that the ship was at least well supplied. Based on the descriptions by the 17th century biographer William Wood, it looks as though they followed the custom of bringing live sheep and pigs to be slaughtered along the way. But early in the voyage, the animals fell ill and died, and the situation soon became dire on the overcrowded ship. The passengers had gone through a great deal even before leaving and were in poor condition from the start. Soon they encountered bad weather and headwinds. Seasickness, vomiting and unsanitary conditions added to their feelings of hopelessness and despair. But in the middle of all this misery, something happened that gave them all renewed hope.

A cruel and brutal sailor had from the very first day taken pleasure in ridiculing and tormenting the immigrants. He cursed profusely as a way of insulting their piety and never missed an opportunity to tell them that he looked forward to throwing half of them overboard as dead bodies before they reached their destination. After that, he told them, he would sell their belongings, and celebrate with the money he made. Some asked him to please stop this harrassment, but he cursed and threatened them even more and thereafter no one dared say anything.

But before they were halfway to their destination, this sailor became ill and died in the most horrible pain. Ironically, he turned out to be the first

200

from the «Mayflower» to be lowered into the sea. The immigrants took this to be a sign that God had not forgotten them.[2]

For two months the little «Mayflower» sailed through autumn storms. When they were just about half way across the Atlantic, the ship sprung a serious leak, and they thought they were doomed. But the immigrants remembered that they had brought some sturdy screws along, and with those they were able to patch the broken plank. But by then they were very low on rations. The butter and cheese turned out to be spoiled and the fish half rotten.[3]

When they reached Cape Cod in Massachusetts in late fall, they gave up the idea of going any further. And on November 11 they went ashore on the «inside» of the keel-shaped island that the Greenlanders had called Kjallarnes—Keel Point.

Life soon began to look brighter once they had firm ground under their feet. «Finally they found water, and this water was the first refreshment they took in New England. They were very thirsty, and they thought it tasted as good as wine and beer used to taste.»[4]

We are reminded of the Vinland Saga. When Leiv Eiriksson came to the same area, the first thing the Norse colonists did was to taste the dew—which the Greenlanders thought tasted sweet.

The first days after the «Mayflower» dropped anchor, four of the immigrants died. After a couple of days a group went out in a barge to scout the area and encountered 4–5 Indians. The natives fled for their lives. The immigrants didn't give much thought to the issue of rightful ownership when they found an Indian corn supply. The Indians had their slash-and-burn fields and small store houses spread over a large area, because they were often attacked by a tribe in Maine that stole their crops. The area's second governor, William Bradford, called the tribe «New England's Vikings».

The winter was mild and nearly without frost, though there was a lot of wind and bad weather. Both fish (Blackfish—globicephala melæna) and seals were beached on Cape Cod's flat, sandy beaches during the storms. The fish were unable to re-enter the water, and the colonists could just pick them up by hand. And they had meat too, when they were quick enough to grab the seals before they made it back into the ocean.

But they were anxious, uncertain and unfamiliar with life in the wilderness. In the evening the landing party made a barricade of logs, sticks and pine branches as protection against the wind, the night frost and possible attackers. They had a large fire in the middle and took turns keeping watch in the opening on the lee side.

One of the first nights was especially frightening. They heard howls that they thought came from lions, and shot several rounds into the dark. Later they learned that there were packs of wolves in the area.

There had been white men before them in this region. From <u>Mourts Relation</u>, published in London in 1632, we have their careful description of November 30:

«When we had gone five-six miles into the forest, we chose another route back. In a flat field we found an elevation, like a grave. But it was larger and longer than other graves we had found, and covered with a wood structure. We opened it.

First we found a mat, and under it a fine bow. Then another mat, and under that a plank—about three quarters of a yard long—with three points at one end, so it looked like a crown. Inside the mat we found bowls, troughs and wooden platters, and some small items that looked like drinking cups. We found yet another fine mat, and under it two bundles—one large and one small. We opened one and found a large quantity of a fine and well preserved powder. In the powder we found the bones and skull of a man. On the head there was still beautiful yellow hair, and some of the skin of the head was also preserved. The human remains were attached to a knife, a package of needles, and two or three things made of iron. They were lying inside a sailor's shirt and trousers made of cloth. The red powder appeared to be a means of embalming. We opened the smaller bundle, and found the same powder and the bones and head of a small child. Among the bones and other things there were strings and ribbons with nice pearls. There was also a bow, three quarters of a yard long, and different toys. We took the nicest things, and closed it up.

We were of different opinion about the embalmed persons. Some said they thought it was an Indian chief or king. Others pointed out that Indians have black hair, and that nobody has ever seen one with brown or yellow hair.»

What the pilgrims had found, was a «Death House»—a privilege reserved only for the most prominent members of Indian society. C.A. Ceram has described this type of culture in detail.[5] «The skeleton was stripped of flesh, whereafter the red powder was applied. Or they let the body lie unprotected for a while, until the flesh began to dissolve, and then

202

they applied ochre on the bones. Only the highest members of the tribe were put to rest with such peculiar pomp and circumstance.

River pearls were their most valuable jewels. Even if they were rare, many graves contained several of them. Some necklaces are valued at thousands of dollars, and equal the value of royal jewels today.»

The chief in the grave out on the old «Keel Point» had three things that set him apart from the tribe's ordinary members. Woven clothes in a style dating from the late Middle Ages, three items made of iron, and a head of beautiful yellow hair. Both he and his son died as Indians of the highest rank.

After a whole month of reconnaissance, the Englishmen went on board the «Mayflower» and sailed the short distance to the mainland. The course was set for what they would later name Plymouth Bay, where their barge nearly broke up in the wind as they approached what is now Browns Banke. Later the ship followed through deeper water.

One of the reasons they decided to settle where they did, was because there had been a farming community in that location before. Much of the area had been cleared. And up on a hill (today Burial Hill) there was a fort with a good view of the surrounding area. The people were gone—most likely they died during the pestilence.[6]

They could not have been Indians—they were slash-and-burn farmers who seared the forest floor in November in preparation for next year's planting in a new location. The Englishmen at first assumed that this had been done because of laziness, to avoid the hard work of clearing fields.[7] And Indians did not construct military forts.

More immigrants died during this early period, while the healthy ones built their first common house. People often cried, and wished that they had never come to these desolate shores. But some liked it. Francis Billington, a hellion on the voyage over, one day climbed up a tall tree and thought he caught a glimpse of a large lake. That climb made him immortal, because the lake is still called Billington Sea.

Based on these accounts there is no doubt that the adjustment to life in the wilderness was difficult. Half of the original 100 colonists died the first summer. But something decidedly positive happened as well. An Indian who was able to make himself understood because of contact with Europeans before the pestilence, took a job with them as an interpreter and advisor. He taught them that the mild winter they had experienced only happened every ten years. They had to prepare for more frost and snow in winters to come. He taught them to plant corn, and was the middleman when they asked the tribe to forgive them for taking their corn out on Cape Cod. But most importantly, he taught them about Indian ways, taught them to understand. One thing that amazed the colonists was how the Indians swam—just like animals in water. They named this style of swimming the «crawl», and the English young people learned how to do it. Later the entire world learned how to «crawl».

The colony at Plymouth Bay was not very successful, though at least the colonists' spirit revived. It would take another thirty years before the 50 colonists had increased to 160 persons.[8]

Actually the colony increased faster than the birth rate would indicate, because new colonists kept arriving from England.

Immigrants back in England fantasized about going to the rich Norse capital «Norumbega», which was supposed to exist on the other side of the ocean. It had become particularly famous because an English ship's boy, David Ingram, claimed he had walked through forests and wilderness from the Gulf of Mexico to New England after having been set ashore by the slave trader John Hawkins. The boy also said that he had visited the incredibly rich city of «Norumbega» before he was rescued by a French ship. Initially even the historian Richard Hakluiyt believed him. But Ingram was soon eliminated from the pages of Hakluiyt's history of discovery, Diverse voyages, published in the last part of the 1500s, because the reality of New England was something quite different. The colonists found rotted and deserted wood buildings, and boats with sails, when they came to the new land, wrote William Bradford, the second governor of Massachussets. But no one tried to explain who might have owned the deserted houses and boats before the English arrived.

New Colonists on Leiv Eiriksson's Turf

The Mayflower people found their community more difficult to establish than they had thought.

After ten years of toil, the leaders journeyed over «The Three Hills» and arrived at the mouth of the Charles River in Boston on September 17, 1630. They immediately realized that this was where they should have started out.

One of the colonists, Roger Clapp, ventured four or five kilometers further up the river, where the salt water stopped at high tide. There he found a dam and a waterfall, with a stone fish trap below. Here the fish could be trapped when the tide fell. It was used by a group of about 300 Indians along the river. But the heavy stone dam was of European construction, and part of the apparent European influence from the 1500s in this area. The place was given the name Watertown.

The French trappers and discoverers who frequented this area one hundred years before the English arrived, reported finding the remains of an old village below.[9] The Englishmen built a settlement in this location and called it Newtown (today Cambridge), but there is no mention of this village in the English papers.

There are several reasons to believe that the Vinlandfarers had their main base here by the Charles River. Just as in the Vinland sagas, we hear in the English accounts about the nice climate, the amazing wealth of birds and eggs, about the grapes, the fruits, the fields, the fine lumber, and later about the headland where the deer gathered so close together that the ground was crusted with their droppings. There the colonists killed up to sixteen animals every day. In the Boston area, no one would be likely to starve to death.

Because of better sailing conditions, and the discovery of a large oyster bank below Newtown, where the famous fish trap was located, the English decided to move the village down the Charles River.[10] The new location closer to the ocean was given the name Boston, after the home town of the leader of this colony.

A mill to grind corn was soon erected on the hill overlooking Boston harbor. But most of the colony's activity continued to be focused on the river. The people who were best off were the ones who had settled in Newtown, writes Wood, who acted as a sort of «roving reporter». The colonists protected their grazing animals from wolves by keeping them on «islands» with moats on all sides. Black cows were left alone, while the red and brown ones were mistaken for deer by the wolves. In the 19th century there were claims that these moats were canals, where the Norse Greenlanders of the Middle Ages floated timber to the sea. One enthusiastic amateur scientist, Eben Norton Horsford, even went so far as to erect a stone tower, «Norumbega Tower», by the Charles River, to mark the place where Leif Eiriksson went ashore in America. At the time people shook their heads over such an idea, but in hindsight it may be that he was not so very far from the truth. The tower still exists.

Because of the new colony, the Indians had to give up the fishing trap at Watertown. By then they had taught the Englishmen to let the fish lie and rot in the fields as fertilizer, after the colonists had had a terrible corn crop in 1631.

In the spring of 1632, after a winter of hunger, it was decided that the ancient fishing trap—or «the weir» as the Englishmen called it—should be improved and modernized.

Wood reports that in the course of two days (two times high tide), 100,000 fish were caught, so the colonists had an abundance of both food and fertilizer. That catch continued for more than two centuries, and the right to the fishing was divided between Watertown on the east side and Brighton on the west side of the river. The administration of the fishing trap was the province of the town clerk of Watertown until the 1800s.[11]

The colonists made a channel from the top of the dam to a water wheel. By releasing the water against the underside of the paddle wheel, there was enough power to run the mill, albeit slowly. A similar mill has been preserved not far from Boston, where interested visitors can still grind corn.

A Replay of Leiv Eiriksson's Harbor Problems

Navigating Boston harbor was a problem for the colonists, just as it had been for the Greenlanders the first time they went ashore in North America. The southern inlet was still partly filled with sand, as it was in Leiv Eiriksson's time. In the middle of the bay there were channels, but also strong currents that made it dangerous to sail there. The Norsemen, in an emergency measure, took to their oars to help maneuver the low clinker-built boats safely past «Straumöya» (Current Island).

The heavy caravel-built English ships could not be maneuvered by rowing, and so they did not try to pass the islands in the middle of the bay. Instead they went up to Deer Point, where sailors rowed ashore on both sides of the small sound that the deer swam across, and with ropes pulled the ships through—thus preventing them from running aground. This was the main avenue of approach to Boston during colonial times.

Solving the navigational challenges was one thing, but it took a while before the colonists began to figure out the Indians.

Every colonist was promised one hundred acres of unoccupied land. According to Governor Bradford's diary, the amount was adjusted according to family size, but nonetheless, the Indians had to give up land.[12] In doing so, they demonstrated a peculiar way of parcelling out land. They took a pinch of soil from each of the four corners of the camp fire, one pinch from the seat of the local chief, one from the land that was to change hands, and one pinch from the neighboring property or area. Two Norwegians, anthropologist Kjell Bondevik, and professor of history, Halvdan Koht, have pointed out that this is a procedure specified in the laws of Gulating, instituted by Håkon Den Gode (Håkon the Good) around the year 950. It was in effect in the Middle Ages in West Norway, the Norwegian possessions in England/Ireland, and on Iceland and Greenland. The two researchers conclude that the Indians must have learned this process from the Greenlanders.[13]

The Indians also had an interesting ball game—which later turned out to have exactly the same rules as the old Icelandic and Greenland ball game «knattleikar». It was a somewhat brutal precursor of modern hockey, which sometimes resulted in injuries. State archivist Ebbe Hertzberg, who studied the matter in Norway, believes the Indians learned the game from their Greenland neighbors[14]—and this author is tempted to say, their Greenland tribe members. Dr. Walther James Hoffman[15] and Fridtjof Nansen[16] reported seeing the game played both on Greenland and among a number of Indian tribes in northeast America.

Pinus resinosa—The Norsemen's Pine

What most of all made America indispensable to Greenland's population, was the Norway Pine (Pinus resinosa). A very hard pine with a reddish color, it is still in high demand around the world, and a luxurious choice for walls and ships' decks. It is very resistant to wind and weather, and grows in a small belt from Newfoundland and New England west to the Canadian lakes and Minnesota. It is still referred to as «Norway Pine». The trees can grow to be 20–25 meters high.

People may have assumed that the tree was named after the town of Norway in northwestern Maine. But in A Natural History of Trees in Eastern and Central North America, Donald Culross Peattie writes that this is not possible. The town of «Norway» got its name in 1797. There are written records to prove that the name «Norway Pine» was in use in 1790.[17] Professor Oddvar Haveraaen of Norway's Agricultural College has investigated the matter together with American colleagues, among them Professor Edward Lutz of Cornwall University and experts at the university's famous plant museum and plant «library». They have found no explanation. Nor has the popular Knowing Your Trees, published by the American Forestry Association, found a source for the name «Norway Pine».

There probably is no other explanation than that this tree, which is not found in any other place on earth, is the pine indigenous to the land of Norumbega, and which the Norse Greenlanders used. By a quirk of fate it has become the state tree of Minnesota, one of the most Scandinavian states in America. There is vigorous resistance to renaming this type of tree «hard pine». It would also rob North America of an important name tradition.

Newport Tower

A very interesting European church ruin in America is a round stone tower in Newport, Rhode Island. It is 24 feet 8 inches in diameter, and rests on eight stone pillars in Roman vaulted style. All measurements in the structure, the diameter of the pillars, the distance from the center to each pillar, etc., is divisible by the old «Skjælland foot», used in Scandianvia and by the Dutch in the Middle Ages.[18] On the inside of the second story wall, there are buttresses thought to have been used as a work bench, table or altar. In a niche in the wall there had been cabinets—some think for money, medicines or the holy vessels of a church. The second story may have been a storage room for valuables, or a shelter for people.

Any art historian can confirm that this ruin belongs to a mighty architectural tradition that arose with the crusades in the 1100s, and died in the course of a single century.[19] The prototypical model was the round church that Emperor Constantine had erected in the year 326 over the Holy Sephulchre in Jerusalem. There is no indication of who erected the tower in Newport. All we know is that a religious order, a regional bishop, or powerful men were always behind the construction of such a building.

The tower in Newport is in size and construction similar to the octagonal tower from the year 1160 which stands in front of the Benedictine monastery of St. Bravo, in Ghent in Belgium. The room among the eight pillars was the lavatory, where the monks washed their hands before every meal. The second story was a storage room for holy things, relics and valuables. The lavatory of the Cistercian monastery of Vernhem in

208

Vâstergötland in Sweden is a similar building.

The Swedish church expert, Dr. Hugo Frölen, writes that the tower in Newport is without a doubt the inner rotunda of a large and correctly constructed round church.[20] And that the building style is the same as the Anglo-Norman style of the Church of the Holy Sephulchre in Cambridge in England, built in 1125, and the fortified round church in Northampton, dating from the same time. Both are tied to the French order of the Templars. La Rotunda in Brescia, just west of Lago di Garda, St. Thomas' church in Bergamo in Italy, and the Cistercian monastery near Drougheda in Ireland, are also typical examples of these types of churches. St. Olav's church in Tönsberg, Norway, was one of Scandinavia's largest round churches.

The Danish archaeologist, Dr. Johannes Bröndsted, writes that the columns and arches of the ruin in Newport are all Romanesque features. And the double «splays» are so typical that no expert in Europe would question that it dates to the Middle Ages.[21] Such doubts have been raised it seems, because there are no sources indicating when the structure was erected.

Once the tower was constructed, the next step would have been to build the outer walls of the church around the inner circle of columns, and then put the roof on top of the entire structure. On top of the Newport ruin there is a foundation for a roof on the outside, and there is evidence of the beginning of construction a few meters outside the columns. But it is likely that this particular church was never finished.

The first to draw attention to the tower was Newport's founder, Sir Edwin Plowden, in 1630. In a letter to King Charles of England he sent a list of twenty-nine reasons for founding a British colony in this area. He first mentions the region's important commodities—the grapes, the plentiful fish «for dryed coad and trayned oyles». Point twenty-seven in the letter addresses how the colony might be defended if it is established: «So the 30 idle men as souldiers or gents be resident in a rownde stone towre and by turnes to trade widt the savages and to keepe their armes and ordinance neate...»[22]

If the church had been finished, Plowden naturally would have written that there was a church ruin there, and not just a tower. Perhaps the builder died before the work was finished? Perhaps they decided that they had started a piece of work that was simply too demanding, since enthusiasm for the crusades was on the wane?

The request for permission to establish an English colony at Newport was granted on July 24, 1632, but for the time being there were no colonists. William Wood visited the area at one point between 1629 and 1633, on his way home to England. He called the present Newport «Old Plymouth» on his map of 1634. He obviously wouldn't have done so unless there were indications of people having lived there. «New Plymouth», the first colony of the Mayflower group, lay on the opposite side of the large peninsula.

A small difference in the height of the columns of the Newport tower has raised doubt as to whether the builders possessed leveling tools. We can dismiss this doubt, by pointing to the similarity to the round church in Bromma in Sweden from around 1100. In the Bromma church, just like the Newport tower, there is on the inside wall, extending most of the way around, a groove about four inches high and two or three inches deep which was evidently used to support the planks of the second floor. But the floor of the Bromma church was pitched toward the middle, where there was a central plank with a channel for water that ran through a hole in the wall.

Why was this done? Probably because it was a fortified church. When the peep holes were open in wind and rain, water would come in through the openings, and it would have to be promptly drained.

The uneven height of the columns on which the beams rested in Newport, may also perhaps be explained by the need for slanted floors to get rid of rainwater.

Verrazzano called Newport «Normans Villa»—the village of the Norsemen—when he was there 100 years before the English arrived. He wrote that this most civilized of people in America had «a European-like structure», and that they tended the grapes in traditional European fashion.[23] Such a thing would not have occurred to the Indians.

The place name «Normans Villa» can be found both on Verrazzano's globe of 1542, and on the well-known map that his brother Hieronymus drew.

When the English colonists finally arrived here in 1637, John Clark and William Coddington—who founded Newport in 1639 together with Plowden—tried to find out from the Indians who had erected the tower. But they knew nothing about it.

More recently theories have suggested that the tower was built by Spaniards, Portuguese or Dutchmen in the 1600s, and that it was originally an observation tower or a light house.[24] But the best known theory is the one that suggests that England's first governor had the tower built and that it represents the remains of a windmill. This because in his testament of December 24, 1677, he asked to be buried «by the path between the house and my stone windmill».

It is true that the colonists for a short while had a windmill rigged on top of the ruin, possibly because the town's regular windmill was lost in a fire in 1675. But it probably was not a very successful arrangement, because in 1678 the ruin was once more just that—a ruin.[25]

Church historians reject the idea that the governor during this busy time of establishing the colony would erect such a strange windmill requiring so much labor employing long forgotten techniques and a style abandoned four hundred years before the English colonists arrived.

To date an area only 10 to 12 feet beyond the columns has been excavated. After World War II an excavation down to the shallow foundation yielded only two clay pipes and a shoe sole from the colonial period.[26]

Greenland had several monasteries, and it would have been natural for such monastic orders to follow settlers to America, since the Greenlanders «used» this land for over four hundred years. On Greenland the ruins of three round buildings have been found.[27]

If the Newport tower is the ruin of a Cistercian monastery, we know that they all have the same form and dimensions wherever they are found.

Americans interested in runes claim to have found the runes HINIRS inscribed on the wall. Henrikus was a bishop of the Western Settlement on Greenland, but never returned from a voyage to America in 1118. It would be reasonable to think that he might have had something to do with the building. But the rune claims are firmly rejected by Scandinavian experts. The Americans have gone a step further, however, and claim to have deciphered a secret rune code with advanced computer technology.[28]

European Ocean Snails and A Norse Coin

A surprising find in North America was a colony of the European ocean snail Littorina littoria, first encountered on the coast of Nova Scotia in the last century. It is not indigenous to America, and scientists think it may have been brought there by European ships that came for lumber in the 1800s. This particular snail is exceedingly slow to multiply, and American scientists speculate that it speeded up in this regard when transplanted. A new colony was subsequently found in Newfoundland. Carbon 14 dating was performed on snail shells found on Indian refuse heaps, and it was

From the excavation at Naskeag Point in Maine, where the Norwegian coin from 1065–80 was found. Mount Norumbega is in the background. From left to right, Elisabeth Warner, Kåre Prytz, Ruth W. Cox, Stephanie Hale and the excavation leader, Steven Cox.

then determined that the snails had come across the Atlantic Ocean in the 1200s and 1300s. Ships probably had been taken ashore and cleaned of snails in the area where they were found.[29]

For many years the two capable amateur archaeologists Guy Mellgren and Ed Runge conducted excavations on the lovely Naskeag Point in Maine—just east of the mouth of Penobscot River, formally known as Norumbega River. Summer after summer the two dug up vestiges of Indian culture by the crate full. They eventually acquired a sizeable collection that they treated in a professional manner. In 1972 Mellgren donated the entire collection to the Maine State Museum. He died in the fall of

1978, and in his will he asked that his ashes be scattered over Naskeag Point.

During the sorting of this collection, experts noticed a coin that Mellgren and Runge had thought was from the reign of the English King Stephen (1135–54), but which was in fact Norwegian. It was from the reign of King Olav Kyrre, who ruled from 1065 to 1092.

The site was immediately declared off limits and kept secret in order to discourage theft, or deliberate planting, of artifacts. The British coin expert Peter Seaby, the Irishman Michael Dolley, and the head of Norway's Mint, Dr. Kolbjörn Skaare, were summoned. All of them quickly concluded that the coin was authentic. Dr. Dolley describes the coin as the oldest European metal find in the United States.[30]

A fragment of the coin was analyzed at the Atomic Laboratory at Kjeller in Norway, and the analysis revealed that King Olav Kyrre was engaged in a bit of monetary chicanery. His silver coin contained only 21.7 percent silver, a trace of gold, and 78.2 percent copper. This agrees with the content found in all the silver coins from this period.[31]

The Maine State Museum assumed the responsibility for further excavations on Naskeag Point in the summer of 1979. In a few square yards thousands of Indian artifacts were found. I was a guest of the archaeologists in September of that year, when the excavations were coming to an end. A major storm had uprooted a number of trees in the area. From the upturned earth, in an area of about 2.5 acres, pieces of flint and flint work rained down when the roots were shaken. The archaeologists at the dig found knives, arrowheads, drills, axes and pipes from a period spanning 2000 years B.C. to around 1700 B.C.—and from another period, beginning around 1000 A.D. and lasting until the European colonists arrived in the 1600s. The leader of the team, Dr. Steve Cox, estimated the find to be the largest Indian trade and market place discovered so far in North America. No more Norse finds have been made, but only a fraction of the entire area has been examined.[32]

It would be reasonable to see this find in connection with the fact that the Norse «capital» in North America on just about all medieval European maps was present day Bangor, on the same river. The place had the fantastic benefit of giving ships a «free ride» of about 40 kilometers on enormous coastal tides. It was the nearest ice-free inland river for the Greenlanders, and one of the best hunting areas in all of North America. In the summertime there were, and are, waterways and lakes in all directions throughout the immense forests all the way to Quebec in Canada. The Spanish also called the river «Rio de las gamas»—the river with game. In the last part of the 1800s, Bangor was the world's largest export harbor for lumber.

The entire lovely point where the coin was found, is now part of the Acadia National Park on Mount Desert Island across the bay.

Swedish Indians in Vinland

The Swedish chancellor and master diplomat, Axel Oxenstierna (1583–1654), was in reality the uncrowned king of Sweden in the early 1600s while the young King Gustaf Adolf participated in conquests and religious wars in Europe. After the humiliating treaty with Denmark in 1613, Sweden had become one of the world's leading powers and without a doubt the strongest military power. Halberds, swords, guns and cannons of Swedish steel were without match, and in addition to that, the country was the world's largest producer of copper and iron.

After its military successes, Sweden had completely cut off Russia along the Baltic, and parts of Poland and Germany had become Swedish. Oxenstierna's foreign policies also included a new war of conquest against Denmark-Norway, and plans to occupy America and initiate trade with the new world. The only problem was that England, the Netherlands and France had already claimed America north of 36 degrees, from the inlet to Chesapeake Bay at the southern tip of the Delaware peninsula.

Several dissatisfied Dutchmen were interested in the Swedish expansion on the other side of the Atlantic, and offered suggestions. The best known is the plan for the «South Company», which was to establish a world wide network of trading stations and colonies south of the 36th parallel. What the plans all had in common, was that they fizzled out before being realized.

After watching ten to twelve years of fruitless planning, chancellor Axel Oxenstierna himself became involved in the matter. It may have had something to do with the fact that he met Hugo Grotius during a visit to Europe in 1634. Grotius had been the top official in Holland, «colonial minister», state historian, and a highly respected man of new ideas in international law. He had left his homeland because of religious political controversy.

Oxenstierna immediately appointed Grotius as Sweden's ambassador to Paris. The jurist Grotius was a champion of the so-called «natural law», and according to this theory, none of the European great powers had exclusive rights to American land. Only the discoverer did.

214

That same year Grotius allegedly managed to get the English king, Charles I, to give Sweden the Delaware peninsula as a «sphere of interest».[33] It sounds surprising, but not unlikely. The unstable Charles I had dissolved Parliament, and gotten himself mired in corruption and financial chaos—prior to being decapitated. And at this point the Swedes were only talking about a trading post where they would buy pelts and sell Swedish goods.

The real plan was to occupy the new area and name it «Nya Sverige»—just like «New Holland» in New York, the English colony «New England» in the old Norumbega, and «Virginia» in the old «Wingan de coe». But it was important to keep this secret until the colony had been established.[34]

The state of Sweden was the formal occupier, but the colony was a private company headed by Oxenstierna, along with two close relatives who were also in the Swedish government. Experienced Dutch colonists were the other majority stock holders. The headquarters were in Gothenburg, Sweden.

During the winter of 1637–38, Dutch seafarers sailed the first two Swedish ships that crossed the Atlantic with a total of 22 Swedish soldiers on board. They followed Columbus' old route via the Canary Islands, and came ashore in Delaware Bay in March.

The Swedes impressed the Indians with several thousand yards of cloth, axes, knives, magnifying glasses, mirrors, necklaces, rings for ears and fingers, and agricultural tools. With the Dutch as their negotiators, the Swedes reached an agreement permitting them to live in the land from the famous 36th latitude up to present day Philadelphia, and as far west as to the sunset. In practice that meant the states of Delaware and Pennsylvania, as well as parts of New Jersey and Maryland. The Indians felt it was a sign of progress that rich white men with valuable trading goods had settled among them. They didn't know anything about the European notion that people could own land, water and air. They thought they would be able to roam the land as freely as before the white man came.

After this one of the ships sailed down to the 36th latitude (36°54'), to the southern tip of Vinland and Antilia. The man in charge of the colony, the German born Peter Minuit, declared the land Swedish, christened it «Nya Sverige» and ordered the cannons to be fired. Thereby it became Swedish. The Dutchmen's role in the enterprise caused outrage in their native Holland where they were just about accused of treason, and their shares were bought out by the Swedes. Oxenstierna was more interested in an all-Swedish colony anyway.

In 1641 the first families, with domestic animals and horses, shipped out from Sweden. Apart from the administrators, most of the colonists were slash-and-burn farmers of Finnish descent. They had spread throughout all the great Scandinavian forests, or «Finnskogene», where they lived primitive and isolated lives. Just about all they needed— utensils, tools, carrying baskets and shoes—they made from wood, animal hides, and birch bark. They brought their East Finnish smoking huts, their saunas and their log house building techniques. Their method of cultivation was to fell the forest one year, burn the trees and the dry forest floor the next, and grow rye in the ashes the third and fourth years. Thirty years would pass before they again would burn the same field.

When the Swedish and Norwegian mining industries and bog iron production blossomed in the 1600s, large quantities of coal and wood were needed. The Finns in the great forests who were displaced by iron smelters, farmers and new communities became destitute. To them, Oxenstierna's colony came as a life saver.

A Dutch captain, who was constantly drunk and who «shunned the Lutheran Swedes like the devil», led the first boatload of colonists across the Atlantic. The forest Finns were astonished at the sight of the stone free soil in Delaware, the herds of deer, huge «catfish» that had to be killed with axes, wine grapes, melons, plums, nuts and chestnuts. The Indians tapped maple syrup in the spring for the whole year, and grew maize instead of rye. The life the red men lived was far better, and much safer, than life in the Scandinavian forests where winter was three times as long. The Indians lived in communities in which all members were responsible for one another. The family clans of the Finns were not very different.

In the spring of 1642 the smoke of the Swedish Finns in Delaware mixed with that of the Indians. The first Indian girls had already become Swedish wives, and Indian widows took new, white husbands. The maize was harvested so early that they were able to plant rye the same year. The Finns introduced carrots, cabbage and onions, previously unknown in the woods of Delaware.

The Indians—tall Lenapes—who lived just like the Swedish and Finnish slash-and-burn farmers, had saunas and the same desire to live a simple life in peace and quiet. Their more blood-thirsty brothers, the Iroquois, threatened on one side, and greedy Dutch and English colonists on the other. Soon Swedish tobacco growers and traders arrived at the river, and claimed that they owned the land and the water in an area as large as Dalarna in Sweden.

The Indians suffered a significant shortage of males because of the attacks from belligerent neighbors and a risk-filled hunting life. The immigrants from Sweden had too many men, so it was a good match. Technically the immigrants were more advanced. They had modern weapons and could make a high quality iron from swampland ore—almost rust free because it contained no sulphur and phosphorous. They were on good terms with the trappers too, and were able to get the Indians the weapons they needed from the world's foremost weapon producer, Sweden.

At this point the European colonial powers sounded the alarm and demanded that «Nya Sverige» be removed. But Sweden mounted a counter attack. In 1642 the country's famous ambassador in Paris, Hugo Grotius, came out with his book De origine gentium Americanarum. Here he asserted that all of North America, down to Mexico, should be considered Norwegian land, because it had initially been discovered and claimed by the Norwegians and had been called «Norumbega» because of the Norwegian colonists. This was contradicted by Holland's Johannes de Laet. But Grotius was considered the authority on colonial rights, and he was never known to voice opinions «on order».

He and Oxenstierna must have discussed the matter in detail, both when these two experts in international affairs met in Paris in 1634, and later.

In Paris ambassador Grotius had written his masterpiece, De jure belli ac pacis («About the Rights of War and Peace»), which has had international credence until the present time. Grotius considered possessions and colonies legal spoils of war, and it was probably a very interesting document to Oxenstierna, who was preparing for war against Norway-Denmark. On top of Oxenstierna's wish list were the Norwegian areas of Jemtland and Hârjedalen. We have no written indication of what else he may have wished for, but the «Norwegian» possessions in America must have been very tempting.

The Swedish colony in Delaware developed very quickly. The tobacco growers earned money as the poison gained popularity in Europe. The Swedish fur traders got most of what the Indians brought out of a wilderness no European had yet seen. The forts were expanded, and Swedish log houses proved themselves superior, both as living quarters and fortifications.

Governor Printz' discipline was hard, and many colonists fled to the Indians and disappeared for good in the wooded hills of New Jersey and the western blue mountains. The boy Lars Thomasson Bure, who was taken care of by the Indians and adopted when he was small, was recognized and reclaimed by his family when he visited the Swedes as an adolescent. He was never happy among his own kin, and returned to his Indian world. It is claimed that he became a chief and later led the tribe to the headwaters of the Ohio River in order to get away from the whites.[35]

He was not the only trusted Swedish Indian. A 1652 peace treaty with the English is signed by «brother-in-law Peter»—a Swedish military advisor who ran off and married an Indian girl, apparently the chief's sister.

Other Swedish slash-and-burn farmers, who were at home in the forests, came with the ships from Gothenburg and became successful farmers in the more populated areas. They had an advantage over the immigrants from England and Holland who were unaccustomed to the forest and «wilderness» life.

In 1655 Holland occupied the Swedish colony. By then Oxenstierna had been set aside by the young queen, and no help arrived from Sweden. The Swedish leaders were sent back to Sweden on Dutch ships. For the Swedish immigrants life became less constricted than when they had to answer to Sweden, and they were highly respected. It became almost a Swedish free state, with its own administration and Lutheran ministers brought from Sweden.

Initially the traders made use of liquor to cheat the Indians of land, rights and merchandise. Later when members of an Indian family wanted to drink, they had to yield their weapons and all their valuables to family members who were not going to participate in the binge. This procedure made it less profitable to make the Indians drunk. On the map of Delaware we can still find the name «Brânnvin Creek» («Liquor Creek»), where a big battle was fought during the American Civil War. This is where a quantity of liquor was poured into a creek by the Indians to rid themselves of the nuisance caused by fire water. The Swedish-Indian culture in many ways was a model one, similar to the French-Indian culture in Canada dating from the 1500s.

The Dutch quietly sent recruiters to the Swedish Finn regions and organized a secret immigration to Delaware via Norwegian harbors.

Eventually four fifths of the colonists used the slash-and-burn farming method, and this was important for the more urban Dutch and English colonists.

In 1664 the Dutch were replaced by the English, and King Charles II entrusted the area to the hands of 2000 English Quakers under the leadership of William Penn. The «urbanized» Swedes were assimilated into the English community, which was named Pennsylvania. The other Swedes ended up on the Indian side in the bloody war against the white intruders. The large Finnish family of Mullikka went to New Jersey, where the names of Mullica Town and Mullica Hills remind us of their presence. Finns Town and Finns Point on the coast are named after the Seneka family. The permanent residents continued to receive Swedish speaking ministers from Sweden until the end of the 1700s.

But foreign ideas gained foothold everywhere. A large donation to the parsonage, for instance, was used to buy the young black girl Peggy for 50 pounds as live inventory. The slave girl was used for different purposes by the ministers, and was hired out for work as well. She bore two girls, in 1725 and 1727. The father is not listed in the church records by the bachelor who then owned her. When Peggy became worthless, she was sold for 7 shillings.[36] Who bought the daughters, is not known.

The English and the Dutch murdered indiscriminately because they needed more land, «clearing» the land of natives and «Swedish Indians». Anything was allowed. During a smallpox epidemic, for instance, clothes and items owned by deceased smallpox victims were laid out so the Indians would find them and become infected.

The worst affected groups migrated west to the enormous prairies, but there they were considered intruders and became evolved in battles against other Indian tribes. The states of Kansas and Arkansas had Swedish-Indian communities, where they were able to breathe a little more freely. But they had to set off on new treks as the white men pressed forward, and conditions became worse and worse. In the beginning of the 20th century, the last wandering Swedish-Indians came to the border of Mexico, where their descendants now live.[37]

Ambassador Hugo Grotius' statement of 1642 is the last time the Greenlanders' centuries long use of America is cited as an argument in the fight over rights to America, or Norumbega.

1. Marsden, in English Historical Review, Vol. XIX, 1904.
2. Bradford, 1972, p. 58.
3. Wood, 1634, p. 5.
4. Bradford, 1972, p. 65.
5. Ceram, 1972.
6. Bradford, 1972, p. 70.
7. Wood, 1634, pp. 13–14.
8. Bradford, 1972, p. 79.
9. Thevet, 1558.
10. Wood, 1634, p. 39.
11. Nelson, 1875.
12. Bradford, 1964, p. 144.
13. Den eldste Noregshistoria, p. 88.
14. Hertzberg, 1904.
15. Hoffmann, 1896, p. 127.
16. Nansen, 1911, pp. 318–319.
17. Castiglioni, Viaggie negli Stati Uniti, vol. II, p. 313: «Pinus sylvistris Norvegica, Norway Pine nel Massachusetts».
18. Syversen, 1979, p. 100.
19. Frölen, 1911, p. 136.
20. Ibid., pp. 17–43.
21. Bröndsted, Johannes, in Tidsskrift for Nordisk oldkyndighed og Historie, 1950.
22. Plowden Papers. Public Record Office, Chancery Lane, London.
23. Verrazzano. See Hagman Hall, 1910, Appendix A, pp. 135–227.
24. Ingstad, 1959, p. 279.
25. Frölen, 1911, p. 42.
26. American Anthropologist, Vol. 57, 1955, p. 35.
27. Rafn, C. «Bemerkninger om en gammel Bygning i Newport», Annaler for Nordisk Oldkyndighet, 1840–41, p. 166.
28. Syversen, 1979, pp. 98–102.
29. Detailed discussion in Science, vol. 134, 1961, pp. 393–94, and Science, vol. 159, 1968, p. 114.
30. Dolley, 1979.
31. Skaare, 1979.
32. Borque & Cox, 1981, pp. 3–28.
33. Johnson, 1927, p. 106.

34. Ibid., p. 75.
35. Linderholm, 1988, p. 115.
36. Ibid., p. 136.
37. Ibid., p. 166.

THE GREAT RIDDLE IS SOLVED

Over the centuries Columbus' voyages to America were forgotten. But eventually his diary was translated into English. The first translation, notable for its solid maritime knowledge, was linguistically worthless. The next translation was the other way around. Over time seven «edited» editions appeared, each worse than the other. Not until our own century did we get translations where the text was left unabridged and unedited.

But by then, the world had long been engaged in a fruitless argument about whether it was Columbus or Leiv Eiriksson who had first arrived in America. As more and more Columbus biographies appeared, new and fanciful theories arose about where he was really headed in 1492.

Finally serious historians more or less gave up. They stated that in 1492 Columbus sailed west and claimed the continent for Spain. They were unable to add much more, because one link was missing—the map that Columbus claimed he had, but which no longer existed.

Norwegian historians had much the same problem with Torvald Eiriksson's saga. There was no map to confirm his journey down to Georgia and the Bahamas. They simply accepted that Torvald Eiriksson's journey began where his brother Leiv Eiriksson's journey had ended.

What no one had dared hope for, happened in 1946 when the British auction firm William H. Robinson received a sizeable portion of Sir Thomas Philips' world famous library and map collection from the early 1800s. When the collection was being cataloged, an unknown map was discovered, signed «Zuane Pizzi…, Venezia 1424». Experts assume he belonged to the well known cartographer family Pizzigano who had introduced the name «Antilia» way out in the Atlantic Ocean, during the time of Pope Urban. It soon became evident that the map in hand was a more complete copy of Pope Urban's map than the stylized versions previously known. It also clearly indicated that the far north had been «experienced», and that there was land drawn in on a latitude corresponding to the coast between Savannah in Georgia and St. Johns River in Florida. Near Savannah a bay was drawn in, with the name «Balmar». Dr. Mario Pei, who later conducted a critical examination of the names I used in my book Lykkelige Vinland («Fortunate Vinland»), suggested that the name means «Vallum Maris»—«rampart in the sea». This is quite in agreement with the information in Torvald Eiriksson's saga, which recounts how the Greenlanders saw mounds or ramparts on a coast of a bay where a massive Indian attack resulted in Torvald's death.

On a position corresponding to the Bahama Islands, the map had one large and four smaller islands, but with no explanatory legend. It is fair to assume it designates a group of islands.

Again we are reminded of Torvald Eiriksson's saga—which tells us that they were on their way to the east when they ran aground and broke their keel in very shallow waters where there were many islands and no animal life.

The paper width of the map made the distance between Europe and America seem shorter, so that the Bahama Islands ended up along the coast of Africa just south of the Canary Islands. The name of the islands is given as «Himadoro». Dr. Armando Cortesao of the university in Quimbra in Portugal was the first to comment on the map, but he could find no explanation for this name. Columbus seems to have associated these islands with a very high mountain, and writes in his diary of November 14, 1492, that they are the easternmost islands on his map.

The geographer who was near the magnetic North Pole in 1360 talked about the high «Himmelradsfjell» that no one should sail past, or they would be swallowed by the ocean currents. On the map that the Pizzigano brothers began in 1367, they drew a mountain or pillar at Chesapeake Bay, designating it as the point beyond which sailors would be caught in darkness and fog and currents. The «Himmadoro» name on the Bahama Islands may indicate that this was the point in the south beyond which no one should go if they wanted to return home. The Portuguese captain, Gill Eanes, was the first to venture beyond this latitude, in 1434.

The map discovered in England was still known to few. In the entire world there were perhaps two or three people who were studying historical geography related to the Vinland voyages and America's discovery, but they were working on different angles. Professor Cortesao, in cooperation with the British Museum, undertook a comprehensive scientific examination of the map. The result was presented in 1954 in The Nautical Chart of 1424, which confirmed that this was the oldest known map of the east coast of America, and was unmatched in accuracy by any other maps in existence before Columbus' voyage in 1492.[1]

Amazingly enough, no one realized that here, suddenly, was a map that agreed with Torvald Eiriksson's saga and with Columbus' sailing route in 1492. All the puzzling things that Columbus wrote about his destination in the diary from day to day in 1492, were explained by this map. Christopher Columbus' navigation and his choice of the southern route were no longer a mystery. And let us not forget that Martin Alonzo Pinzón went all the way to the Vatican to have the map's existence confirmed before he accepted Columbus' plan and became the next in command of the expedition.

But this epoch making geographical and historical piece of news was overshadowed by a so-called «Vinland map» claimed to date from 1440. A media show surrounding the map attracted the attention of the entire world, and it rose in price from month to month. Uncritical journalists were not aware that Andrea Bianco's map of America from 1436 already adorned a wall of the Doge Palace in Venice as «America map no. 1». The commotion around the «Vinland map» didn't quiet down until it was revealed that it had been drawn with ink in the 1950s.

Meanwhile the map that had been found in England had received a more muted reception. In 1955 it was sold to the James Ford Bell Collection at the University of Minnesota, where it is now kept.

The originator of this map was the geographer who traveled west in the 1360s, and whose acquaintance we have already made. It is obvious that the map designer had himself seen the coast down to Chesapeake Bay. He also added the Georgia-Florida coast and the Bahama Islands in their correct positions, apparently after having had them described by others. In the copy of the voyage account in the British Museum, it says that this geographer noted everything the Greenlanders told him, and that he then «measured the information with a geometric instrument used to draw maps». This is what I think we are seeing south of Chesapeake Bay.

The Norumbega Name Fades

The name Norumbega is still alive in many areas of New England. Far into this century the steamboat «Norumbega» was in regular traffic between Mount Desert Island and the Maine coast.[2] In the hot debate over who first reached America, it was assumed that the name meant «something Indian». When Norwegian researchers began to take an interest in the Vinland voyages in the last century, they didn't take issue with this assumption, even if both American and Canadian citizens suggested otherwise. The oldest name in North America cannot be found in any Norwegian history book or lexicon. But it is absurd to overlook a cultural heritage because of modesty or misguided politeness. It is interesting to note that the official guide for the state of Maine explains the meaning of the name as «The Norsemen's Land».

In December, 1988, the Norumbega map was first officially exhibited in Portland, Maine. At the same time a «Norumbega Conference» was held, with 300 professional American historians, archaeologists and historical geographers in attendance. They concluded that the name Norumbega included present day New England and the maritime Canadian provinces, Baffin Island, and the arctic regions. And that this region had been under Norwegian administration and law up until about year 1500.[3]

Locally it will be necessary to make an effort to preserve the name, because it is facing competition with newer names of our era. In Bangor there is a Norumbega Parkway, and a Norumbega Mall by the lively Kenduskeag Stream, just above where the tidewater turns. In 1982 a young policeman was unable to tell me the location of Norumbega Mall, until he had called an older colleague over the radio.

But every New Year's Eve American youths are reminded of their land's Norse past. Mountain climbers from all over the United States gather on Mount Desert Island in Maine, where they keep vigil to see the first rays of sun fall on the easternmost point of the United States—on Mount Cadillac, Mount Sargent, Mount Penobscot and Mount Norumbega.

1. Cortesao, 1954.
2. Joy, Barbara. The History of Mount Desert Island, I-X.
3. Summary by Albert G. Hahn.

BIBLIOGRAPHY

Alfrædi islenzk, I–III. Old Icelandic manuscripts, published by Kr. Kålund, Copenhagen 1908–18.

American Bureau of Ethnology and Archaeology. 14th Annual Report, Part I, 1892–94, Washington 1896.

Annales Islandi, Vol. I, 1922.

American Anthropologist, Vol. 57, 1955.

Amundsen, Roald. Nordvestpassasjen, 1907. New edition, Oslo 1972.

Anghiera, Pietro Martire. De Orbe Novo, 1511. Modern English edition by F.A. MacNutt: The Eight Decades of Pietro Martire d. Anghiera, London and New York, 1912.

Arber, A. The Travels and Works of Captain John Smith, Edinburgh, 1910.

Archivo Vaticana Diversorum, Alexander VI, Arm 29. T 50. Fol. 23.

Aschehougs Verdenshistorie, Vols. 1–15, 1985.

Ausfürliche Nachricht von den Salzburgischen Emigranten... Viertes Stück, 1740. Houghton Library, Harvard University.

Baardsson, Ivar. Det gamle Grønlands beskrivelse. Edited by Finnur Jonsson, Copenhagen 1930.

Benediktsson, Jacob. Islendigabok and Landnámabok, in Islenzk fornrit, Reykjavik 1968.

Bereton, «A Briefe and True Relation of the Discouerie of the North Part of Virginia» in Burrage, H.S. English and French Voyages 1534–1608, London 1906.

Beste, George. A True Discourse of the Late Voyage of Discouerie for Finding a Passage to Cataya, London 1578. Newer edition with foreword by W. Stefansson, London 1938.

Biggar, H.P. in The English Historial Review, 1917.

Biggar, H.P., A Collection of Documents Relating to Jaques Cartier and the Sieur de Roberville. Canadian Archives Publication No. 14, Ottawa 1930.

Bjørnbo. Cartographica Groenlandica. Medd. om Grøland, XLVIII, Copenhagen, 1912.

Borque, Bruce and Cox, Steven. Investigation of the Goddard Site 1979. Maine State Museum, 1981.

Boxer, Charles. The Portuguese Seaborne Empire, London 1969.

Bradford, Ernle. Columbus, London 1973.

Bradford, William. History of Plymouth Plantation 1606–1640. New edition by W.T. Dawis, New York 1964.

Brøgger, A.V. Vinlandsferdene, Oslo 1937.

Brøndsted, Johannes. Norsemen in North America Before Columbus. Report from the Smithsonian Institution, Washington, 1953.

Caldwell, Joseph R. «The Archaeology of Eastern Georgia and South Carolina» in Griffin (ed), The Archaeology of the Eastern United States, Chicago 1952.

Canadian Historial Review, vol. XXXVIII, 1957.

Capestrano, Johannes A. Haupte Zeitschrift für Deutsches Alterthum, IV.

Cappelens verdenshistorie, Vol. X, 1984.

Carson, Rachel L. Havet som omgir oss, Oslo 1952.

de las Casas, Bartholome. Historia General del Mundo. Madrid, 1612.

de Castaneda, Pedro. The Coronado Expedition diary, edited by G.D. Winship, in 14th Annual Report of the American Bureau of Ethnology and Archaeology, Part I, 1892–93. Washington 1896.

Castiglioni, W. Viaggie negli Stati Uniti, Vol. II.

Ceram, C.W. Der erste Amerikaner. Hamburg 1972.

Champlain, Samuel. Les Voyages du Sieur de Champlain. Paris 1613.

Clissold, Stephen. The Seven Cities of Cibola. London 1961.

Collinson (ed.). The Three Voyages of Martin Frobisher. Hakluyt Society, London 1867.

Collis, Maurite. Cortéz and Montezuma. Oslo 1955. The Colonial Conferences between Britain and the Netherlands, London 1940 and 1954. Ed. W.J.M. van Eysinga.

Columbus, Christopher. Diario de Colon. Copy from original by Las Casas, Madrid 1972.

Columbus, Fernando. Historia del Signor D. Fernando Colombo dell Ammiraglio D. Christoforo Colombo suo Padre, 1537. Modern edition: Buenos Aires 1918.

Cortesao, Armando. The Nautical Chart of 1424. Lisbon 1954.

Cortesao, Armando (ed.). Portugalliae Monvmenta Cartographica. Lisbon 1960.

Cortesao, Jaime. Os decubrimentos Portugeses, No.41.

Cortéz, Hernando. Letters from Mexico. New York 1971.

de Costa, B.F. Ancient Norumbega or the Voyages of Simon Fernandez and John Walker to the Penobscot River 1579–80. Albany 1890.

Dee, John. The Private Diary of Dr. John Dee, and the Catalogue of his Library of Manuscripts. The Cambden Society, 19, London 1842.

De Lollis. Raccolta Columbiana, II, Rome 1892–94.

Den eldste Noregshistoria. Translated from Latin by Halfdan Koht, Oslo 1921.

De Ro, Peter. A History of America Before Columbus. Philadelphia 1900.

De Witte, Charles-Martel. Les Bulles Pontificales et l'expansion portugaise au XVe siécle. Louvain 1958.

Dictionary of National Bibliography, Vol. XIV.

Diplomatorium Islandicum, Volume IX.

Diplomatarium Norwegicum, Vols. XII, XVII and XIX.

Diplomatarium Norwegicum, 1352 and 1360.

Documentos Inéditos del Archivo de Indias, Vol. XXII, Añode 1512, Sevilla.

Dolley, Michael, in NNF-NYTT. Meddelelser fra Norsk Numismatisk Forening, No. 2, 1979.

Driver, Harold. The Indians of North America. Chicago 1961.

Eirik den Raudes saga. Modern edition: Soga om Eirik Raude, by Ivar Eskeland, Oslo 1976.

Encyclopædia Britannica.

English Historical Review, Vol. XIX, 1904.

la Farge, Oliver. A Pictorial History of the American Indians. London 1956.

Fell, Barry. America B.C. New York 1976.

Flateyarbok. Printed edition, Copenhagen 1944–45.

Flomannasaga. New edition by Gudny Jonsson, Islendinga sogur, 12, Reykjavik 1953.

Fritzner, Johan. Ordbok over det gamle norske språk. New edition: Oslo 1954.

Frolén, Hugo F. Nordens Befestade Rundkyrkor, Vol. I, Stockholm 1911.

Gathorne-Hardy, G.M. The Norse Discoverers of America. Oxford 1921.

Grágás. Translated and published by V. Finsen, Copenhagen 1852–70.

Grimberg, Carl. Menneskenes liv og historie. Oslo 1955–58.

Grotius, Hugo. De origine Gentium Americanarum, 1642. Newer edition: Wittenberg 1714.

Grønlands annaler. Notes about Greenland made by the learned farmer Bjørn Jonsson. New edition by Olafur Halldorsson, Reykjavik 1978.

Grølands historiske minnesmerker, I–III. Documents about Greenland's history. Reprint: Copenhagen 1976.

Hakluyt, R. Diverse Voyages Touching the Discovery of America and Its Islands Adjacent, 1583. Facsimile edition: Hakluyt Society, London 1850.

Hagmann Hall, E. «Giovanni da Verrazano and His Discoveries.» New York Scenic and Historic Preservation Society, 15th Annual Report, Albany 1910.

Halldorsson, O. Olavs saga Trygvassonar en mesta. Copehagen 1958.

Hansische Geschichtsblätter, vom Hansischen Geschichtsverein 65/66, 1940–41.

Harrison, W.E.L. in The Mariner's Mirror, Vol.XVI, 1930.

Harrisse, Henry. Recueil de voyages et de documents etc., I–II, Paris 1882–83.

Heggestad, Leiv, Hødnebø Finn and Simensen, Erik. Norrøn Ordbok, Oslo 1975.

Helland, A. Norges land og folk. Oslo 1900–09.

Henning, R. Von Rätselhaften Ländern. Swedish edition, 1926.

Henriksen, Vera. Mot en verdens ytterste grense. Oslo 1988.

Hertzberg, Ebbe. «Nordboernes gamle Boldspil». Historisk skrift tilegnet professor Daae. Christiania 1904.

Hewson, J.B. A History of the Practice of Navigation. Glasgow 1951.

Historia Norwegiæ. New Norwegian edition by Halvdan Koht, Oslo 1921, and standard Norwegian edition by Astrid Salvesen, Oslo 1969.

Hodge, F.W. and Lewis T.H.: Spanish Explorers in the Southern United States 1528–43. New York 1907.

Holmsen, Andreas. Norges historie til 1660. Oslo 1949.

Holtsmark, Anne. Islendingabok. Oslo 1967.

House of Lords MS. Microfilm in State Paper. Domestic Elisabeth S. P. 12.

Ingstad, Anne Stine. Det nye land med de grønne bygder. Oslo 1975.

Ingstad, Helge. Landet med de kalde kyster. Oslo 1948.

Ingstad, Helge. Landet under leidarstjernen. Oslo 1959.

Isachsen, Gunnar. «Nordboernes ferder to Nordsetra», in Norsk geografisk selskaps årbok, 1906–07.

Isachsen, G. and F. in Norsk Geografisk Tidsskrift, Vol. IV, 1932.

Jane, Cecil. The Voyages by Columbus. Hakluyt Society, Vol. 65, London 1930.

Janes, John and Davis, John, in Hakluyt, R. The Principal Navigation of the English Nation, London 1589.

Jordens Folk. Edited by Edward Evans-Pritchard, Vol. III, Oslo 1976.

Joy, Barbara. The History of Mount Desert Island, I–X.

Kielland, Thor B. in Kulturhistorisk Lexikon Før Nordisk Medeltid, Vol. I.

Kolsrud, Oluf. Olavskyrkja i Trondheim. Oslo 1914.

Kongespeilet. Bokmål edition by A.W. Brøgger, Oslo 1947 and new Norwegian edition by A. Hellevik, Oslo 1963.

Krarup Nielsen, A. (ed.) Jordens erobring. Vol. IV, 1930–31.

Kulturhistorisk Lexikon för Nordisk Medeltid.

Laet, Johannes de. Note ad Dissertationem Hugonis Grotii, Amsterdam 1643.

Landnamabok. Modern edition by Jacob Benediktsson, Reykjavik, 1968.

Lappenberg, J.M. An die Alterthumsforscher Deutschlands und des Nördliche Europas. Hamburg 1834.

Larsen, Sophus. La découverte de l'Amerique Septentrionale en 1472–73 par les Danois et les Portugais. Paris 1926.

Linderholm, H. Nya Sveriges historia 1638–1655. Stockholm 1988.

Lowery, Woodbury. The Spanish Settlements Within the Present Limits of the United States 1513–61. New York 1911.

Løvenskiold, Hermann L. «Falkefangst» in Aschehougs konversasjons-leksikon, 1972.

The Mariner's Mirror, Vol. XVI, 1930 and Vol. LIV, 1968.

Magnussen, Finn, in Nordisk Tidsskrift for Oldkyndighet, 2. rekke, 1813.

McGovern, Thomas. «Cows, Harp Seals, And Churchbells. Adaption and Extinction in Norse Greenland.» Human Ecology, 8 (3), 1980.

McManis, R. European Impressions of the New England Coast. University of Chicago Dept. of Geography Research Paper, 1972.

de Medina, Pedro. Libro de grandezas y cosas memorables de Espana. Seville 1548.

de Meras, Gonzalo Solis. Pedro Mendéres de Aviles. Adelanto Governor and Captain of Florida. Diary edited by Jeanette T. Connor. Florida State Geographical Society, No.3, Deland, Florida 1923.

Mercator, Gerhardus. THEATRUM orbis terrarum, 1595. Facsimile edition, Amsterdam 1968.

Moore, Clarence B. Mound Investigation. New York 1897–98. Summary in Caldwell 1952.

Morcken, Roald. «Norse Nautical Units and Distance Measurements», The Mariner's Mirror, Vol. 54, No. 4, Cambridge 1968.

Morgan, E. The Founding of Massachusetts. Historians and the Source. London 1964.

Morison, Samuel E. Portuguese Voyages to America in the Fifteenth Century. Cambridge, Massachusetts 1940.

Munch, P.A. Det norske Folks Historie. Christiania 1852–64.

Munch, P.A. Pavelige regnskaps- og dagbøker. Christiania 1864.

Munk, Jens. Navigatio Septentrionalis . Copenhagen 1624. Facsimile edition, Oslo 1960.

Nares, G.S. Narrative of a Voyage to the Polar Sea During 1875–6 in H.M. Ships Alert and Discovery. I–II, London 1878.

Nansen, Fridtjof. Nord i taakeheimen. Oslo 1911.

Navarrete, Martin F. Coleccion de los viages y descubrimentos que hicieron por mar los Españoles desde fines del siglo XV. I–III, Madrid 1825.

Nelson, R.: History of Waltham. Boston 1875.

Njáls Saga. Standard Norwegian edition by: Hallvard Lie, Oslo 1952, new Norwegian edition by: Aslak Liestøl, 1965.

Nordenskiöld, A.E. Om bröderna Zenos resor och de eldsta kartor öfver Norden. Stockholm 1883.

Nordisk Tidsskrift for Oldkyndighet, 2. rekke, 1813.

Norges gamle Love. Christiania 1846–95.

Næss, Almar. Hvor lå Vinland? (With English summary.) Oslo 1954.

Nørlund, Poul. Buried Norsemen at Herjulfsnes. Copenhagen 1924.

Olaus Magnus. Historia om de Nordiske Folken, 1555.

Olsen, Magnus. «Kingitórsoakstenen og sproget i de grønlandske runeinnskrifter.» Norsk tidsskrift for sprogvitenskap, 5, 1932.

Ortelius, Abraham. Theatrum Orbis Terrarum. Amsterdam 1587.

Ortelius, Abraham. Theatrum Additamentum, IV, 1590.

Osterman, H. Niels Egedes beskrivelse af Grønland. Copenhagen, 1939.

Pedersen, Alf Bjarne. Bein- og hornskurd. Oslo 1966.

Polo, Marco. The Travels of Marco Polo. Translation by Aldo Ricci, London 1931.

Purchas, Samuel. Purchas his Pilgrimes, 1625. New edition, Glasgow 1906.

Prytz, Kåre. Lykkelige Vinland. Oslo 1975.

Prytz, Kåre. «The Antilia Chart of 1424 and Later Maps of America», Norsk Geografisk Tidsskrift, 31, Oslo 1977.

Quattlebaum, P. The Land Called Chicora. Gainesville, Florida, 1956.

Quinn, D.B. The Roanoke Voyages 1564–90, I–II, London 1955.

Quinn, D.B., Cumming, W.P. and Skelton, R.A. The Discovery of North America. London 1971.

Ramskau, Torkild. Solsteinen (with English summary). Copenhagen 1969, 1982.

Rasmussen, Knud. «Nordmendenes bebyggelse av Nord- grønland for 1000 år siden.» Tidens Tegn, May 8, 1920.

Ravenstein, E.G. Martin Behaim—His Life and His Globe. London 1908.

Rimasafn. Edited by Finnur Johnsson, Copenhagen 1905–1912.

Roussel, Aage. Meddelelser om Grønland, Vol. 89, Copenhagen 1941.

Rygge, Elisabeth Wiese. «Beinskurd», in Aschehougs konversasjonsleksikon, Oslo 1972.

Salomonsen, Finn (ed.). Grønlands fauna. Copenhagen 1981.

Scisco, L.D. «Tracks of Ponce de Leon in 1513», American Geographical Society Bulletin, XLV, New York 1913.

Scott, John F. A History of Mathematics from Antiquity to the Beginning of the Nineteenth Century, I–II, London 1958.

Science (US), 1961 and 1968.

Shetrone, Henry Clay. The Mound Builders.

Skaare, Kolbjørn, in NNF-NYTT. Meddelelser fra Norsk Numismatisk Forening, no. 2, 1979.

Smith, John. My First Voyage to Norumbega Now Called New England, in Arber, E. Travels and Works of Captain John Smith. Edinburgh 1910.

Steinnes, Asgaut. «Ein Nordpol-ekspedisjon i 1360», in Syn og Segn, Oslo 1958.

de Stobnicza, Johannes. Introductio de Ptolemei Cosmographiam. Cracow 1512.

Storm, Gustav. «Om opdagelsen av Nordkapp og veien til det hvite hav» Norsk geografisk selskaps årbok, V, Christiania 1893–94.

Sturlasson, Snorre. Edda. Norwegian editions by G.A. Gjessing, Oslo 1899, and Ivar Mortensson Egnund, Oslo 1928.

Swanton, J.R. «The Indian Tribes of North America», Bureau of American Ethnology Bulletin, 145, 1952.

Taranger, Absalon (ed.). Norges Historie. Oslo 1915–17.

Thevet, A. Les singularités de la France antarctique. Paris 1558.

Thorne, Robert. Letter in British Museum, Cotton MS, Vit.c., VII, 329–45.

Thwaites, R.G. (ed.). The Jesuit Relations and Allied Documents, 1–73, Cleveland 1896–1901.

Tooley, Ronald. A History of Cartography. London 1969.

Tordesillas, Herrera y. Novus Orbis. Seville 1558.

Tornøe, J. Kr. Columbus in the Arctic? Oslo 1965.

Tsukernik, David Y., in Tornøe, 1965.

Tunis, Paul. Amerikas indianere. Danish edition, Copenhagen 1953.

Ulloa, Louis. La genèse de la découverte de l'Amerique. Paris 1928.

da Verrazano, Giovanni. See Hagmann Hall 1910.

Vinbladet. Oslo 1989.

Voksø, Per (ed.). Norges Fjellverden. Oslo 1980.

Waring, Antonio. The Waring Papers. Edited by Stephen Williams. Papers no. 7, 9, 12 and 18A. Harvard University Press 1972.

Wassermann, Jacob. Columbus. Norwegian edition: Oslo 1955.

Webster's English Dictionary.

Williamson, James, A. The Cabot Voyages and Bristol Discovery Under Henry VII. Cambridge 1962.

Winsor, Justin. Narrative and Critical History of America, I–II, London 1886–89.

Wood, William. New England's Prospect. London 1634.